APR 16

P9-CFK-075

WINTER
is
COMING

'Much has been written about the historical resonances of *Game of Thrones*, but never quite like this. There is deep scholarship at work here, paired with an immersive understanding of the strange and yet strangely familiar lands of Westeros and Essos. Carolyne Larrington is the perfect guide: in luscious prose, she leads us through the Seven Kingdoms and on across the Narrow Sea, at each step exploring the echoes and parallels to be found in our own medieval past. Beautiful, haunting and thought-provoking, this is at once a celebration and an enrichment of George R. R. Martin's world. What more could a fan want?'

Helen Castor, Bye-Fellow of Sidney Sussex College,
Cambridge and bestselling author of *Blood and Roses*
(2004), *She-Wolves: The Women Who Ruled England before
Elizabeth* (2010) and *Joan of Arc: A History* (2014)

WINTER

is

COMING

THE MEDIEVAL WORLD OF

GAME OF THRONES

Carolyne Larrington

I.B. TAURIS

LONDON · NEW YORK

Published in 2016 by
I.B.Tauris & Co. Ltd
London • New York
www.ibtauris.com

Copyright © 2016 Carolyne Larrington
Reprinted in 2016

The right of Carolyne Larrington to be identified as the author
of this work has been asserted by the author in accordance
with the Copyright, Designs and Patents Act 1988.

All rights reserved. Except for brief quotations in a review, this
book, or any part thereof, may not be reproduced, stored in or
introduced into a retrieval system, or transmitted, in any form or
by any means, electronic, mechanical, photocopying, recording or
otherwise, without the prior written permission of the publisher.

Every attempt has been made to gain permission for the use of the
images in this book. Any omissions will be rectified in future editions.

References to websites were correct at the time of writing.

ISBN: 978 1 78453 256 7
eISBN: 978 0 85772 931 6

A full CIP record for this book is available from the British Library
A full CIP record is available from the Library of Congress

Library of Congress Catalog Card Number: available

Text designed and typeset by Tetragon, London
Printed and bound in Great Britain by T.J. International, Padstow, Cornwall

For John

CONTENTS

LIST OF ILLUSTRATIONS

LIST OF ABBREVIATIONS

BOOKS IN *A SONG OF ICE AND FIRE* SERIES
(Citations are by chapter number)

GT: *A Game of Thrones*
CK: *A Clash of Kings*
SS: *A Storm of Swords*
FC: *A Feast for Crows*
DD: *A Dance with Dragons*

GAME OF THRONES TV SHOW
(Cited by season and episode, e.g. (1.1) = Season 1, Episode 1)

SEASON ONE

1. 'Winter is Coming'
2. 'The Kingsroad'
3. 'Lord Snow'
4. 'Cripples, Bastards, and Broken Things'
5. 'The Wolf and the Lion'
6. 'A Golden Crown'
7. 'You Win or You Die'
8. 'The Pointy End'
9. 'Baelor'
10. 'Fire and Blood'

SEASON TWO

1. 'The North Remembers'
2. 'The Night Lands'
3. 'What is Dead May Never Die'
4. 'Garden of Bones'
5. 'The Ghost of Harrenhal'
6. 'The Old Gods and the New'
7. 'A Man without Honor'
8. 'The Prince of Winterfell'
9. 'Blackwater'
10. 'Valar Morghulis'

SEASON THREE

1. 'Valar Dohaeris'
2. 'Dark Wings, Dark Words'
3. 'Walk of Punishment'
4. 'And Now His Watch is Ended'
5. 'Kissed by Fire'
6. 'The Climb'
7. 'The Bear and the Maiden Fair'
8. 'Second Sons'
9. 'The Rains of Castamere'
10. 'Mhysa'

SEASON FOUR

1. 'Two Swords'
2. 'The Lion and the Rose'
3. 'Breaker of Chains'
4. 'Oathkeeper'
5. 'First of His Name'
6. 'The Laws of Gods and Men'
7. 'Mockingbird'
8. 'The Mountain and the Viper'
9. 'The Watchers on the Wall'
10. 'The Children'

SEASON FIVE

1. 'The Wars to Come'
2. 'The House of Black and White'
3. 'High Sparrow'
4. 'Sons of the Harpy'
5. 'Kill the Boy'
6. 'Unbowed, Unbent, Unbroken'
7. 'The Gift'
8. 'Hardhome'
9. 'The Dance of Dragons'
10. 'Mother's Mercy'

PREFACE

This book is about what happens when a scholar of medieval literature and culture watches the HBO show *Game of Thrones* and reads George R. R. Martin's series, *A Song of Ice and Fire*. It's not intended to chase up Martin's sources or to spot direct influences on David Benioff and Dan Weiss, the show's creators; rather, it pays tribute to the remarkable world-building that the books and show achieve, creating a world (the 'Known World' in fan parlance) which strikes all sorts of resonances with the cultures of medieval Europe and Asia. If you like, this book is about what happens when medievalist *Game of Thrones* fans get together, discussing what Westeros and Essos have in common with both the historical medieval world and the altogether more arcane and vivid world of the medieval imagination: parallels, reminiscences, shared structures and understandings.

Winter is Coming assumes that you are up to date as far as the end of Season Five of the show. The divergence between show and books, which didn't matter all that much until recently, has now become considerable. In terms that those of us who edit medieval texts would use, we should probably now talk of two different recensions. It's the same story (kind of), but the divergences are much larger than might be covered by the term 'version'. In effect, the show's chronology has now reached the end of *A Dance with Dragons*, even if some storylines have developed very differently, and they contain a good number of cliffhangers to be resolved in Season Six. I've tried to keep spoilers from the books to a minimum; though I haven't flagged up every time I explain that someone is called something else in print, I've tried to dodge saying too much about the books' plots where they diverge from the show. So, in the terms of that invaluable *Game of Thrones* news site, Winter is Coming, the Unsullied (those who haven't read the books) needn't fear to learn too much.

Spoilers are signified by a picture of a raven in the margin, with a line showing the extent of the spoiler, as follows:

Serious spoiler

Medium spoiler

Minor spoiler

And here's an explanation of terminology: the Known World is what the folk at A Wiki of Ice and Fire call the planet on which the story is taking place; the show and the books are self-evident terms, but when I refer to the *series*, I mean the narrative as manifested – in its different ways – across TV and print.

I'd like to thank various people who have encouraged this project – or labour of love. Elizabeth Archibald was at my side when I started to watch the show on a plane in 2012; she too has succumbed to the allure of the books and has contributed many insights to what follows. Eleanor Rosamund Barraclough and John Henry Clay share the medievalist perspective, chewed over at dinner on more than one occasion. My students – Tim Bourns, Violet Adams, Harry Palmer and Scott Oakley – have illuminated many plot points and nuances. Mikayla Hunter and Emma Charatan were attentive and engaged readers of early drafts, and I owe much to their suggestions. Frieder Missfelder has sent me useful links and engaged in enthusiastic discussion, bringing in a different historical perspective. My thanks also to Jesus Hernandez for his permission to reproduce Fig. 11. Former students Christina Cortes, Jon Day, Kelly McAree and Imogen Marcus were all happy to spend our last alumni get-together talking *Game of Thrones*. My god-daughters Eleanor and Cara Shearer equalled the wikis in their encyclopedic knowledge of the books. My colleague Patrick Hayes has had more influence on my thinking than might be expected from a mere modernist. Alex Wright of I.B.Tauris persuaded me to write this after an impassioned discussion about medievalism in the show one lunchtime, and I owe him much gratitude for the happy hours of rereading and rewatching that ensued – even if a second viewing of 'The Red Wedding' was even more traumatic than the first. Thanks too to the folk at the Winter is Coming news site, and the legions of fans who have made the Wiki of Ice and Fire and the Game of Thrones Wiki such invaluable resources to writers like me.

INTRODUCTION

Tyrion: 'The wide world is full of such mad tales. Grumkins and snarks, ghosts and ghouls, mermaids, rock goblins, winged horses, winged pigs … winged lions.' Griff: 'Kingdoms are at hazard here. Our lives, our names, our honor. This is no game we're playing for your amusement.' Of course it is, thought Tyrion. The game of thrones. (DD, 8)

'Grumkins and snarks' and kingdoms at hazard: *Game of Thrones/A Song of Ice and Fire* encompasses both high fantasy, with its dragons and manticores, its White Walkers and blood-magic, and also very real questions about the politics of kingship, religious faith and social organisation. Like Tolkien's Middle Earth, *Game of Thrones/A Song of Ice and Fire* constructs its fantasy out of familiar building blocks: familiar, that is, to us medieval scholars. These blocks are chiselled out of the historical and imaginary medieval past, out of the medieval north, with its icy wastes, its monsters and its wolves; out of the medieval west, with its recognisable social institutions of chivalry, kingship, its conventions of inheritance and masculinity; out of the medieval Mediterranean, with its hotchpotch of trading ports, pirates, slavers and ancient civilisations; and out of the medieval fantasies of the exotic east, where Mongol horsemen harried fabled cities of unimaginable riches, and where bizarre customs held sway among strange tribes on the edges of the known world – and even beyond.

The codes which govern the Baratheon monarchy, the clan system of the Dothraki, the Brotherhood of the Night's Watch and the responsibilities of the Warden of the North: all these chime with the kinds of social and cultural organisation found in medieval Europe and Central Asia. George R. R. Martin's world-building draws primarily upon medieval European history (the fifteenth-century English civil uprisings known as the Wars of the Roses are often cited as a major inspiration), but he also makes use of the customs of earlier warrior cultures (the Celts, Anglo-Saxons and Vikings), of the history of the Mongols, whose courage and ambition brought into existence the largest land empire the world has ever seen, and he draws on the folklore and beliefs that were widespread in medieval Europe. From the cultures of high medieval Europe, Martin borrows and adapts overarching concepts such as the Catholic Church and chivalry; from further afield, the Mongols – hybridised with some Native American societies – inform the Dothraki.

How far is the recent history of the Seven Kingdoms a reworking of the fifteenth-century Wars of the Roses? Martin has declared that the struggle for domination between the descendants of Edward III was an inspiration for the politics of Westeros, and the chime of Stark and York, Lannister and Lancaster is a suggestive one. Yet, filtered through Martin's powerful imagination and the epic vision of show creators David Benioff and Dan Weiss, the facts of history are transmuted into something richer, stranger, more archetypal. Take the Princes in the Tower, Edward and Richard, the two sons of the Yorkist king Edward IV. After their father died suddenly in early 1483, their paternal uncle Richard, Duke of Gloucester, took charge of the boys, aged twelve and nine. They were lodged in the Tower of London, in preparation for Edward's coronation as Edward V; then – mysteriously – they disappeared, and Uncle Richard seized the throne.

Bran and Rickon were never in line for the Iron Throne, of course (though Bran becomes heir to Winterfell), but the motif of the supposed death of two innocent children is refracted more than once in the series: in Elia Martell's children as well as Catelyn's youngest sons. Similarly, Cersei has been compared with Queen Margaret of Anjou (1430–82), the consort of the Lancastrian Henry VI; but, although Margaret also invested everything in her child, given the incapacity of her husband, she was very much less able to impress her personal will on the equivalent of the Small Council.

1. The Princes in the Tower

And Cersei can – and has been – as profitably be compared with a good number of other troublesome and feisty medieval queens: Eleanor of Aquitaine (*c*.1122–1204), Isabella (1295–1358), queen of Edward II, the late sixth-/early seventh-century Merovingian queen Brunhild of what's now northern France; the list goes on. Cersei has very human qualities (her drinking habits, her demented jealousy of Margaery), but her name echoes that of the enchantress of Greek epic: Circe, who turned men into animals but who was outwitted by Odysseus. Cersei, our 'green-eyed lioness', too wields a kind of magic over the men who surround her. And her incest with Jaime points to a mythic dimension: the divine golden twins, two halves of a single soul – or so Cersei claims to Ned:

> Jaime and I are more than brother and sister. We are one person in two bodies. We shared a womb together. He came into this

world holding my foot, our old maester said. When he is in
me, I feel ... whole. (*GT*, 45)

High politics then are infused with elements of myth and folk tale;
the contest for control of Sansa, as the heiress of Winterfell, played
out by Lord Baelish, the Boltons and by Sansa herself, is at stake in
Season Five. Whoever has Sansa in their power has a good claim to
be Warden of the North, yet, while she's in the clutches of Ramsay
and Roose, she is also the beleaguered fairy-tale princess, imprisoned in the tower, praying for rescue by – whom? Neither Theon/
Reek nor Brienne and Pod are exactly the stuff of a maiden's – or
a knowing no-longer-maiden's – dreams.

Just as what seems historical and real is in dialogue with the
traditional and folkloric, the series' supernatural speaks equally
to real-world concerns. Dragons are wondrous creatures, 'fire
made flesh', but they are also dangerously destabilising factors in

2. *Queen Margaret of Anjou*, detail

the geopolitics of the Known World. Daenerys is not really able to control them, and we've seen and read too much about the damage they can do: from the terrible ruins of Harrenhal to the deserts of the Disputed Lands. Could Westeros really be conquered using the equivalent of a tactical nuclear weapon? And what would then be left to rule over? In more human terms, the debate about the logistics of the future conquest of Westeros – through dragon-terror, through the massed forces of the Unsullied, through a battle for hearts and minds that Jorah for one is sceptical about – runs through the series. 'The old Houses will flock to our Queen as she crosses the Narrow Sea,' claims Barristan Selmy. 'The old Houses will flock to whichever side they think will win, as they always have,' ripostes Jorah as the Targaryen faction debate launching the invasion in the wake of Joffrey's death (4.5). And Jorah is likely to be right.

The White Walkers/Others too, the most alien, horrifying and unappeasable forces in the Known World, speak of changing conditions in the far north, of mass movements of people unable to live with the consequences of climate change in their traditional homelands. These are not just concerns contemporary to us; medieval people who lived in marginal societies – like the Scandinavian colonists in southern Greenland in the fifteenth century – found that even a small change in average temperatures spelt the extinction of a whole way of life. Sometimes the history of Westeros and contemporary politics mesh together in uncomfortable ways. 'You're fighting to overthrow a king, and yet you have no plan for what comes after?' Talisa asks Robb Stark when she is trying to understand his perspective on the War of the Five Kings (2.4). Is it better, as Barristan avers to Daenerys, to answer injustice with mercy, and not to crucify 163 Masters of Meereen? Or, as Dany responds, to meet injustice with justice – but whose? (4.4). 'Has the Crown suddenly stopped needing the gold, troops and wheat which my House supplies?' Olenna Tyrell asks pointedly in her interview with

Cersei about Loras's imprisonment (5.6); what resources remain available to large urban populations under changing political and climatic circumstances, and what kinds of compromise will be required to obtain them? These are all real questions, no less real for being posed within a fictional space. Many of the answers involve familiar economic factors: the depletion of precious-metal resources (the mines of Casterly Rock), the financial difficulties contingent on the denial of credit (how the Iron Bank deals with default), the effects of local legislation on global trade (radiating from Slaver's Bay as far as Volantis); all these contemporary and real-world constraints operate in the Known World too, from the west of Westeros to the furthest reaches of Essos.

Both the books and the show frame their narratives through shifting points of view: the intricate plots follow the perspectives of particular characters, showing or narrating what happens to them, and, in the books, telling us what they are thinking and feeling. In the show such interior psychological processes become clear through the actors' expressions and through dialogue; characters need someone else to talk to in order to give voice to their feelings. Daenerys's status as *khaleesi*, queen and Mother of Dragons means that she is usually conscious of her dignity; even with Sers Jorah and Barristan she finds it difficult to open her heart and speak as one human being to another. The characters who are granted Point Of View status are often – and this is not coincidental – sympathetic and likeable: indeed, we'd probably shudder to see the world through the eyes and mind of young Joffrey. What we are never shown, however, is how the world looks from the position of the non-Westerosi characters: we neither hear their reflections on their own cultures nor do we share their views on Westeros, regarded with an outsider's critical eye (the one exception is discussed in Chapter Five). From time to time Lord Varys, Master of Whisperers, offers in his silky tones his perspective as an outsider, for he was slave-born in Lys. But Varys is too often playing an unfathomable double game for us to rely on his words and viewpoint. And so, whether we are in the Free Cities, among the Dothraki or in the cities of Slaver's Bay, like Daenerys the readers and audience are restricted to Westerosi perspectives on the Essos folk whom we encounter.

This exoticising attitude to the inscrutable east is by no means restricted to modern, or even colonial-era, western thinking. Its roots go a very long way back, into the early romances about Alexander the Great and his campaigns of conquest in Asia; the earliest Greek version dates from the third century CE. *The Wonders of the East* is a title given by editors to an Old English prose text found in the same manuscript as the great poem *Beowulf*, dating from around 1000. Here we learn (just after a discussion of the Donestre, a cannibal race) of

> a place where people are born who are in size fifteen feet tall and ten broad. They have large heads and ears like fans. They spread one ear beneath them at night, and they wrap themselves with the other. Their ears are very light and their bodies are as white as milk. And if they see or perceive anyone in those lands, they take their ears in their hands and go far and flee, so swiftly one might think that they flew.[1]

For all we know, such folk (traditionally called the Panotii) may live on the scarcely explored continent of Sothoryos, along with Amazons, Blemmyae (men with faces in their chests), unipeds and other monstrous-yet-human figures. And I, for one, would very much like to see them.

At some point in the late 1350s or 1360s, an author (or rather a fictitious author) claiming to be Sir John Mandeville, knight of St Albans, wrote an account of his voyages in a work known as *Mandeville's Travels*. Hugely influential, translated into all the major (and a good number of minor) European languages, preserved in nearly 300 manuscripts, the book even accompanied Christopher Columbus on his voyage to the Indies (West, not

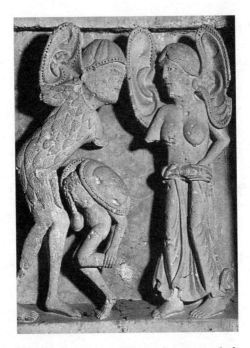

3. A Panotii couple, a thirteenth-century relief
in the Basilica at Vézelay, France

East, as it turned out). 'For many man hath gret likyng and
desire to hyre nywe thynges,' 'Mandeville' opines – and he's
not wrong.[2]

'John Mandeville' relates how he journeyed from southern
England to Jerusalem and the Middle East, then onwards to India,
East Asia, Java, China and all the way to the Gates of the Earthly
Paradise and to the Fountain of Youth, before he turned home-
wards once more. In reality, *Mandeville's Travels* was the work
of a writer who probably did not travel much further than the
nearest library, where he found the sources for his travelogue. He
brought together contemporary pilgrim guides – what to see in
Jerusalem and alternative routes for getting there; recent accounts
by Franciscan friars of their travels across Central Asia to the court

of the Great Khan; traditional knowledge drawn from standard encyclopedias; tall tales as old as Herodotus; and the missionary Odoric of Pordenone's bang-up-to-date narrative about his travels in India and China. Urban legends and anthropological facts, the fabulous and the well-observed all jostle together in Mandeville's text. Together, his disparate reading produced a work which, through its compiler's learning and imagination, brought alive medieval geography for thousands of readers, and explained the world – or *a* world – to them.

And that's the intention of this book: to try to explain the Known World, its customs, inhabitants, power plays, religions and cultures through a medievalist lens. Like Mandeville, we'll be travelling on a long, dangerous and exhausting journey, from the icy wastes north of the Wall and the mighty castle of Winterfell to the shadowy eastern city of Asshai, from the modernity of the mercantile city state of Braavos to the ancient ruins of doomed Valyria. And yet we don't need to turn off our TVs, lay aside our copies of the books and bid a sorrowful farewell to our loved ones, for, like Mandeville's exploration, our journey takes us only through the world of imagination.

Before we set off, however, a little orientation is in order. The cultures of the Known World, mostly but not exclusively framed by the norms of Westeros, share a good number of deep-seated cultural beliefs: about rank and gender, about honour and face, hospitality, justice, weapons and the habits of dragons. Chapter One outlines the ways in which these central concepts operate. In Chapter Two, we enter Westeros where the series does: at Winterfell, 'the heart of the north'; we range both on this and the other side of the Wall to explore this distinctive and dangerous terrain. Chapter Three leads us down the kingsroad to King's Landing, to the complex, shifting alliances at court and its uneasy relationship with the Faith, and then on to the smiling lands of the Reach, to desert Dorne and to Stannis's forbidding seat in sea-girt Dragonstone. With Chapter Four we set sail across the Narrow Sea, to visit the varied Free

Cities which lie along its Essos coastline and to hear the persuasive preaching of the Lord of Light. And in Chapter Five, we take horse eastwards, across the Dothraki Sea, to Slaver's Bay and its cities, to mysterious Qarth and the Shadowlands beyond. And then, finally, we turn for home. In the Epilogue – not to be read by the Unsullied – I leave behind the Known World, and what we know within it, to gaze into the future. Like Maggy the Frog's prophecy, what I see there may – or may not – come true. And, like Cersei, you are free to believe or to reject my vision.

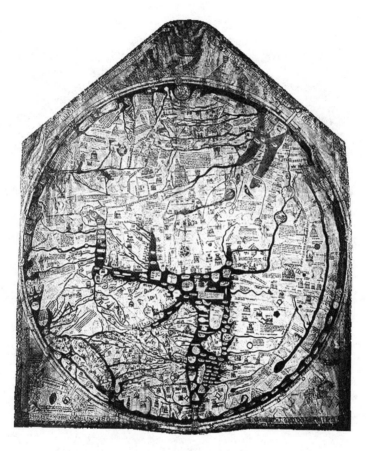

4. The Hereford Cathedral *mappamundi* (map of the world)

5. *The Iron Throne*

CHAPTER 1

THE CENTRE

> *Gilly: 'Is this every book there is?' Sam: 'They say the*
> *Citadel has the largest library in the world [...] in*
> *Oldtown.' Gilly: 'I'm sorry I don't know things.' (5.5)*

The Citadel, the headquarters of the Order of Maesters in Oldtown, has the largest library in the Known World, recording crucial knowledge in the manuscripts and scrolls that are carefully preserved there. This chapter offers a crash course in some of the most important things that Sam knows and Gilly doesn't about the world south of the Wall. It introduces some of the central concepts, the world views and social rules in the Known World: information that we'll need before we embark on our long journeying through Westeros and Essos in the next chapter. Most of the peoples of Westeros and Essos adhere to these beliefs and operate according to these social codes. Nevertheless, there are times – many times – when these beliefs are challenged and the codes interrogated. Those who raise awkward questions are often outsiders in some sense: Varys, Petyr Baelish or Jorah Mormont, and especially Daenerys. In the first section, we investigate the old, well-established principles which particularly affect individuals: genealogy, Houses, honour and face, oral tradition and speech acts, and the broadly patriarchal view of love, gender and sexual politics. In the second section, we look at larger social structures: hospitality, justice and vengeance, war and weapons – and last of all, that powerful game-changer, dragons and their lore. Where there are striking parallels in medieval culture, I'll bring them forward. This will allow us to probe more deeply into these important constituents of the world in which our characters move.

RANK, BIRTH AND HONOUR

Who someone is, both in the medieval world and in the world of *Game of Thrones*, depends absolutely on who their parents and their grandparents were. For lower-class characters social mobility is not easily won; Varys's astonishing social ascent, from slave-born baby in Lys via a youth as a castrated child-beggar and prostitute in Myr to membership of the Small Council of the Seven Kingdoms, is quite dizzying. His semi-criminal activities – fencing stolen goods in Pentos, creating a network of informers throughout Essos – spread his reputation as the Master of Whisperers across the Narrow Sea. Lord Varys holds no land, belongs to no House and his title is entirely honorific. Few other major characters have had such a meteoric rise; even Lord Baelish inherited land and a title, though the House of Baelish is relatively recently established, and Littlefinger (his derisive nickname) is always keenly aware of his social inferiority both to the Tullys, with whom he was raised, and to the Starks. How Lord Baelish parlayed his wits and abilities to rise to the position of Master of Coin – in some ways comparable to the positions the fourteenth-century poet Geoffrey Chaucer held in the civil service of Edward III and Richard II – is rather interesting, and we'll take a closer look at him in Chapter Three.

For the craftsmen, sellswords, farmers, sailors and prostitutes of the main kingdoms and cities of Essos and Westeros, parentage merely serves to confirm them in their social role. Bronn is the obvious exception. Among other subcultures, when a man identifies himself as his father's son he makes clear his lineage and offers one good reason why he should be respected: Shagga of the Stone

Crows feels that it's imperative to make clear on every possible occasion that he is the son of Dolf. So too, when he speaks formally, Drogo recalls that he is son of Bharbo (a name which encodes the barbarism which the Andals ascribe to the horselords). Before the emergence of surnames, and indeed still in modern Iceland, using a patronymic was the only way to distinguish someone from others bearing the same given name. The narrator of *Beowulf*, for example, in the Old English poem named after that hero, is in the habit of mentioning Beowulf's father Ecgtheow. Here the reference doesn't just distinguish the hero from other Beowulfs, but reminds the poem's original audience – and the characters within the poem – of stories about Beowulf's father. When Beowulf's patronymic is revealed to King Hrothgar of the Danes he is immediately able to place him: as the son of a man whom Hrothgar had helped in his younger days, a realisation which makes it easier for the beleaguered Danish king to accept young Beowulf's help against the monster Grendel.

Bloodline is everything for the members of the Great Houses, and their relative standing is determined by the length of their history. The Starks have been Kings in or Wardens of the North for over 8,000 years, since the time of Brandon the Builder, who not only built Winterfell but, more impressively, the Wall. Other Great Houses can trace their ancestry back to the Andal invasions, or in the case of the Targaryens, since before the Doom of Valyria. Like the medieval aristocracy, the members of the Great Houses believe that their privilege, their authority and their ideological understanding of themselves as 'noble' is transmitted through blood. This belief isn't just confined to Westeros; it's not for nothing that the Dothraki use the phrase 'blood of my blood' among themselves. Nor is the notion of the power of blood just metaphorical, for the actual blood of kings has a particular efficacy in Melisandre's eyes, and perhaps in the cult of the Red God she serves. Leeches containing the blood of Gendry, Robert Baratheon's bastard son, are flung on a brazier by Stannis while he curses his rivals: Robb Stark, Balon Greyjoy and Joffrey, Stannis's apparent nephew. Does this seal their fates? Melisandre might claim so, but we can identify more proximate causes for their deaths. Still, blood-magic is powerful and for that reason generally taboo; its outcomes – such as the vegetative state of Drogo, the hatching of the dragons, the *maegi*'s prophecy to Cersei, the murder of Renly – are uncertain and perilous.

Legitimacy is crucial, knowing who one's family is is essential, and thus bastards and those whose ancestry is hidden or obscured are the ones to be watched. The bastard has much, maybe everything, to prove. Jon Snow's illegitimate birth shapes his fate entirely; it lies behind his decision to join the Night's Watch and his eventual succession to its command. In part, his decision to join the Watch is fuelled by his hero-worship of his uncle Benjen Stark, but it's mostly driven by his realisation that there's no role for him in Winterfell. He cannot hope to inherit a holdfast nor to find any role within the castle that is commensurate with those of his brothers. Roose Bolton's vile bastard Ramsay is also a Snow until Roose adopts him formally as his son and heir. Ramsay's efforts to make himself worthy to bear his father's name often clash with his sadistic instincts, but the scene in which Roose legitimises him (4.8) suggests very strongly how Ramsay has longed for his father's acceptance. Similarly, the implications of Joffrey and Tommen's illegitimacy exclude them from rightfully occupying the Iron Throne. It's not their incestuous origin that is problematic, but rather that – unlike their black-haired elder brother, who died of a childhood fever (recalled by Cersei in 'The Kingsroad', 1.2) – they are not of Baratheon blood. Although the many bastards that Robert sired among the lower classes of King's Landing do not present much of a threat to the throne, Joffrey, like King Herod, or indeed King Arthur in Sir Thomas Malory's fifteenth-century account of his life, the *Morte D'Arthur*, decides it is safer to eliminate all potential rivals.

According to Malory, Merlin prophesies that Arthur's incest-begotten, May-born son will cause the downfall of the kingdom. Arthur is thwarted in his attempt to eliminate Mordred, for the ship carrying the baby from Orkney (where Arthur's half-sister gave birth to him) to London is shipwrecked en route; the baby is washed ashore and reared by a fisherman. Arthur places the other May-born boys in a boat and sets them adrift: they all perish. Yet Merlin's prophecy can't be circumvented, for Mordred nevertheless survives and plays out his fated role. Just so, Cersei believes that all Robert's children are dead, but Gendry has survived, despite Melisandre's best efforts. In the show he is elided with Edric Storm, another of Robert's bastards, and has escaped from Dragonstone with Davos's help. In the books, Gendry is working as a smith at the inn at the crossroads where so many fateful encounters take place, and his eventual destiny remains a matter of speculation. To be the only surviving son, legitimate or not, of the House Baratheon lends him a particular aura. Ned Stark saw something special in Gendry, and offered to train him himself: 'if the day ever comes when that boy would rather wield a sword than forge one, you send him to me' (1.4). So in medieval romance it sometimes happens that the experienced knight can tell that the young man pretending to be altogether ordinary must be better born than he claims. In Malory's 'Tale of Sir Gareth', Gareth, son of the King of Orkney, decides to hide his identity when he comes to Camelot, and is allowed at his own request to work in the kitchens for a year before asking to be assigned an adventure. Gareth wants to dissociate himself from his brothers and father and be honoured for his skills and character, not his lineage. Sir Lancelot becomes his mentor, and though he's sure that Gareth is nobly born, he politely goes along with the subterfuge and takes it upon himself to knight Gareth at the year's end. In another tale in Malory, a cowherd's son, who is fascinated by chivalry – and who is a hopeless agricultural worker – is revealed by Merlin to be the illegitimate son of King Pellinore. Arthur knights young Tor and he becomes a valued and effective member of the Round Table.[1] Whether such social promotion awaits Gendry is hard to predict; in the show we've no idea where he went after Davos released him from the dungeons.

To be noble, then, is to be a better person than the commoners. The aristocracy, or so they like to believe, behave better, keep their promises, are courageous, unflinching and generous when they can be. For men, military skills are crucial, whether as knights or as straightforward warriors like Ned and Robb Stark. Noblewomen lead more restricted lives, as pawns in the creating of alliances through marriage and as mothers, but also as advice-givers and strategists (particularly within a domestic setting). They are expected to be beautiful and intelligent, but also obedient and modest. Where Westeros differs from the medieval model, however, is that there seems to be no appeal to the gods to decree or endorse the status quo. Medieval thinkers argued that God had created the different estates – those who fight (the nobility), those who pray (the Church) and those who work (the peasantry). Doubtless God approved of the emerging bourgeois groups of craftsmen, trades-men, merchants and civil servants who were not quite classifiable within the old model, though how far his approval extended to the so-called 'fourth estate', women, is questionable. A clear religious underpinning to Westeros's class system is absent; most charac-ters' relative disaffection from religion will be discussed further in Chapters Two and Three. In the southern Seven Kingdoms, where Faith in the Seven prevails, nobility is tightly bound up with the concept of chivalry, conceived in near-identical terms to the medi-eval understanding of knightliness. Chivalry and its implications will be discussed further in Chapter Three.

Membership of a lineage endows nobles with what is perhaps the most important constituent of individual characters: their sense of personal honour. Honour – particularly for a man – revolves around keeping his word, not allowing others to insult him and remembering the history of his House. If he is a bastard, he begins at a disadvantage; if he has no surname, for example, his chances of acquiring honour are very limited indeed. Theon is excluded from some of the responsibilities which go with membership of House Stark, by reason of his ambiguous status – one that's revealed only gradually in the early episodes of Season One. His position as hostage compromises his sense of honour, particularly in the face of his father's unyielding view of what constitutes Greyjoy honour, with terrible political and personal consequences.

Individuality has less to do with the essential, irreducible core identity that we moderns believe ourselves to possess. As in the medieval period (before the twelfth-century thought-revolution, sometimes characterised as 'the birth of the individual'), membership of social groups forms people's identity in the Known World. Who someone is depends first on gender and then on rank; on who their parents, kin-group and House are, which gods they worship, whether or not they are a knight, where they live, and which candidate they regard as the rightful occupant of the Iron Throne. But if a man's character has an irreducible core, it probably lies in his estimation of his own honour.

Honour is closely bound up with ideas of truth and morality, of doing what someone thinks is right. It's not clear, given the different religions which hold sway across the two continents, that morality is necessarily very closely tied to religious belief – though we'll come across some exceptions below. Honour is mutable, negotiable, and can be lost, won, sacrificed or leached away by the challenges faced in the turmoil of the Seven Kingdoms. Across the sea in Essos, or so Barristan Selmy reflects, '[i]n the viper's pit that was Meereen, honor seemed as silly as a fool's motley' (*DD*, 55). Indeed, one of the strongest points of contrast between eastern and western cultures, discussed at length in Chapter Five, is the western notion of personal responsibility, a guilt ethic (not particularly dependent on the notion that the gods, old or new, are watching us) and a strong sense of shame with regard to the social codes of the nobility. In the east, ethics are situational; people tell Daenerys what they think she wants to hear and they dissemble in pursuit of their goals. Hizdahr zo Loraq's probable involvement with the Sons of the Harpy is a case in point; Daario Naharis is fairly sure of it and recommends killing him and all the other Masters. Daenerys's sense of honour forbids execution without proof. Not that Essos has a monopoly on double-dealing, but Walder Frey and Roose

Bolton's breach of ethical norms at the Red Wedding damages their reputations irretrievably; Robb feels terrible guilt at breaking his promise to marry a Frey girl. Hizdahr, in contrast, is not a player in the Westerosi honour game, and has little compunction about lying to the queen. The Green Grace, the high priestess of the old Ghiscari religion practised in Meereen, who advises Daenerys from an insider's perspective, is absent from the show, leaving the *khaleesi* reliant on counsel from other incomers, or locals with their own axes to grind.

Ned Stark's sense of honour, manifested as his commitment to revealing the truth about Cersei's children, brings him to grief. Visited in his prison cell by Varys, Ned is given the chance to save his life by denying the truth; he will be allowed to take the black and retreat to the Wall. Ned angrily rejects the offer: 'You think my life is some precious thing to me, that I would trade my honour for a few more years of what … of what? … I learned how to die a long time ago' (1.9). For Ned, though, the lives of his daughters do turn out to be more important than his honour, and he makes a public and dishonouring confession of his treason – all to no avail.

The idea of face is an integral part of honour: respecting the social standing of another man and expecting him likewise to offer respect to you. If a man fails to respond to insult, then he loses face, and with it authority. Khal Drogo's authority over his *khalasar* depends crucially on face; he is quick to anger, and brooks no challenge to his orders. Daenerys's influence on him weakens his standing in his men's eyes; although they accede to his boast that they will cross the Narrow Sea, Daenerys's intervention to save Mirri Maz Duur, and her readiness, drawing on her relationship with the Khal to bolster her power, to give orders which the *khalasar* resent, finally bring about Drogo's downfall. Though he wins his fight with Mago, his festering wound means he can no longer stay on his horse – 'A khal who cannot ride is no khal' (1.9) – and his authority vanishes. The blood-riders in the *khalasar* are quick to abandon their dying leader and his *khaleesi*.

Over the course of his marriage to Daenerys, Drogo learns patience; he puts up with Viserys for longer than might be expected. But Viserys's final demand that Drogo keep his word, and his drunken breaking of the taboo against carrying weapons in Vaes Dothrak, cannot be ignored. Drogo's punishment of his wife's petulant brother, by giving him the golden crown which he craves, takes ironic note of Viserys's obsession, but it also shows his ruthlessness and ingenuity. Viserys has counted on the prohibition against shedding blood in Vaes Dothrak to allow him to abuse Drogo with impunity, but Drogo immediately sees how to circumvent the taboo, to answer Viserys once and for all, and by visiting a terrible death upon him he gains face not only with his *khalasar* but with Daenerys herself.

Kings have more latitude than ordinary mortals when they are offered disrespect; Robert will take teasing from Ned where he stands on his dignity with others. Joffrey, on the other hand, has no sense of humour, and his fundamental insecurity on the throne manifests itself before he is even crowned. The minstrel Marillion, whom we first encounter in the inn where Catelyn and Tyrion's paths cross, is horribly punished by Joffrey for composing a bawdy ballad about Robert, the boar and the 'lion in the king's bed'. Marillion's lyrics are indeed near the knuckle, indicating that Cersei's secret is now the talk of the city. Joffrey's ruthlessness and sadism come together, and he has Ilyn Payne rip out the minstrel's tongue.

ORAL TRADITION

The Houses of Westeros have their mottos, or House Words, which epitomise the House's self-image. 'A Lannister always pays his debts' is not in fact the Word of House Lannister – that's 'Hear me roar' – but the first phrase is heard far more often, whether on the lips of the Lannisters or as said about them. 'Winter is coming', the Word of House Stark, is the most resonant of the House Words; 'We do not sow' sums up the relentless refusal of the Greyjoys to countenance any other life but that of raiding, an ideology challenged by Asha in her bid for her father's throne. The anodyne 'Growing strong' of House Tyrell encodes a warning which Cersei can hear all too clearly; the ambitions of Margaery's House vault ever higher as House Stark, House Baratheon and House Tully's fortunes sink. Each House also has a sigil, an emblem which symbolises its values. The narrative opens with the sigil of House Stark made real: the Stark children acquiring their direwolf pups, each one powerfully linked to its owner's fate. The lion, kraken, stag and hideous flayed man embody the identity of the Houses they represent. The sigils are also vital for recognition in a largely preliterate society, fulfilling the same function as medieval heraldry: the Tudor rose, the different lions of England and Scotland, the French fleur-de-lis. So the Mountain tries to frame the Tullys by leaving a sack of bloody fish at the scene of his depredations when he ravages the Riverlands; the River-man who brings his grievance to Ned as Hand doesn't understand the word 'sigil', but he can confidently interpret the

6. Shields showing heraldic devices

symbols left as a signature.

In societies in which there is no writing, or very limited quantities of it, as in the European Middle Ages, a man's word was extremely important. Speech acts – vows, promises or oaths – take on a particular importance when agreements are not underpinned by written contracts, and they are often reinforced by the presence of witnesses, or by the invocation of God. When the time comes to fulfil the promise or keep the oath, the witnesses, whether human or divine, stand ready to remind the swearer. So Khal Drogo invokes 'the Mother of the Mountains' when he swears to give his child the Iron Throne and finally to fulfil his promise to Viserys and Daenerys:

> I will take my khalasar west to where the world ends, and ride
> the wooden horses across the black salt water […] I will kill
> the men in iron suits and tear down their stone houses […] I
> swear before the Mother of Mountains as the stars look down
> in witness. (1.7)

Drogo's dramatic performance, shouting and stamping, raising his arms and calling on gods and men to witness, makes it impossible for him to renege on his promise; only death can prevent him from fulfilling his pledge to do what no Dothraki has ever done before: to take his *khalasar* in ships over the 'poison water' to attack Westeros.

In the Old English poem *Beowulf*, there's a scene in which the hero Beowulf vows, before his own men and the Danes in the court of Denmark's king, Hrothgar, that he will kill the monster Grendel, who ravages the royal hall, or he will die in the attempt. 'I will perform warrior-like brave deeds / or wait for my final day in this mead-hall!' he swears. And, before he lies down to rest, Beowulf ramps up the tension by boasting that he won't use a sword or other weapons against the monster, challenging Grendel to try his physical strength against the human hero. During the fight, when Grendel and Beowulf are locked in combat, and the warrior has tight hold of Grendel's hand, he summons the final burst of adrenaline that's needed to tear the arm right off by remembering his *æfenspræce*, his speech earlier in the evening. And, for the monster, 'a gaping wound became clear on his shoulder / sinews sprang apart, the joint burst open.' Grendel is doomed.[2]

The oath of the Night's Watch, with all that entails, must not be sworn lightly. The first season opens with the terrifying events that cause Will (Gared in the books), the Brother of the Watch, to flee southwards from the Wall. The consequences of his flight are clear: deserters and oath-breakers must die, and Ned Stark carries out the execution himself. When news reaches Jon Snow that Robb has called up his bannermen and is marching southwards, Jon comes close to discounting his oath – 'I should be there [...] I should be with him' (1.9), despite Maester Aemon's wise words. Jon's through the gates of Castle Black and out in the forest when his friends and fellow oath-takers, Grenn, Pypar and Sam, catch up with him. When they recite the provisions of the oath to Jon, reminding him of what he swore in the presence of the Old Gods, he realises at last the seriousness of what he has promised. Though he will later break some other provisions of the oath, Jon finally grasps the truth of the argument that Jeor Mormont, Maester Aemon and his friends have been making: the Brothers of the Night's Watch are his family now. Oath-breaking is to be taken very seriously indeed; Jaime can never live down the nickname of 'Kingslayer'. He can neither deny its truth nor undo the event that gave rise to it, however justified the killing of the Mad King might have been in the light of the atrocities Aerys committed.

Sworn brotherhood was an important institution in medieval Europe. It originated in Germanic areas, and there's quite a bit of evidence pointing to various kinds of warrior bands swearing loyalty until death on the battlefield. In medieval England men would enter into sworn-brotherhood agreements, replacing or augmenting their own family ties with a freely chosen friend and companion. They would enter into this kind of pact by taking the Eucharist together, swearing to mutual love and the obligation to avenge the brother if he were killed. In 1421, two squires in Henry V's army, Nicholas Molyneux and John Winter, swore a compact in the church of St Martin at Harfleur in France. Their oath augmented *lamour et fraternite* (the love and brotherhood) which already existed between them, by becoming *freres darmes* (brothers in arms). Molyneux and Winter agreed to arrange ransom for one another if either were captured, to stand hostage for the other, and to pool their gains of war so that they could be invested later back in London.

How formal is the promise made between Robb and Theon when the Greatjon proposes that Robb be proclaimed King in the North? Theon asks if he is Robb's brother, 'Now and always', and Robb returns, 'Now and always' (1.10), a phrase that Theon repeats.[3] Theon's carried away by the drama of the moment; he doesn't pause to wonder whether he can carry his House (and his irascible father) along with him, but rather seizes the opportunity to change his status with regard to the other members of House Stark. Maester Luwin and Robb himself have at times reminded Theon that he's essentially a hostage in Winterfell, standing surety for the Greyjoy House's loyalty to the throne, and Theon has been hurt by his exclusion from the sibling group. Theon's tragedy stems in part from his failure to keep the full provisions of this promise in mind, but the fact that he swore it, and believed what he swore, lies behind his decision to abandon his pursuit of Bran and Rickon when he has control over Winterfell.

Promises given in medieval romance are often regretted. The 'rash boon', as the motif is called, is often promised without full awareness of the consequences. So in one Welsh tale, the First Branch of the *Mabinogi*, Lord Pwyll grants an unconditional boon to a petitioner at his wedding feast – and the man promptly asks for both his wife and his feast! Pwyll cannot refuse, though his wife is smart enough to think up some conditions which ultimately save the day – and her husband's face. And so too poor Shireen promises Stannis that she will do *anything* he asks if it will help him in the campaign against Winterfell: a promise with consequences that the loving daughter could never have foreseen.

PRIMOGENITURE

The principle that the eldest son inherits is a settled convention in all Westeros. Not so in Dorne: Arianne Martell counters when Arys Oakheart argues for Tommen's primacy over Myrcella. '*Why*? What god made it so? I am my father's heir. Should I give up my rights to my brothers?' (*FC*, 13). Earlier in the battle for the Iron Throne, the fact that Robert is not the father of Cersei's children means that Stannis, Robert's next brother, must be the true heir. Like many a medieval younger brother, Renly is less than impressed by the convention that the throne should pass to the next eldest. Loras Tyrell, who plays Lady Macbeth to Renly's doubting ambition, declares that 'Stannis has the personality of a lobster!' and launches a vigorous attack on the primogeniture principle (1.5). Renly has more progressive ideas about the role of the king than either of his brothers, and claims that he would govern with more kindness; a claim that will never be put to the test. So crucial is primogeniture in the Westerosi way of thinking that Daenerys assumes that it extends to the Dothraki too; she is horrified to learn from Jorah that her son will have no status among the *khalasar* if Drogo dies. Rather, Jorah warns, the new *khal* will have the child killed as a potential rival.

The idea that the eldest son should inherit the throne, or, if not of royal stock, should inherit the title and estates, leaving nothing for the younger brothers, took legal hold in Europe in the eleventh century. Previously, at least in England, kings had been chosen by the royal council from among the eligible males in the dynasty; if an elder brother was deemed unsuitable as a ruler, a younger might be chosen instead. Family property was shared out among the sons, while the daughters were given dowries when they married. This kind of inheritance system, known as 'partible inheritance', had the advantage of providing for all the surviving siblings, but over generations it tended to weaken the family position by dividing and subdividing land and other property, so that any one individual held a rather small share. The introduction of primogeniture was intended to solve the problem by giving everything to the eldest, making it necessary for younger sons to seek their own fortunes by going on Crusades, entering the Church or finding an eligible heiress to marry. The strict version of primogeniture did not last particularly long in France: the sometimes unhappy fates of younger brothers led to its modification by the twelfth century. Younger sons might now be given castles, manors or estates, held from the eldest rather than owned outright. This practice served to some extent to keep property together.

The Black Death which ravaged Europe in the years after 1348 reduced its population by an estimated 40 per cent. This catastrophe considerably eased the pressure on land; in England many families, from the wealthier members of the peasant class upwards, found themselves now able to obtain land and houses to settle on their surviving children, so that all might now marry. In medieval fiction, particularly in romance, the younger brother is often depicted as accepting his role – after all, he has known from his earliest years that, barring accidents to his elder brother, he cannot expect much from his father – and he sets off into the world to make his fortune, leaving his fraternal rivalries behind him. There's one English romance, though, the late fourteenth-century *Tale of Gamelyn*, in which brothers fall out just as badly over inheritance as Stannis and Renly. The trouble is caused by Gamelyn's father who, against all his barons' advice, decides to leave to his youngest son a portion three times what he leaves to the two elder brothers. The middle brother Ote is loyal to young Gamelyn, but John, the eldest, conspires to have him outlawed and to seize his inheritance. Ote goes bail for his brother's appearance in court; he's on the verge of being hanged by John because Gamelyn has not turned up when the youngest brother bursts in, swearing that it's John and not Ote who will hang. And indeed Gamelyn *does* hang John; the enmities and jealousies caused by the father's eccentric disposition of the patrimony are incapable of peaceful resolution.[4]

WOMEN, HONOUR, SEX AND MARRIAGE

> Oberyn: 'We don't hurt little girls in Dorne.'
> Cersei: 'Everywhere in the world they hurt little girls.' (5.4)

The women of Westeros and Essos are, like their medieval sisters, subject to the rule of the patriarchy. Noblewomen's value lies chiefly

in their function to unite different families, and their lot is generally to be married off strategically by their kindred with a view
to forming alliances and making good on promises. Such lack of
agency was typical of aristocratic marriage patterns in the medieval
period. Noble girls were betrothed young and often married as
soon as they reached puberty ('flowered', in Westerosi terms). So
Catelyn is married to Ned after the death of Brandon (Ned's elder
brother); love grew only gradually within their marriage. Daenerys
is traded to Drogo on the promise of military support for Viserys's
bid to seize back the Iron Throne; unexpectedly, Drogo shows her
tenderness on their wedding night in the books, if not in the show.
Sansa, a key pawn in the marriage game, is affianced to Joffrey, wed
to Tyrion (a marriage dissolved for lack of consummation), only to
be offered (in the show) by Littlefinger to Ramsay. The rape inflicted
on Sansa on her wedding night must have been the lot of many a
medieval bride; a virgin would have little idea of what awaited her
in the bedchamber. For in medieval Europe, sexual violence was
endemic, as it is in Westeros; only male protection could guarantee
a woman's safety outside the home. As Martin himself notes,

> Rape and sexual violence have been a part of every war ever
> fought, from the ancient Sumerians to our present day. To
> omit them from a narrative centered on war and power would
> have been fundamentally false and dishonest, and would have
> undermined one of the themes of the books: that the true hor-
> rors of human history derive not from orcs and Dark Lords,
> but from ourselves.[5]

Margery Kempe, of whom we'll hear more in Chapter Four, left
us what's probably the first autobiographical account by a woman
in English, composed in the first half of the fifteenth century.
She recounts a sexual assault on her committed by the Steward
of Leicester; in her many travels across Europe Margery went in
constant and justified fear of rape by strangers. Her religious faith

made her unwilling to have sexual relations with her husband after the birth of her first child. Nevertheless, the contemporary view of marriage legitimised her husband's forcing himself upon her: thirteen further children resulted. In the end Margery enlisted Jesus's help to negotiate with her husband and she managed strategically to bribe her way out of unwanted marital relations by paying off her husband's debts before she set out for Jerusalem.[6]

Widows, at least in England, were regarded as no longer under the authority of their father or brother, particularly if they had sons, and they found it easier to avoid unwanted second marriages. In late medieval Italian cities, however, where women tended to marry men much older than themselves, widowhood often came early. In such instances, the widow's brothers would reclaim their sister and her dowry in order to make another strategic marriage for her. And very often the first husband's family would keep the children from the marriage; the sorrowing woman would thus lose children and husband at a stroke. It's unsurprising, then, that as widow and queen mother Cersei can't stand up to her father when he orders her to marry Loras Tyrell to double the bonds between the Lannisters and the most powerful House in the Reach, but her habit of obeying her father dies hard. Over the medieval period, particularly as the Church began to emphasise the importance of women's consent when a match was contracted, the understanding that mutual respect and affection made marriages stronger and happier for both the participants began to grow. Husbands who went off to the Crusades for a decade needed to be sure that their wives could manage affairs competently; the unofficial influence and wisdom of wives and mothers could change the fates of nations.

Eleanor of Aquitaine, one of the most formidable queens England ever had, aligned herself with her sons when they revolted against their father, Henry II. Margaret of Anjou, Henry VI's queen, had to contend with a long delay before she produced an heir, her husband's physical and mental collapse, and the rising power and ambition of the House of York: factors which brought about the

Wars of the Roses. Often compared with Cersei, Margaret could not rule the kingdom herself: the Duke of York was chosen as Protector during the king's illness. His criticism of the way the king's party, supported by the queen, had managed the kingdom's affairs both at home and in the wars with France made open conflict inevitable. Yorkist victories, culminating in the coronation of Edward IV in 1461, meant many years of diplomatic campaigning for Margaret in hopes of recovering the throne for her husband or son. It would take ten years for her to achieve French support for the bid of the Earl of Warwick ('the Kingmaker') to restore Lancastrian rule; it seems likely that her hopes lay in the acceptance of her son as an effective king. The restoration was short-lived: Yorkist and Lancastrian armies met at the Battle of Tewkesbury on 4 May 1471. Edward, Margaret's son, was killed and Henry VI died in prison: Margaret's hopes were crushed. She spent the next five years in the custody of Alice de la Pole, dowager duchess of Suffolk and the grand-daughter of the poet Geoffrey Chaucer. Alice had been a friend and supporter of Margaret in their youth; perhaps this made conditions more bearable. After the payment of a sizeable ransom and the renunciation of all her property in England, Margaret returned to her native France in 1475, where she died seven years later. Her story is a particularly dramatic one, but its outline is echoed in the fates of very many medieval queens.[7]

Female honour is conceptualised rather differently from male honour in Westeros. The insult 'whore' is bandied about a great deal, and both women and men take offence at it. Ned almost strangles Petyr Baelish when he claims, quite truthfully, that Ned's wife is within his brothel. Petyr has taken Cat there to keep her arrival in King's Landing secret, but Ned construes it as an appalling insult to her and his honour. Sexual purity is key in determining noble female honour, while sexual freedom is the prerogative of men and of wildling women. Osha says she's had men who would eat Theon up and use his bones to pick their teeth; Ygritte is absolutely insistent that she has the right to choose even the 'crow' Jon Snow as her lover. No shame seems to attach to male promiscuity, though Cersei is offended by Robert's behaviour and Catelyn finds it impossible to come to terms with the apparent infidelity on Ned's part which brought Jon Snow into her family. It's only Tywin Lannister who feels that keeping a mistress is unworthy behaviour for Tyrion when representing his father as acting Hand of the King; Tywin's hypocrisy in this regard – in taking Shae as his own mistress – is an important factor in his death.

As in medieval European cities, brothels are an essential part of Westerosi life. The Bishop of Winchester owned the land where the best-known brothels of medieval London stood, in Southwark, and profited considerably from the rent they paid him; local prostitutes were sometimes known as 'Winchester geese'. There's a brothel at the gates of Winterfell, where we first encounter Tyrion enjoying a beer and a blow job; Littlefinger's wealth is maintained by his brothels in King's Landing: houses which cater for every kind of sexual taste, he boasts to Varys. Littlefinger's establishments present

7. A scene in a bathhouse doubling as a brothel

a shuttered front to the street, but inside they are luxurious, with plump, tapestried cushions, gauzy curtains, thick hangings and curving arches, offering prospects of secluded spaces beyond in an invitingly Mediterranean style. Baelish tutors his employees in the art of pleasing their clients, but only, it seems, verbally. When Ros and her friend invite him to join them, he refuses, for his heart belongs elsewhere, he says. The brothels of Mole's Town, up near the Wall, keep the Brothers of the Night's Watch satisfied; after all they have sworn to take no wife, not to practise complete chastity.

Medieval houses of ill repute often offered bathing facilities; the opportunity to remove one's clothes, climb into a nice warm tub of water with the woman of one's choice and then move from the bath to the bed and back again compounded the pleasures which such places had to offer. Wine, rich food, music and conversation could be had in high-class establishments. Brothels which served the lower classes, such as the Mole's Town establishment, were grubbier, depending on regular trade and a quick turnover. The Winterfell brothel lies somewhere between the two extremes; it's not as stylish as a Baelish house, but the hospitality there seems to suit Tyrion well enough.

Let's now take a close look at the woman who most strongly challenges Westeros's (and medieval Europe's) misogynist stereotypes: Brienne. She's an impressive fighter – whether against Jaime Lannister, or (in the show) the Hound. She is haunted by her failure to prevent the killing of her beloved Renly, though it's hard to see how any man might have fared better against the supernatural shadow-assassin. Brienne has striking counterparts in medieval and early modern romance: Britomart, the virgin female knight of Spenser's *The Faerie Queene* (1590s), and her forerunner, Bradamante, in the Italian epic romances *Orlando Innamorato* (1495) and *Orlando Furioso* (1516). Both women are effective warriors; they range through the romance world taking on all comers. But both are extremely beautiful, and each is in love with a noble knight: Bradamante with the Saracen Ruggiero, whom

8. Bradamante, in an early woodcut

she marries after he converts to Christianity, and Britomart with Artegall, the knight who symbolises Justice in the poem. Artegall (equal to Arthur) is bewitched and imprisoned by an enchantress called Radigund. Only Britomart can rescue him, and she does so, defeating and killing Radigund without compunction. Merlin prophesies that Britomart and her beloved will be the ancestors of a long line of British kings and queens and there's every expectation that this will come to pass, though the poem is unfinished.

No such happy heterosexual and traditional resolution looks likely for Brienne's story. She's strong and not unattractive, but she's also big and threatening. Her intense love for Renly has left little room for other romance in her heart; she establishes respectful and affectionate bonds with Jaime and Pod, but most other men treat her with open or scarcely veiled contempt. The treacherous big-mouth, Ser Shadrich, encountered while Brienne is travelling with a couple of gallant if hopeless hedge knights, addresses her with extreme rudeness: 'You're a fine strapping wench.' Brienne registers the insult, but lets it pass; later Shadrich calls her 'woman', and she reflects, 'Woman was marginally better than wench' (*FC*, 4). 'Wench' is very markedly a term for a lower-class woman in medieval

English; May, in Chaucer's 'Merchant's Tale', becomes indignant when her old and blind husband tries to bribe her to remain faithful to him: 'I am a gentil womman and no wenche,' she protests. Brienne has her moment to avenge Renly when she comes face to face with Stannis in the aftermath of the Battle of Winterfell, a moment which may bring closure to the guilt she has felt for failing him.[8]

In the second half of this chapter we turn to larger social structures embedded within the cultures of the two main continents. We will start with the near-universal obligation of hospitality, then examine the law and its relationship to vengeance and justice. After that comes warfare and its rules, and a man's relationship with his weapons. And finally we'll consider those ultimate weapons, the vectors of mass destruction of the *Game of Thrones* universe: the dragons whom Daenerys has hatched and reared, and whom she loves as a mother.

GUEST-RIGHT

Hospitality is, in real-world societies, a central obligation of human interaction. If someone enters your house, you take responsibility for their welfare. You feed and shelter them, exchange conversation with them, and on their departure send them on their way, very often with parting gifts. And the guests in turn should accept what's offered, conform to the customs of the house, go on their way in due time and with grateful thanks. Yet hospitality is rarely so simple, whether in the Known World or in medieval narratives. The Latin word *hospes* (a host or a guest) is closely related to *hostis* (an army); host, guest and hospitality, but also hostility, are thus aligned with one another. When guests arrive under your roof they can bring unknown complications, pre-existing enmities, from which a good host will have to defend them, or – as in the visit of Robert and his in-laws to Winterfell – the hosts may discover things about their guests that must not be known to others. The guest is vulnerable; he or she must take on trust the goodwill of the host and hope to be safe. Medieval romance often makes use of the topos of the 'Imperious Host': an uncouth and dangerous man who acts churlishly towards his guests. In one tale, involving the Arthurian knight Sir Gawain, Gawain and his party arrive at a castle, hoping for shelter for the night. Usually those who take lodging with the monstrous giant, the Carl of Carlisle, are lucky to escape with their lives. However, Gawain disarms the Carl with his courtesy, while his two companions, Bishop Baldwin and the king's foster-brother Sir Kay, act rudely and give offence. Gawain's perfect obedience enables him to disenchant the Carl, who is really a bewitched knight, and he is rewarded by marriage to the Carl's beautiful daughter. Those who failed the obedience test, the Carl reveals, have been executed by him, but now he is restored to knightliness and humanity he will build a chantry chapel in which to pray for the souls of those he has slain.[9]

In Westeros and Essos both, the norms of hospitality are breached in dramatic fashion by hosts and guests. In Qarth, Daenerys's dragons are stolen and members of her *khalasar* murdered. At Winterfell, Catelyn is all the more outraged when she wrongly believes that Tyrion was responsible for sending an assassin to kill Bran because he had entered her home as a guest. Her public accusation that Tyrion had conspired to kill Bran is effective in rallying the various bannermen who owe fealty to the Tullys when she and Ser Rodrik accidentally come across Tyrion at the inn on the kingsroad. Worse still – infamous, indeed – are the terrible events at Edmure Tully's wedding to Roslin Frey:

> The Red Wedding they're calling it. Walder Frey committed sacrilege that day. He shared bread and salt with the Starks. He offered them guest-right. The gods will have their vengeance […] Frey will burn in the seventh hell for what he did. (4.3)

So comments a Riverlands farmer to Arya and the Hound, speaking of Walder Frey's horrific exaction of vengeance for Robb's failure to keep his oath to marry a Frey girl. Walder's strategic position in the Seven Kingdoms, holding the Twins, the two forts which control the only bridge across the river Trident for hundreds of miles, has given him an unwavering belief in his own importance. When Robb's love for Talisa (in the show – in the books his marriage to Jeyne Westerling plays out rather differently) causes him to break the promise made by Catelyn on her son's behalf, the old man's pride is nettled. Thus Walder plays straight into the hands of the Boltons, who have already been suborned by the Lannisters, despite the fact that their House is sworn to the Starks. Only the leader of the House whose sigil is the grisly Flayed Man would be cruel enough to turn the joyous occasion of a wedding into a massacre: Catelyn, Robb, his pregnant wife Talisa, numerous northern soldiers and even Grey Wind, Robb's direwolf, are slaughtered, and the bodies of the Starks desecrated. Grey Wind's head is cut off and sewn onto Robb's torso; Catelyn's corpse is flung unceremoniously into the river.

It's hard to think of real-life, or even fictional, parallels to the horror of the Red Wedding. In Chaucer's 'Man of Law's Tale', the Sultaness, mother of the Sultan of Syria who has converted to Christianity to marry the lovely Constance, daughter of the Emperor of Rome, is enraged by her son's apostasy. Pretending nevertheless that she will also convert, the Sultaness, 'the cursed crone' as the narrator calls her, arranges a feast for the bridal couple and then conspires with her council that 'the Sowdan and the Cristen everichone / Bene al tohewe and stiken at the bord' (the Sultan and everyone of the Christians / Be slashed to pieces and stabbed at the table). Constance is placed in a rudderless boat and set adrift at sea. The Emperor takes horrible vengeance on the Syrians: his army 'brennen, sleen and brynge to meschance' (burn, slay and bring to misfortune) the Sultaness and her confederates. At the end of the tale, he and his daughter, her new husband and her son are reunited after further misadventures.[10] From a later period, we might also think of the infamous Glencoe Massacre of 1692,

9. *The Black Wedding*, an early twentieth-century illustration

in which a party of soldiers, many of whom were associated with the Campbell clan, accepted hospitality, in the Highland tradition, from the MacDonalds. The next morning the guests murdered 38 of their hosts, beneath the clan-chieftain's roof and more widely in Glencoe. MacDonald homes were burned to the ground, and another 40 clan women and children died of exposure. The Glencoe Massacre was infamous, not just for the number of victims from a single clan, nor for the subterfuge involved, but primarily because the killings fell under the Scots law of 'murder under trust': a particular category of murder deemed more heinous than ordinary murder. The subsequent inquiry had to exonerate King William, who had signed the order for the massacre, and there was little sense that the perpetrators had been brought to justice. The massacre provided potent propaganda for the Jacobite uprisings of 1715 and 1745. Martin has also invoked the Black Dinner of 1440, in which the young sixth Earl of Douglas and his little brother were invited to a feast at Edinburgh Castle by ten-year-old King James II of Scotland. At the end of the dinner, the head of a black bull, symbolising the boys' ancestor, the famous Black Douglas, was thrown onto the table; the two brothers were dragged outside onto Castle Hill, subjected to a mock trial for treason and swiftly beheaded; the ostensible host, the young king, was a cat's paw for the larger political ambitions of Sir William Crichton, the Lord Chancellor of Scotland, who, like Tywin, the Hand of the King, perceived a significant threat to the monarchy and the stability of the kingdom in the Douglases' power.

There's little sense, whether in the show or in the books, that the ancient, cynical and merciless Walder Frey faces either widespread opprobrium or any kind of justice for his betrayal. The Houses of Stark and Tully are in complete disarray and the Lannisters remain in the ascendant. However much scandal Walder's treachery has caused, no executive power can bring home the heinousness of his behaviour to him. Yet even the characters with whom the narrative encourages us to side are tempted to break the laws of guest-right. Jon Snow gets himself admitted to Mance Rayder's tent, ostensibly to parley, but with a poorly worked-out covert plan to kill the King-beyond-the-Wall, even at the cost of his own life – a kind of suicide attack. Jon is not quite guileful enough to disguise his intentions from Mance; his glance lingers on a knife as they are eating and Mance realises what's in Jon's mind. Taxed with the immorality of breaking the hospitality laws, Jon comes to his senses, but before he can decide how to get out of the impasse, Stannis's army appears. Jon's close call with committing as serious a breach of guest-right as that which killed his family is part of his ethical training. From his early days on the Wall, too quick to take offence, too ready to consider breaking his oath, yet brave, ingenious and finally states-manlike in his treatment of the wildlings, Jon's learning is one of the series' great themes.

JUSTICE AND VENGEANCE

Law codes tend to be among the earliest texts created when a society gains the technology of writing. Even before literacy arrived in pre-Christian Iceland, laws were codified, and a third of them were recited by the Lawspeaker every year at the Assembly (the Althing), so that they might be remembered, discussed and, if need be, modified. Medieval Iceland was famously known in the rest of Europe as the land without a king; who, then, European lords asked themselves, could effect justice? The Icelanders conducted lawsuits, outlawed criminals, arranged for compensation negotiations and the payment of fines for criminal or civil violations of law at the annual Assembly. It's clear, though, both from the sagas and from contemporary history, that it was hard to press one's rights against one's own chieftain, or if one could not put together an alliance of powerful supporters. Elsewhere in Europe, the law was the king's law, and his officials would enforce it on the ground. Important cases might be heard in the king's presence, witnesses called and judgement given, to be enforced by the king's authority. So in King's Landing, the king, or his Hand, hears cases and receives deputations from aggrieved subjects. The accused is allowed to call witnesses, though this avails Tyrion little in his trial for the murder of Joffrey. The odds are clearly stacked against him by his father and his sister, still grieving for her dead son. Although Jaime and Tywin cook up a deal whereby Tyrion could join the Night's Watch, Cersei unleashes Shae as a hostile witness. Tyrion's mistress claims that Sansa had prevailed upon Tyrion to murder Joffrey for her. With Tyrion's consequent tirade against the court and his family, and their ingratitude for his heroic conduct at the Battle of the Blackwater, all chances of mercy vanish.

As in his previous trial in the Eyrie, Tyrion claims the right to trial by combat; his hopes that Bronn, the sellsword who saved him on that occasion, will fight for him again are dashed when Bronn reveals that he has been bought off with a marriage into the nobility: 'I like you [...] I just like myself more,' he deadpans (4.7). Oberyn Martell acts for Tyrion, hoping to achieve vengeance for his sister Elia, raped and murdered by the Mountain, Gregor Clegane, at the culmination of Robert's Rebellion. The Mountain is Cersei's champion in the trial by combat; despite fighting stylishly, and indeed almost winning, Oberyn assumes too soon that he is the victor, and the Mountain, recovering from an apparently debilitating blow, makes short work of him, gouging out his eyes in a memorable scene.

Trial by combat was a genuine medieval custom, one which probably originated in Germanic areas. The two parties in dispute, or their representatives, fought in single combat; the winner of the duel was regarded as having won his case. The obvious flaws in the procedure meant that the practice fell out of favour, in England in the fifteenth century and in France in the mid-fourteenth century.

Judicial duels were a staple of romance narratives; in the late twelfth-century French romance *Yvain*, or *The Knight of the Lion*, Sir Yvain and Sir Gawain fight to a draw to establish the rights of an elder and a younger sister in a case involving their inheritance from their father. The elder sister claims the whole estate under the new laws of primogeniture, just taking hold in France at that point; the younger sister is left without even provision for a dowry. The king finally arbitrates a fairer division of property.[11] In Malory's *Morte D'Arthur* Sir Lancelot fights two judicial combats on behalf of Queen Guinevere. On the first occasion she has been falsely accused of poisoning a dinner guest; despite only arriving at the

10. Trial by combat, in a German manuscript

last moment for the fight, Lancelot overcomes the accuser and the poisoner's true identity is revealed. On the second occasion, Guinevere is accused of having committed adultery with one or more of ten injured knights who are recovering from their wounds in her antechamber. Her accuser, Sir Meleagant, has found blood all over the queen's bedding and leaps to the obvious conclusion. But the blood has in fact come from Lancelot's lacerated hands; he broke the bars at the queen's window to be with his beloved. Lancelot very deliberately manoeuvres Meleagant into formulating his accusation with specific regard to the ten wounded knights, and he easily defeats Meleagant in combat on this technicality.[12]

Small wonder, then, that when Arthur's nephews bring a formal accusation of adultery before the king, Arthur decides against allowing a public accusation of the couple, for Lancelot will fight in the queen's defence and inevitably win. Instead, the queen and her knight are caught in a compromising position; Guinevere is seized and condemned to death at the stake, a fate from which Lancelot rescues her in defiance of the king and his laws. Meleagant had declared to Lancelot that 'God will have a stroke in every battle', and indeed, in Arthurian romance, the ethical validity of trial by combat depends on knights only taking up arms to defend the truth. Once Lancelot's chivalric morality has become corrupted, as in his duel with Meleagant, Arthur's justice system is shown to be irredeemably compromised, a critique that reflects poorly on his kingship.

So too in the two trials involving Tyrion. The Knights of the Vale are desperate to please their widowed lady and, like Penelope's suitors in *The Odyssey*, hopeful of replacing Jon Arryn. 'Waiting and simpering on the stairs like buzzards, waiting to get their claws into me', as the ungrateful Lysa puts it (5.5), they are eager enough to fight on her behalf against the dwarf. Bronn makes fairly short work of his opponent by ducking and diving, feinting and retreating. As long as Cersei can command the Mountain as her champion, no right can prevail against her obsessive belief about the death of her son. In this society, trial by combat has less to do with God (or the Seven) operating to make sure that justice prevails in human affairs. The champion is normally expected to spend the night before the fight in religious vigil, but it's hard to imagine the Mountain invoking the Seven's protection, and such niceties are dispensed with in Bronn's fight in the Eyrie. Rather, trial by combat calls for a man to possess physical strength, fighting skill and courage – or to be able to wield social capital: to have the social standing, the gold or the charisma to command the greatest champion. As queen mother, Cersei has two out of three; Tyrion has only his charm, which isn't sufficient. Fortunately for him – at least in the immediate situation – the old blood-feud which prevails between Oberyn, the Mountain and the other members of his family provides him with a champion.

The call for vengeance when a family member is killed is endemic in honour societies like Westeros, a culture which remembers, through stories passed down through generations. They were kept alive in ballads like 'The Rains of Castamere', that anthem of Lannister ascendancy, frequently invoked in the books and so memorably sung as a signal to start the massacre of the Red Wedding. Honour requires that revenge be sought for such losses, the more so when the original victims were killed in some dishonourable way. Vengeance is pursued by the Houses that suffered collateral damage in the final phases of Robert's Rebellion, notably among them the Martells. Arya too holds in mind a long list of those against whom she will take revenge sooner or later; her nightly recital points to the importance of list-making and memorisation in a largely oral culture. The names on Arya's list vary: Joffrey, Cersei and Ilyn Payne have first billing, while in the books Arya commemorates her traumatic experiences at Harrenhal by naming the chief torturers commanded by the Mountain: the Tickler, Polliver (who stole Needle from her) and Raff the Sweetling, among a good many others. Polliver was the first of these to be killed by Arya herself; in the books she kills the Tickler in the same fight.

Vengeance is primarily foregrounded in the strand of the story that links the deaths of Elia and Oberyn Martell; the Dornish – particularly of course, the Sand Snakes – are obsessed with revenge against the Lannisters and the Crown, and it's not clear what game Doran Martell is playing in sending Trystane (in the books Nymeria Sand) to take up the Dornish seat on the Small Council. One act of revenge shapes the story arc of the whole cycle: the vengeance taken by Robert Baratheon for the abduction of Lyanna Stark by Rhaegar Targaryen. This move catalysed resistance to Targaryen rule and precipitated the rising known as Robert's Rebellion. Robert believed his fiancée to have been stolen away and raped by the married Targaryen prince, and he recalls with pride the day when he killed Rhaegar at the Battle of the Trident: 'In my dreams, I kill him every night. A thousand deaths will still be less than he deserves' (*GT*, 4). Like Helen of Troy, Lyanna may have been more complicit in the abduction than her future husband and male kinfolk were led to believe; that Lyanna and Rhaegar spend the war in the Tower of Joy in the Red Mountains of Dorne recalls Sir Lancelot's Castle, Joyous Garde, where he takes Queen Guinevere after he has rescued her from the stake. While the name could be ironic, it also suggests that Rhaegar and Lyanna genuinely loved one another – a possibility endorsed by Barristan Selmy's account of Rhaegar (5.4). By the time Ned comes to rescue Lyanna, after Rhaegar's death at Robert's hands, his sister is dying. The promise that she extracts from Ned haunts him to his dying day. Although Rhaegar, Lyanna, her brother Ned and Robert the avenger are all dead by the end of the first book and first season, the final implications of Robert's vengeance are not yet fully played out. Lyanna's kidnap fuelled the rebellion – though as the madness of Aerys became increasingly apparent, his overthrow might only have been a matter of time. Yet the change of dynasty, with Robert's ascent to the throne and his fateful alliance with the Lannisters, fundamentally shaped the Seven Kingdoms in which the story unfolds; the secret of what passed between Ned and Lyanna in her final moments may be revealed at the series' end.

Vengeance begets vengeance, as Ellaria Sand (in contradistinction to her role as chief architect of revenge in the show) points out to the older Sand Snakes after their father's death:

Oberyn wanted vengeance for Elia. Now the three of you want vengeance for him […] If you should die, must El and Obella [her daughters] seek vengeance for you? Is that how it goes, round and round forever? I ask again, *where does it end*?' (*DD*, 38)

In early Western European societies, blood-feud was rife. Even where Roman law prevailed, or where Christianity took hold, it was hard to persuade men to resort to law instead of killing to avenge their losses. Many of the most famous Icelandic sagas have blood-feuds, reciprocal killings, associated legal cases and the eventual settlement (often when most of the original participants in the feud are dead) at their centre. *Njáls saga*, probably composed in the thirteenth century, unpacks an almost forensic account of how and why the patriarch Njal, his wife, sons and grandson came to be burned alive in their farmstead, despite the fact that Njal had never raised a sword against anyone. The causes of the feud go back more than 50 years, and the resolution of the vengeance taken for Njal and the other victims by Njal's son-in-law Kari takes a good few years to achieve. Yet at the end of the saga, when the score-settling and savagery has played itself out, Kari marries Hildigunn, the niece of the Burners' ringleader and the woman who arguably set the final act in motion when she charged her uncle with avenging the death of her husband.[13] For the Icelanders who heard or read the saga, the minutiae of who kills whom, how justifiable that killing was, what the requisite compensation might be and whether the feud could end or must claim further victims, gave an intense and dispassionate insight into the lives of their ancestors. And for the modern reader, the drama and tragedy of the sagas, whether *Njáls saga* or other classic Norse sagas such as *Laxdœla saga*, *Gísla saga* or *Grettis saga* (for they all have blood-feud at their heart), remains profoundly moving and deeply shocking.

Feud and vengeance are central to the greatest medieval tales, for such stories epitomise the tensions between individual honour, family loyalty, the place of a kin-group in their social hierarchy, and the support they can command. Such stories have a moral core, too; they probe into the ethics of aggression. Whom is it licit to kill? Who makes an honourable target for vengeance? Revenge is not always the province of men (as we'll see in Chapter Three). In the first movement of *Njáls saga* the hero Gunnar, facing impossible odds, is fighting off the men attacking his home. Nevertheless, he is prevailing – until his bowstring is sliced through. Turning to his wife, he asks for two locks of her hair to restring the bow. 'Is anything important to you at stake?' she asks, indifferently. 'My life,' answers Gunnar. 'Then,' says Hallgerd, 'I shall remind you of the slap you gave me, and I don't care how long you defend yourself.' And though Gunnar fights bravely, he cannot finally overcome the difference in numbers, nor his wife's malice.

Cersei presses hard when it comes to vengeance for the so-called Purple Wedding, even if she pursues the wrong parties in Tyrion and the missing Sansa. The Lannisters seem far from suspecting Olenna Tyrell's role or Littlefinger's plotting, but given the depletion of Lannister resources and the shortages which mean that King's Landing is dependent on supplies from Tyrell lands, it's probably expedient for Tywin not to ask *cui bono?* – who stands to benefit most from Joffrey's death? For the answer is surely Margaery. Vengeance for the Red Wedding looks to be a long time coming. Arya is on the other side of the Narrow Sea, Bran is pursuing his own mystical adventures and Edmure Tully, the only competent male adult of House Tully, is Walder Frey's hostage – and now bound to him by the obligations of a son-in-law. It's not unknown for a son-in-law to attack his father-in-law: the story of Ingeld, whose marriage with King Hrothgar's daughter was intended to create peace, is alluded to in *Beowulf*. Although the bride may be fair, as

Beowulf himself drily foretells, the ancient rivalries between Ingeld's tribe and the Danes will break out anew, war will be declared and the great hall of Heorot will be burned to the ground.[14] Vengeance is a dish best served cold, it's sometimes said; whether punishment or reconciliation awaits those behind the Red Wedding massacre is hard to predict.

WAR AND WEAPONS

Ever since Ned Stark's execution, war has raged in one part or another of the Seven Kingdoms. There have been some pitched battles: the Stark–Lannister confrontations which resulted in the capture of Jaime, and of course the great naval battle of the Blackwater. Mostly, however, war has been pursued by harrying. Although women and children are not normally regarded as combatants, women are often raped and murdered, children slaughtered and prisoners tortured in an endless cycle of cruelty. In the early twelfth century, when the English throne was contested by Stephen and his cousin Matilda, it truly seemed, in the words of a contemporary chronicler describing the 'nineteen long winters' of the Anarchy, as if 'God and his angels slept'. So too in Westeros: scorched-earth tactics, burning farms, killing cattle, looting supplies, rape, murder and pillage are endemic to the campaigns. Nobles are relatively unaffected by battle, unless, like Jaime, they actively command troops in the field and are captured. Medieval convention would have deplored the Starks' treatment of Jaime; a noble prisoner was normally kept in reasonably comfortable conditions while ransom was negotiated, not in an open-air draughty cage. More usually, the aristocracy would shut themselves inside their castles and wait out the warfare at the gates. 'A smart commander doesn't abandon defensive advantage,' Roose admonishes Ramsay when he plans a sortie against Stannis's army, encamped close to Winterfell (5.8). But although the Norman castle-building programme in England and Wales worked very well for the new aristocracy after 1066, in Westeros the tactic of withdrawing behind castle walls risks the alienation of the common folk who bear the brunt of the invaders' violence, as Robert points out to his wife.

In these warrior cultures, whether in the north, the Southlands or across the sea in Essos, a man's relationship to his weapon is crucial. While the Dothraki wield their *arakh*s ('for a man on horseback a curved blade is a good thing, easier to handle,' as Jorah explains (1.3)), in Westeros the primary weapon is a sword. The very best are forged of Valyrian steel, a rare commodity of particularly good quality: it holds its edge like no other metal, and has a distinctive rippled pattern. The secret of forging new Valyrian steel, using dragon-fire, died in the Doom of Valyria, but the metal that survived can be reforged without losing its virtue: 'Only one metal could be beaten so thin and still have strength enough to fight with, and there was no mistaking those ripples, the mark of steel that has been folded back on itself many thousands of times' (*SS*, 32). So too, in early Anglo-Saxon England (fifth to sixth century CE), the old swords brought over from the continental homelands were regarded as superior. It took time for the smiths, transplanted into a new landscape, to discover supplies of iron ore and to locate the charcoal needed to raise the forge temperature high enough to make strong, flexible steel, neither too brittle nor too pliant. Old English poetry often mentions the serpentine design in the best-quality swords; this was produced by pattern-welding, twisting and fusing individual rods of steel together, forging and reforging them for suppleness and strength, exactly the technique which perished with the smiths of Valyria.

In *Beowulf*, the swords which are particularly valued are the old ones; they carry with them the *mana*, the aura of those who have been killed by them in past battles; they are redolent of victories won. When an enemy is defeated, the victor takes his sword and makes his defeat part of the weapon's history. Beowulf borrows the

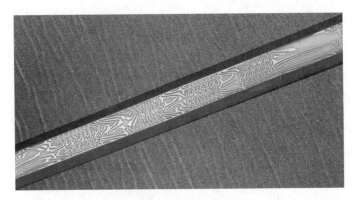

11. A modern Viking-style pattern-welded
sword, made by Jesus Hernandez

famous sword Hrunting for his battle against Grendel's Mother, although no metal can pierce her hide except for her own ancestral sword, displayed on the walls of her den. For the first time in its history, the poet observes, Hrunting fails. Beowulf's own royal sword Nægling proves unable to prevail against the dragon that is his nemesis, and it shatters on the monster's skull.[15]

Medieval swords often have names, signifying a relationship which is closer to that of human and animal than human and inanimate object. Arya may have had to drive her beloved direwolf Nymeria away, but she holds on to Needle as long as she can, and her recovery of it in killing Polliver signifies a major turning point in her fortunes. Ned's great sword Ice, also of Valyrian steel, marks his first and last moments in the story. We see him draw it from its wolfskin scabbard to execute Will for his desertion from the Night's Watch, and Ilyn Payne uses it to behead its owner at Joffrey's command. So mighty is Ice that Tywin has it reforged into two new swords by a smith from Volantis, one of the three smiths who still know how to work Valyrian steel. The first sword, characteristically named 'Widow's Wail' by its new owner, is presented to Joffrey as a wedding gift. The second is given to Jaime, who in turn gives it to Brienne to take with her in her search for Sansa. Brienne names the blade 'Oathkeeper' in honour of the oath she swore to Catelyn. And Longclaw, the Valyrian sword of House Mormont, given by Lord Jeor, Commander of the Night's Watch, to his son Jorah, is recovered by him when Jorah flees Westeros. Longclaw is equipped with a new pommel, ornamented with the direwolf of House Stark to replace the bear of the Mormonts, and presented to Jon Snow. This is a poignant moment for both giver and receiver; Jeor has abandoned hope of seeing his son again, for Jorah's dishonour – selling poachers into slavery – cannot easily be purged. In giving the sword to Jon Snow, Jeor in effect signals that the young man should be his successor, just as Sam had foretold, and he becomes a kind of second father to him. Swords are charged with an emotional power which goes far beyond their function in war.

DRAGONS

Effective as Valyrian steel may be – Catelyn's hands were cut to the bone when she seized the blade of the assassin sent to murder Bran – it isn't clear whether it can withstand dragon-fire without melting. For dragons, long thought to be extinct, are the ultimate strategic weapon of the Known World. Dragons gradually diminished in size as they slid towards extinction: the great dragons which brought the Targaryens from Valyria declined into pathetic creatures scarcely the size of a horse. The dragon eggs given to Daenerys as a wedding present by Illyrio Mopatis at first seem to be mere curios, but Daenerys is powerfully drawn to them; while Viserys sees them simply as currency to buy ships and men, his sister is experimenting with heating them. Fire alone isn't enough, though, to hatch a dragon egg; the circumstances in which Daenerys succeeds in bringing her 'children' into the world are dark and terrifying. Intense fire, produced by Drogo's funeral pyre, and blood-magic – the death of Mirri Maz Duur, burned alive on the pyre – combine with Daenerys's own steely determination to bring dragons back into the world and back under Targaryen control.

The advantages of dragons are very clear: they give those who control them the capacity to wage aerial warfare and to deploy a firepower that's analogous to a nuclear device. What Aegon's dragons did to Harrenhal, destroying the largest castle in the Seven Kingdoms and roasting its inhabitants in the Kingspyre Tower, is powerfully visible, both in the scenes set there and in the collective memory of the Westerosi. To ancient and blind Maester Aemon, born Targaryen, dragons appear in his dreams: 'I see their shadows on the snow, hear the crack of leathern wings, feel their hot breath. My brothers dreamed of dragons too, and the dreams killed them, every one' (*FC*, 26). But dragons are hard to train, and harder still to rear. Rhaegal, Viserion and Drogon, whose names speak of the men who have meant most to Daenerys, don't at first thrive, for they need to discover their own fire-breathing capacities in order to cook their own meat. And as they grow, they require ever-larger prey: sheep, cattle and – unfortunately, for they do not discriminate – children. Daenerys learns how to control them up to a point, speaking to them in High Valyrian (*Dracarys!* – the command to throw flame – points to the roots of the words for the creature in Western European languages as derived from Latin *draco*). Their capacity to catch fish, diving underwater, throwing their catch up in the air and grilling it is impressive, for water tends to extinguish a firedrake's flames. Daenerys eventually has to face up to the damage they cause if allowed to fly freely. Drogon escapes the indignity of confinement in the underground dragon-den of Meereen, but his unhappy brothers are imprisoned there after Daenerys becomes aware that their depredations have caused children's deaths. In the books, the sense that Daenerys has lost control of her dragons has important political consequences: Brown Ben Plumm, the captain of the Second Sons mercenaries, defects to Yunkai, further weakening her position within Meereen.

When first hatched, the dragons were charming little creatures, letting out faint squawks and clinging loyally to the 'Mother of Dragons': 'Have you ever heard baby dragons singing? It's hard to

12. A dragon from a medieval bestiary

be a cynic after that,' Jorah tells Tyrion (5.6). In Germanic tradition and British folklore it's invariably the case that the cute little serpent grows into a dangerous nuisance. In the *Saga of Ragnar Hairy-Breeches*, young princess Thora is given just such a little snake by her father. If the beast is to grow and thrive, a new gold coin must be placed under it every day. By the time Thora is of an age to marry, her dragon is sitting on a considerable hoard, and, moreover, eating a whole ox every day. It seems fond enough of her, for it encircles her bower, but it's clear to her father, and perhaps to Thora herself, that it must be disposed of. Thora's hand in marriage is advertised as a reward for whoever can kill the dragon, and the bold Viking Ragnar, son of the Danish king, comes to try his luck. This dragon spouts poison rather than flames, so Ragnar has some special trousers made for him that are coated in pitch, and a spear with a detachable head. Wearing his pitch-covered clothes, he rolls in sand before he advances on the dragon, stabbing it twice with his spear. As the creature dies, a huge tidal wave of poisonous blood strikes the retreating Ragnar between the shoulders, but his cleverly made clothes protect him. He returns to claim the credit for the dragon-killing, for he retains the shaft which fits the spearhead embedded in the dragon's body, and claims his princess.[16]

Other Germanic dragons prove to be fond of gold; the dragon in *Beowulf* knows (like Tolkien's Smaug) to the last item how much treasure he has in his hoard, and when a goblet is stolen the dragon flies out by night and wreaks fiery revenge, burning down Beowulf's hall and laying waste his stronghold. This creature (the origin of Smaug) is a firedrake like the dragons of Valyria; he also has poisonous breath, and it takes two mighty heroes, Beowulf and his young companion Wiglaf, to overcome him. Tolkien's and Beowulf's dragons have a vulnerable spot which the hero must identify, but Known World dragons are more strongly and comprehensively armoured, as Tyrion well knows:

> *Dragons are not so easy to kill as that. Tickle him with these* [crossbow bolts] *and you'll only make him angry.* The eyes were where a dragon was most vulnerable. The eyes, and the brain behind them. Not the underbelly, as certain old tales would have it. (*DD*, 57)

Dragons are hard to raise, then, and I suspect that the dragons will turn out to be difficult to deploy as aerial transport and as weapons of war. Men don't normally ride on dragons' backs in medieval tradition, but there's an intriguing reference to the practice in a thirteenth-century Norwegian text known as *Konungs skuggsjá* (The King's Mirror). In this, a father and son are discussing various marvels. The father is making the argument that marvellousness is relative: that in Norway men habitually use skis to get about, but this would seem marvellous to people from other lands. The son adds that he has heard that in India men ride on dragons. The father is doubtful: dragons are nasty venomous beasts, he demurs, though he concedes that it is possible to tame wild animals under certain circumstances.[17] The Indian dragon-riders are mentioned in one of the versions of the famous twelfth-century *Letter of Prester*

John. This was a document which purported to have been sent by the legendary Christian king Prester John, who was thought to live in India. In the letter (in reality a monkish forgery), Prester John writes that he has heard of the plight of the Christian Crusaders fighting against Islamic forces in the Near East and offers to come to their aid. 'Dragons are fire made flesh. And fire is power,' says Quaithe the shadowbinder (2.5). Our last glimpse of Daenerys with Drogon reveals her to be far away from Meereen, in the midst of the great grassland, the Dothraki Sea. She has learned to ride her baby, but how she will make use of the dragons whose blood runs also in her own veins is one of the challenges which has yet to be resolved.

This chapter has, perforce, dwelt mostly on the customs, history and traditions of Westeros, for it's that continent which is at the centre of the books: the Iron Throne of Westeros is the stake in the great game in which, as Cersei says, 'you win or you die'. Westeros is more densely imagined than Essos, as we'll see, depicted very much in terms drawn from medieval European society, and the 'Point of View' characters whose experiences focalise the narrative are immersed in its culture. For the Westerosi, the cities and people of Essos are strange, exotic, even barbaric; their languages are obscure, their customs incomprehensible. The regions of Westeros, the north and the south, are much more knowable, in some respects almost familiar to us. Although the south initially gives the appearance of a secure confederation of kingdoms, it is riven with rivalries, unseen threats, plots and dangers: these lie in human hearts and minds, rather than externalised in the 'snarks and grumkins', in Tyrion's phrase, that live beyond the Wall. And the north, always uneasily trying to hold in balance the polity south of the Wall and the strange beings north of it, is like its Warden: stark, unforgiving, masculine and wild. And it's there, at the mighty castle of Winterfell, that our journey through the Lands of Ice and Fire will begin.

13. *Jon Snow and Ghost*

CHAPTER 2

THE NORTH

*Tyrion: 'I don't believe that giants and ghouls and White
Walkers are lurking beyond the Wall.' Benjen: 'You've never
been north of the Wall, so don't tell me what's out there.' (1.3)*

WINTERFELL

We start our epic journey through the north of Westeros,
but not at the Wall, where the series starts with a small
troop of Rangers riding out of Castle Black. Rather
we begin at Winterfell, home and power centre of the Starks, the
Wardens of the North. It's a busy, thriving castle community when
we first see it, with strong grey ivy-clad stone walls, a few ruined
towers in the outer curtain wall and a huge communal hall where
the household assembles for feasts and to take counsel. Within the
walls are the blacksmith's forge, a practice space for sword-fighting
and archery. At its gates there's apparently a brothel, in which we first
meet Tyrion, drinking ale and taking his pleasure with red-haired
Ros. Beyond the walls lies the Godswood, with its strange silver-
white trunks and blood-red leaves, and the dark pool which reflects
the thoughts of those who come to commune with the gods there,
'an island of peace in the sea of chaos that Winterfell had become'
(*GT*, 53). Elsewhere in the castle demesne there are hot springs
which heat Winterfell's glasshouses; these assure the food supplies
when winter comes to the north. Winterfell is enormous – though

not as big as Harrenhal – and its fortifications suggest to those who dwell there that it's impregnable: its double range of walls with a moat lying between them should repel all attackers. That Theon manages to take control of it with a small band of Ironborn is only possible because he has intimate knowledge of the castle and because its garrison is elsewhere, dealing with the feint attack at Torrhen's Square. Winterfell's architecture is reminiscent of the great Norman concentric castles built by Edward I, most notably in Wales: Caernarfon, Beaumaris, Conwy and Harlech. It's very different from the Red Keep of King's Landing, in the midst of the city. A square-keep castle like the Tower of London, with Maegor's Holdfast at its centre, the Red Keep contains numerous halls, towers (such as the Tower of the Hand and the White Sword Tower, headquarters of the Kingsguard), dungeons, secret passageways, a godswood and a sept.

The social organisation of the north is markedly different from the southern customs of King's Landing. The north keeps to older ways, not just as far as religion is concerned (of which more below), but in Lord Eddard Stark's rule over his people. Ned is a lord, not

14. Caernarfon Castle, Gwynedd, North Wales

a king, and his dominion over his castle, household and lands is much closer to that of an Anglo-Saxon earl than the later medieval model of kingship which prevails in King's Landing. Ned's closest companions live in the castle with him, but he can also call upon his bannermen, a loose confederation of lords who owe their allegiance to him and who will come when summoned to battle. Ned has Maester Luwin (more on the Order of Maesters in Chapter Three) at his side to offer advice, but there's no bureaucracy, no civil service to run the territory for him. Although, as Ser Rodrik Cassel, the Master-at-Arms, notes to Catelyn when he brings news of Will (Gared in the books), the deserter from the Night's Watch, 'law is law, my lady', it's a different kind of law that prevails up here. Ned tells Bran, 'The man who passes the sentence should swing the sword', and he carries out Will's execution himself (1.1). There's no headsman, and apparently no legal apparatus; the summary execution is simply carried out in the king's name.

The north is a place for warriors, not knights: when Jaime suggests, courteously but pointedly, that there may well be a tournament to celebrate the appointment of the new Hand of the King, Ned brusquely rejects the invitation to take part. It may well be true, as Ned explains, that it's not good strategy to let one's enemies see one's fighting technique in advance of battle for real, but it's also the case that the men of the north have little time for the rituals of chivalry. The grace and showiness of Ser Loras, the Knight of the Flowers, dazzles Sansa when she witnesses her first tournament as Prince Joffrey's betrothed, but she shrinks from the needless bloodshed – and her father doesn't even bother to attend. Ser Rodrik is unusual in holding the title of knight, but there's advantage in having a fighter who knows the ways of chivalry as well as the techniques of hand-to-hand fighting as your Master-at-Arms, the sergeant who trains the young men to become warriors.

Northern fighters use the older style of interlinked chain mail, a flexible and comfortable form of armour, rather than the heavy and limiting plate armour of the southern knights, or they may wear

leather breastplates. Ned wields the most famous great-sword in
Westeros: Ice. Made of Valyrian steel, the sword is so large that it can
only be swung using both hands, and thus precludes using a shield
for defence. Ice, then, is ceremonial rather than a battle sword, used
when no resistance is expected or offered. Anglo-Saxon swords were
considerably smaller than the rather impractical weapon associated
with Ned; often pattern-welded (as discussed in Chapter One), they
were the most important and symbolic attribute of Anglo-Saxon
noblemen. Around 37–40 inches in length, the swords were used
for cutting and slashing – much as we see in Ned's fight with Jaime.
They did not lend themselves to the nimbler thrust-and-parry rapier
work that Arya learns from Syrio Forel. Her slender Braavosi-style
rapier, Needle, as Jon Snow remarks, won't take a man's head off,
but as long as Arya sticks her opponents with the pointy end, it
makes an effective enough weapon.

DIREWOLVES

*There's not been a direwolf sighted south of
the Wall in two hundred years. (GT, 1)*

The sigil of House Stark is a grey direwolf on a white ground; as
Theon notes, they normally prowl north of the Wall. When the Stark
boys find a dead female direwolf and her living pups on the way
back from Will's execution, the adults are uneasy. The dead animal
seems to be a portent – but of what? That winter is coming? That
House Stark faces extinction? And how should we interpret the
antler, the weapon of the stag, sigil of House Baratheon, embedded
in its throat? By the end of Season One and *A Game of Thrones*, it's
clear that the direwolf did indeed foreshadow disaster.

The dire wolf (in two words) was in fact an extinct prehistoric
wolf, a creature from the Pleistocene era, the *canis dirus*, which once
roamed the plains of North Dakota. These beasts were considerably

larger than the present-day wolf, but they didn't reach the extraordinary size of the Westerosi direwolf. The wolf, dire or not, is an enduring symbol of terror in the Western European imagination. The wolf howl in the dark forest, the noiseless padding of the creature around the winter homestead, even the big, bad wolf of fairy tale all speak to an ancient fear of what awaits us out in the wilderness. The wolf has particularly terrifying associations in Norse mythology, for cosmic wolves race across the sky in eternal pursuit of the sun and moon. And one day – the day of Ragnarök, the end of the world – they will swallow up their prey. The monstrous, mighty wolf Fenrir was bound with a magic fetter by the Norse gods until Ragnarök.[1] His huge jaws are propped open with a sword so that he cannot bite, and from his maw runs a river of slaver and spittle. Yet the direwolves, those creatures of fear, whose very name encodes foreboding, are the devoted companion creatures of the young Starks and of Jon Snow. Their attrition rate is fairly high: Robb's beast, Grey Wind, dies with him; Sansa's Lady is unjustly executed in Nymeria's stead, but Bran's Summer, Rickon's Shaggydog and Jon's Ghost are still with us. And Nymeria herself, Arya's direwolf, who was driven away in order to save her life, is still at large, leading a pack in the Riverrun region. Arya maintains a subconscious connection with her. Even in far-off Braavos, Arya has wolf-dreams, and she can warg into Nymeria's body; it's thus that she discovers Catelyn's body floating in the Trident and drags it out (*SS*, 65).

The concept of warging (as the show calls it), or skin-changing (as in the books), is inherently related to the supernatural bond between human and wolf. The word itself comes, via J. R. R. Tolkien, from the Old Norse term *vargr* – meaning both wolf and criminal – and is related to the Old English word *wearh*, 'outlaw', one which still retains an association with the wolf. Tolkien's wargs were monstrous wolves, ridden by orcs, a concept Tolkien took from Norse tradition, for in Norse poetry the wolf can be metaphorically described as 'the trollwoman's steed'. Wolves were regarded as extremely antagonistic to people, living beyond human communities in social groups and preying on their flocks and indeed, in the aftermath of battle, on the bodies of the dead. In both Norse and Old English, wolves belong (like ravens and eagles) to the Beasts of Battle, animals who know, presciently, when carnage is in the offing. Licking their chops in anticipation, wolves head to the slaughter in order to feast. An effective and courageous war leader is characterised in Norse as 'one who gives the wolf breakfast', one who provides plentiful corpses for the creatures to devour.

Outlawry was an effective punishment for early medieval societies; the guilty man was sent away from human habitation on penalty of being killed on sight if his enemies saw him. Less drastic than execution or maiming, outlawry allowed a man leisure to think about his crimes and, it was hoped, he might eventually be readmitted to society, having seen the error of his former ways. Outlawry was dangerous and uncomfortable, especially in Iceland, where outlaws were banished to the desolate centre of the island or to the deserted islands along its shores. Finding food was hard; stealing the local farmers' sheep was one way of surviving, though this inevitably led to friction with the settled population. Although there were no actual wolves in Iceland, outlaws were regarded as metaphorical wolves, predators on the sheep of law-abiding folk, and it's not hard to see how the connection between wolves and wicked men came about in both languages. Old English outlaws would typically take to the fens and marshes where, like the crannogmen of the Neck, they could hide out from those who wished to pursue them.

Norse belief also included ideas about shape-shifting and animal transformation. As with the Starks, the capacity to take on wolfish identity ran in the family; the grandfather of the Icelandic poet and fighter Egil Skalla-Grimsson was called Kveldulf (Evening-Wolf). Kveldulf didn't adopt wolf form, according to the saga about his grandson; he simply grew more bad-tempered and unsociable as the day wore on. Kveldulf's son Grim could at times be possessed by a wolfish rage; in one such attack he almost kills his own son.[2] In other sagas, men's spirits appear in dreams in wolf form, or in other animal shapes, and in the thirteenth-century *Saga of the Volsungs*, the heroes Sigmund and his son Sinfjotli, outlaws living in the forest, come across a hut where two men are sleeping and wolfskins are hanging on the walls. The father and son put on the skins and become wolves, werewolves in effect, slaying animals and men. Finally they fight with one another in wolf form, until Sigmund kills Sinfjotli by biting through his throat. Fortunately a pair of weasels, who also fight one another to the death, show Sigmund the qualities of a certain leaf that revives the dead, and he brings his son back to life. The skins can only be taken off on certain days each month, and so the two wolves wait out the remaining time, then climb out of the skins and burn them so that they cannot bring harm to anyone else.[3]

Sigmund and Sinfjotli become wolves in effect once they put on the wolfskins. They understand one another's wolf-howl speech, and they retain some part of their human consciousness. At the same time they give free rein to lupine instincts in loping through the forest and killing men. Since they are hiding out in their enemy's forest, killing his men may be as gratifying to human as to wolf; Sigmund is certainly struck by a very human grief and remorse when he has slain his son. In other medieval werewolf stories, from Brittany and England for example, the werewolf can change back into human form if he can find his human clothes. While in a wolf's form, he thinks and acts like a wolf; when human he regards his dual nature as a curse. In these tales, the werewolf's wife is horrified to learn his secret; she steals his clothes, condemning him to remain in wolf form. By acting unwolfishly, the unhappy animal manages to persuade the king to bring him to the court as a kind of pet. There he behaves himself well until his wife and her new lover present themselves; then he leaps at her and tears off her nose. Although the court argues that the wolf cannot be trusted, the wise king sees that there's a deeper story. Under torture the wife and lover admit their crime and are suitably punished; the wolf is given clothing and thus reverts to his human identity.[4]

15. A werewolf gargoyle, Moulins Cathedral, France

These wolves clearly retain human essences beneath their shaggy skins, but the fusion of human and animal raises interesting metaphysical questions of consciousness and responsibility. Both books and show reveal Bran's growing control over his shape-shifting. His human body stays exactly where it is at first, in bed in Winterfell, while his consciousness occupies Summer's body, going where his direwolf goes and seeing what it sees. Later he learns to control or direct the body in which he is lodged. At first it's Summer's, but later he takes over Hodor and silences him when he cries out in fear of thunder, threatening to betray the group's location (3.9). Disturbingly and riskily, Bran wargs into Hodor at Craster's Keep, causing him to kill the appalling Locke, Roose Bolton's crony and the man who severed Jaime's hand (4.5). While this action facilitates the party's escape it raises serious ethical questions about identity and moral responsibility: *who* actually killed Locke?

Some wildlings can also skin-change. The capability is restricted to those who, like the Starks, are descended from the First Men. Orell's eagle is good for travelling long distances across the icy wastes and for spying on enemy movements. So too, in Norse myth, the god Odin is able to make a quick getaway from the giant Suttung, from whom he has stolen the mead of poetry, by assuming eagle form. The giant also transforms himself into an eagle and pursues the god; he almost succeeds in catching him (which is why eagles have rather short tail-feathers). The other gods, waiting in Asgard, see Odin's desperate flight from his pursuer and quickly prepare vats to catch the mead. Meanwhile, Odin repels Suttung by squirting some of the mead back at him from his anus, and the giant bird's momentary hesitation is enough for Odin to swerve over the walls while his pursuer abandons the chase. Odin vomits up the mead which he has held in his craw, and it's available to gods and men as poetic inspiration. The mead he ejected behind has landed where anyone may take it, and thus it's fallen to the lot of bad poets everywhere.[5]

Both books and show give quite substantial explanations of wargs and their relation to prophetic knowledge, 'greensight'. In the show it's Jojen Reed who has the task of explaining his unfolding capacities to Bran and to warn him of the dangers of spending too long enjoying the freedom of moving in Summer's body (3.2; 4.2). Jojen himself, one of the crannogmen, has greensight, and he is vital in helping Bran understand his new destiny and in bringing him to the Three-Eyed Raven. In *A Dance with Dragons* (Prologue), Haggon, who raises and trains Varamyr Sixskins, the most impressive of the Free Folk's skin-changers, explains the ethics of skin-changing. There's no eating humans as meat, no mating with wolves when in wolf form, and no occupying human bodies. Varamyr himself, the greatest skin-changer of them all, has little truck with such ethics; he kills Haggon and various other innocents. And when his human body is dead, he lives on in the form of a wolf, One Eye. This provision, called 'Second Life' in the books, preserves Varamyr's life, but he can no longer escape the wolf's shape and his human consciousness will gradually fade away – the danger feared by the Reed siblings for Bran.

Haggon's rules point up the problems of policing the boundary between human and animal; an animal becomes cannibal and commits bestiality when the creature eats its human prey and has sex when inhabited by a skin-changer. An interesting Welsh tale, 'Math, Son of Mathonwy', in the *Mabinogi*, composed probably in the twelfth century, tells the tale of two brothers who are punished for their crimes against their magician uncle, King Math. With his magic staff he transforms them into male and female deer and they head off into the forest together, returning after a year with their offspring. Each year for three years, Math transforms them into a different species: deer, boar and lastly wolves, and swaps over their sexes. The young are given human form and names which reflect their erstwhile animal origins: Hydwn (Little Deer), Hychdwn (Little Pig) and Bleidwn (Little Wolf). Once the brothers are restored to human form, one disappears from the story altogether, while the other brother, Gwydion, recovers his position as his uncle's right-hand man as if nothing had happened. The brothers' crime – conspiring to start a war in order to get the opportunity to rape the king's virgin – is reflected in their sentence; they transgressed against human law and are shamefully punished. Whether the animals know that they are human is unclear; if they retained human consciousness, they might have desisted from mating with one another, but perhaps their animal instincts, like the homing instinct that brings them back to the court each year, are too strong.[6]

RAVENS: DARK WINGS, DARK WORDS

It's in Winterfell too that we first learn how ravens form the communication network of Westeros, flying from maester to maester bearing urgent messages. They carry letters rather than communicating verbally, though of course ravens can, like parrots, be trained to imitate human speech. Some ravens are apparently

intelligent enough to find their way to different castles. The books
tell us how a messenger raven is transported by road back to its
place of origin; the show is less concerned with the practicalities
of raven communication systems. The ravens often bear serious
news: already foreshadowed by Bran and Rickon's dreams, the
wonderfully understated impact of the tidings of Ned's death at
Winterfell is underscored by the arrival of a raven and the silent
appearance of Maester Luwin crossing the castle courtyard, holding a letter. ('Dark wings, dark words', as the proverb has it.) The
ravens have an important strategic function: for news to travel by
messenger the thousand miles from the Wall to King's Landing, let
alone as far south as Dorne, would take months, if the messenger
ever managed to get through the badlands around the Neck. The
raven permits news to travel quickly and confidentially, and thus
speed up reactions to events – like Ned Stark's execution – of
political moment.

16. Odin and his ravens, from an eighteenth-century Icelandic manuscript

In Norse myth Odin has two ravens, Hugin and Munin, whose names correspond to something like 'Thought' and 'Memory'. The two birds fly out over the world every day and return with news; perching on the god's shoulder, they impart their intelligence into his ear. Odin tells us that he fears for them when they are on their travels, lest the birds, which symbolise his own intellectual faculties, do not return.[7] The raven is also a 'beast of battle' in Norse, and can speak; one poem from around 900 shows a raven and a Valkyrie in conversation, praising King Harald Fairhair of Norway for his victory at the Battle of Hafrsfjord.[8] Ravens are said to have been carried on the ships on which Norwegians migrated to Iceland; when they failed to return to ship the sailors knew that land was close ahead. This tradition seems to be borrowed from the story of Noah's Ark; there Noah looses a raven to see if the flood waters have sunk enough, but the bird is distracted by all the carrion and fails to return. A dove proves more reliable. There's surely a joke, then, in the claim that King Baelor – 'the blessed' Targaryen, the religious zealot – intended to replace ravens with doves. However, he found them wholly unreliable, according to the account in *Black Wings, Swift Words*, written by Archmaester Walgrave, the Citadel's communications expert, and the ravens retained their role.

The Crannogmen

Before we head up to the Wall, we should drop in on two more northern peoples: the crannogmen and the Ironborn. First we'll ride out of Winterfell's South Gate, down the kingsroad as far as the Neck, with its treacherous marshes and fens, its water snakes and lizard-lions (an alligator-like creature, the sigil of House Reed) who lurk like logs, unseen beneath the waters. Here, in the south-ernmost part of the north, live the crannogmen. Their homes are reed-thatched huts, built on stilts or on floating islands made of bundles of reeds, and they live by catching fish and frogs. From their fen fastnesses they can harass anyone who passes across the narrow causeway of the Neck; poisoned arrows and sneak attacks are their weapons. The names of their Houses reflect their environment: alongside the dominant House Reed are House Fenn, House Quagg, House Peat and House Boggs.

The crannogmen take their name from the artificial islands on which they live; these are known as *crannog*s in Irish and Scots Gaelic. They were used from the Neolithic period until as late as the eighteenth century, and archaeological remains of such settlements can be found in Scotland. The crannogmen's guerrilla warfare recalls the resistance of the fen dwellers of East Anglia to the Norman invaders; from their islands among the marshes eleventh-century Englishmen waged long campaigns against their new overlords. The most prominent of the resistance leaders was Hereward the Wake (Wake = 'watchful'), who operated in the fenlands around the Isle of Ely. The contemporary evidence for Hereward is patchy; some of it is contradictory, and some – a battle with an enormous bear, and the rescue of a princess – is obviously fictionalised folklore. Even discounting these 'Bear and the Maiden Fair' elements, the outline of Hereward's life suggests strong affinities with several *Game of Thrones* plot lines. Returning from the continent where he'd been exiled before the Norman Conquest, Hereward discovered that the Normans had seized his ancestral estate; they had killed his brother and set his head on a spike outside the hall. Hereward killed fifteen of them almost single-handedly and retreated to the fens. Here he harassed and raided the Norman landholders, joined forces with some Danes sent over by King Sveinn Estridsson (for the Danes still had a claim to the English throne) and sacked Peterborough Abbey. The abbey's treasures may have been returned after a direct intervention from St Peter, or they may have been removed to Denmark. Hereward and his ally Morcar, Earl of Northumbria, made a last stand in Ely but were routed by the Normans. Whether a treacherous monk of

Ely revealed a safe route through the fens to the enemy, or whether
the Normans employed a witch to bring Hereward to his knees,
isn't clear, but Hereward was forced to flee. Sources differ as to
whether he made his peace with William the Bastard and lived
out his life in England or whether he was later killed by Norman
knights while lurking in the fens as an outlaw.[9]

The sketchy details of Hereward's career inspired the extraordinary book by Paul Kingsnorth, *The Wake*, published in 2014 and
longlisted for the Man Booker Prize. Written in a reimagined form
of Old English, the novel tells the story of Buccmaster, an Anglo-
Saxon whose response to Norman violence in his Lincolnshire
village is to mount an ultimately futile guerrilla campaign and
to revert to worship of the old gods of Anglo-Saxon paganism.
These – at least in their local forms – are to be found deep in the
fen waters, where the Christians had sunk them. Buccmaster vows
himself to them once again by diving down at the secret fenland
spot where they are submerged. Older savage gods, Odin and
Wayland the Smith, a figure who shares Buccmaster's craft, drive the
Englishman's battles against the French, culminating in a climactic
showdown in the neighbourhood of Ely.[10]

THE IRONBORN

Hereward may well have had Anglo-Danish ancestry; certainly
this would explain his alliances with the northern earl Morcar
and Sveinn's expeditionary force. It's much harder, though, to
imagine any such alliance between the crannogmen and the
Ironborn, whose domain in the Iron Islands lies to the south
and west of the Neck. There we'll head, to take ship across the
turbulent waters off Cape Kraken, across Ironman's Bay to Pyke.
Here the Greyjoy seat is built across several rock stacks, jutting
spear-like up from the sea and connected by dangerous swaying
rope bridges. Ferocious seaborne raiders, the Ironborn have many

affinities with the Vikings of the eighth to eleventh centuries. Their military power is underpinned by their slim, beautifully designed warships in which they strike at will along the coastline. The Iron Islands are rugged and hard terrain, lacking in natural resources. Balon Greyjoy's proud boast is that 'we are iron-born, we are not subjects; we are not slaves, we do not plough in the fields or toil in the mine. We take what is ours' (2.3). The Scandinavian raiders who brought terror to Europe for three centuries may have left their homelands because population pressure made it hard for them to sustain a living by agriculture on the thin soils and limited flatlands of the Norwegian fjords. But when a man's Viking days were done, if he survived, he was happy to retire to a farm in Iceland or Norway and raise a family.

The Ironborn despise farmers, then, and, at least as Balon words it, they much prefer raiding to trading. When he discovers that Theon's splendid neck-chain was bought rather than stolen, Balon tears it from his son's neck, snarling, 'that bauble around your neck, did you pay the iron-price for it, or the gold? [...] I asked you a question – did you pull it from the neck of a corpse you made or did you buy it, to match your fine clothes?' (2.2). Not many Vikings would have agreed with Balon. The Ironborn seem surprisingly drab in their clothing and adornments; no Viking would have torn Theon's gold from him unless he intended to start a fight on the spot. Vikings loved their bling, as anyone who was able to get to the Vikings exhibition at the British Museum in 2014 will know, and they loved to show it off. And they were equally alive to the possibilities of trading, whether in treasure, in commodities or in humans. Early in the medieval period the Vikings played an important part in the slave trade across Russia and the Middle East, providing women and eunuchs for the courts of the eastern empires. Slav boys, who were often literate and therefore useful in Byzantine bureaucracy, were a good source of income for the Scandinavians who travelled down the Volga to the Black Sea; women, seized from the British Isles and sold in Norway, found their way to Iceland. Victarion Greyjoy, whose point of view is deeply grounded in the Ironborn moral code, reflects on his people's practice of selling into slavery those who prefer to surrender rather than die in battle: 'Victarion had only contempt for such weaklings. Even so, the selling left a foul taste in his mouth. Taking a man as thrall or a woman as a salt wife, that was right and proper, but men were not goats or fowl to be bought and sold for gold' (*DD*, 56).

Medieval Scandinavians valued other skills beyond fighting. Rögnvald, Earl of Orkney in the twelfth century, boasted in a memorable verse:

> I am good at board games;
> I know how to use nine skills;
> I lose my memory of runes quite slowly;
> I am practised at reading and smithing.
> I can travel on skis;
> I can shoot and row, pretty usefully.
> And there are two other things I know:
> harp-playing and making poems.[11]

King Olaf Tryggvason, King of Norway in the late tenth century, was said to have been able to run along the oars of a longship being rowed at full speed. So too can Balon, though he lacks Rögnvald's other, more cultured accomplishments: 'At thirteen he could run a longship's oars and dance the finger dance as well as any man in the isles' (*FC*, 1). The finger dance, a game played by stabbing daggers between outstretched fingers, wouldn't have held much appeal for Vikings.

The political and military successes of the Viking-age Scandinavians – settling northern England, founding Dublin and establishing Normandy – were enabled by the capacity of their ships to travel far up the great rivers of Europe, journeying from the Baltic to Byzantium via the river systems of what is now Russia. And, like the Ironborn, they raided along the coastlines of all

17. The Oseberg Viking ship in the Viking Ship Museum, Oslo

northern Europe. They were also formidable fighters on land; the Great Army swept across northern England in 865, intending to conquer rather than to raid. Their campaign lasted fourteen years, and by the end of it the Scandinavians, under their leader Guthrum, controlled the Danelaw: the whole of England north of a line drawn from the mouth of the Mersey to the Thames Estuary. Had it not been for Alfred the Great's resistance, they might have taken the whole of England under their control, as the Danish kings Canute and Sweyn Forkbeard were to do in the early eleventh century.

The Great Army took horses from those they defeated and thus were mobile enough to achieve military success inland, away from the rivers and coastlines where they could easily regroup on their ships. The Ironborn are much less effective when away from the water; Theon's capture of Winterfell is achieved through a clever initial strategy, thought up by Theon and Dagmer Cleftjaw: they lure out the forces of the castle by staging a diversionary attack on Torrhen's Square. Asha (Yara in the show), well trained by her father, recognises that the Ironborn cannot hold Winterfell, and begs Theon to leave with her. Later, once her forebodings have been realised and Theon and Winterfell have been captured by the psychotic Ramsay Snow, Asha mounts a daring expedition to rescue her brother from the Dreadfort. Using longboats and smaller craft, Asha's force successfully makes its way upriver and into the castle. But Theon's psychological subjugation is so complete that he refuses to answer to his own name; Asha outruns Ramsay's dogs, retreats to her ships and gets away.

Balon's campaign of vengeance against the north, attempting to undo the humiliation visited on him by Ned Stark when his two elder sons were killed in Robert's Rebellion, thus has limited success. The Ironborn hold Winterfell briefly, plus Torrhen's Square, Deepwood Motte and Moat Cailin at the height of the campaign, but Moat Cailin is won through Ramsay's deception; Deepwood Motte falls to Stannis and Asha is captured. Torrhen's Square alone remains in the hands of Dagmer Cleftjaw, an Ironborn captain. Balon's death, whether accidental or caused by his brother Euron, leaves the Ironborn campaign in disarray:

> My brother Balon made us great again, which earned the Storm God's wrath. He feasts now in the Drowned God's watery halls, with mermaids to attend his every want. It shall be for us who remain behind in this dry and dismal vale to finish his great work. (*FC*, Prologue)

So declaims Aeron Greyjoy when he calls for a kingsmoot to determine the succession. The religion of the Ironborn is very different from any version of Viking religious practice that we know of. Balon's people worship the Drowned God, who protects them in their voyages. His adversary and antithesis is the Storm God, who is bent on destruction; when tempests rage the two gods are locked in conflict. The Ironborn are initiated into the religion via a kind of baptism; they are immersed in seawater and symbolically drowned. Thereafter, 'what is dead can never die'; they hope to gain immunity from death at sea by this initiation ceremony.

After death, as Aeron proclaims, the Ironborn will journey to the Drowned God's halls. Here the heroes will feast while mermaids serve them. This post-mortem belief does have some affinities with the Viking belief that warriors would enjoy an afterlife of fighting by day and feasting by night; the Valkyries would serve them mead and ale at a feast presided over by Odin. Pre-Christian Scandinavians believed that Ran, the goddess of the sea, caught sailors in her net and dragged them to the bottom of the ocean. Her spouse is Ægir, and their daughters the waves which sometimes sport with the ships that cross their domains and sometimes overwhelm them, tearing down their masts and surging over the gunwales.[12] Norse belief consistently envisages death as feminine: Hel, goddess of death, rules over the hall where those who did not perish in battle are sent. Valkyries choose who will fall in battle, and conduct them to Valhalla. The Ironborn are a highly misogynist and gendered society, judging by their attitude towards Asha as a possible ruler, so perhaps it is not surprising that there is no place for the female in their religion. No more than the Ironborn would Vikings have tolerated a female leader; Asha's bid for the throne would have been just as doomed if she'd been the only daughter of a Viking chieftain.

Nevertheless, Asha is granted a great deal of autonomy, wielding power over men and ships, for her older brothers are dead and Theon has long been away. She is also more strategically effective than Theon, recognising the limitations to longship-based sea power. But Asha can't escape patriarchal control, any more than her counterpart in Norse legend, Alvild the Pirate. Alvild had, from her girlhood, been protected by two poisonous snakes, given her by her father. Inevitably they grew enormous and troublesome; a hero was sought to rid Denmark of the creatures. A certain Alf presented himself and slew the serpents, and Alvild was all ready to marry him, when her mother criticised her for being willing to accept the first good-looking young man to come along. Stung, Alvild rejected Alf and, so Saxo, a Danish chronicler writing around 1200, tells us, 'began to lead the life of a savage pirate'. Moreover, 'many girls of the same persuasion [...] enrolled in her company.' Alf set out in search of his bride, sailing far across the seas around Scandinavia, until, quite by chance, he and his men ran into Alvild and her crew. Battle was joined; the Danish men were 'filled with astonishment when they found what graceful, shapely limbed opponents they had'. And of course the women lose; Alvild's helmet is struck off by Alf's companion, 'but seeing the smoothness of her chin, [he] realised that they ought not to be fighting with weapons, but kisses.' Very soon Alvild is back in female clothing, respectably married, and she becomes a mother. Her Viking days are decisively over.[13] In later medieval Scandinavia, tales of maiden-kings, women who took male names, dressed as men and successfully led armies, became very popular; the maiden-king would always finally be overcome by the man she was destined to marry, resuming female clothing and habits when gender norms were reasserted. So too Asha is married off in her absence; though she takes lovers freely while campaigning, she is left little room for manoeuvre except when she's out in the field.

It's time now to turn to the Wall, to take a closer look at that enormous structure, the inescapable fact that everyone in the north has to come to terms with. Let's head now with Jon Snow, Benjen and the ever-curious Tyrion up to Castle Black to take a closer look at it.

CASTLE BLACK AND THE WALL

Like Jon we fall silent at our first glimpse of the Wall, taking in its huge scale, its dull icy gleam, grey, striped with white, a band of faint pink light lying across the top: Jon's destiny (1.2). The Wall was built with the aid of giants, or so legend has it, to secure the northern border of the Seven Kingdoms. Martin has claimed that it originated in Hadrian's Wall, built to keep the bloodthirsty Scots and Picts out of the northernmost part of the Roman Empire.

18. Hadrian's Wall, Northumberland

Yet at 700 feet high and 300 miles long, the Wall dwarfs the Romans' achievement. It was was erected to keep the White Walkers/Others at bay, but for the Free Folk the Wall represents an impenetrable barrier between them and the green lands of the south, confining them to the wilderness and making them vulnerable, come the onset of winter, to the depredations of the Others. The folk of the south have forgotten the original reason for the Wall during the long summers, and now see it as a barrier keeping undesirables out of their territory. This Wall now speaks to many other walls in the real world: the Berlin Wall, the wall between Israel and Palestine and the border between the US and Mexico. The Free Folk, as Osha points out, just happened to be on the wrong side when it was built, and keeping them out has now become the Wall's *raison d'être*: 'You know nothing, Jon Snow. This Wall is made o' blood,' says Ygritte (*SS*, 30).

In King's Landing the Wall is regarded as a convenient place to send criminals and dangerous people, and no one apprehends its strategic importance. In the north, though, it's an existential fact which can't be ignored. And, surprisingly, it's beautiful, as Jon learns to recognise:

> *The Wall has more moods than a woman.* On cloudy days it looked to be white rock. On moonless nights it was as black as coal […] but on days like this, there was no mistaking it for anything but ice […] every crack and crevasse limned by sunlight, as frozen rainbows danced and died behind translucent ripples. (*DD*, 53)

When he becomes Commander of the Night's Watch, Jon has strategic decisions to make about the Wall, the garrisoning of the various fortresses along its length and negotiation with the Free Folk and their de facto leader, Tormund Giantsbane, Mance's successor. Jon's experiences among the wildlings, in particular his affair with Ygritte, has shown him that although the Free Folk are ideologically hostile to the people of the south, they are also refugees, asylum seekers, hoping to escape the aggression of the White Walkers/Others. Jon is not a man with particularly liberal sympathies, but he has learnt to be pragmatic, and he has closer affinities with the Free Folk than with Stannis and Melisandre. Jon's dilemmas engage with larger human-rights questions; whether the real human peril caused by the awakening of the White Walkers/Others and the onset of winter – in effect, by climate change – can be humanely resolved remains to be seen.

THE NIGHT'S WATCH

> *Night gathers, and now my watch begins. It shall not end until my death. I shall take no wife, hold no lands, father no children. I shall wear no crowns and win no glory. I shall live and die at my post. I am the sword in the darkness. I am*

*the watcher on the walls. I am the fire that burns against
cold, the light that brings the dawn, the horn that wakes
the sleepers, the shield that guards the realms of men. I
pledge my life and honor to the Night's Watch, for this night
and all the nights to come. (Oath of the Night's Watch)*

The Night's Watch is one of the Known World's many military orders, a sworn brotherhood of men dedicated only to service on the Wall. Desertion and oath-breaking is punished by death, as in the case of Will, the very first character we meet. Jon Snow is more fortunate: though he heads out into the forest south of the Wall to join Robb's campaign against the Lannisters, his friends pursue him and bring him back before his dereliction becomes desertion. The Lord Commander is understanding: 'Honour made you leave; honour brought you back.' 'My friends brought me back,' replies Jon sulkily. Quick as a flash, Mormont ripostes, 'I didn't say it was *your* honour' (1.10). Like other senior members of the order, Mormont has a clear view of how the bonds between sworn brothers should operate, creating new emotional ties, a new family in a network of mutual trust and affection. Earlier, Maester Aemon had asked Jon, 'Tell me, did you ever wonder why the men of the Night's Watch take no wives and father no children?' 'No.' 'So that they will not love […] love is the death of duty' (1.9). And, at least among Jon's friendship group, their love for one another reinforces duty and obedience.

Medieval Christianity understood the advantages of harness-ing military power to particular objectives through the creation of fighting orders. The most important of these orders were the Knights Templar and the Knights Hospitaller, both established as a result of the west's gaining of the Holy Land as a consequence of the First Crusade. Jerusalem was recaptured from Muslim forces in 1099, and Christian pilgrims began to flock to the sites where Jesus had walked. Though Jerusalem was secure, the rest of the territory was not, and thus in 1118 the French knight Sir Hugues de

Payens proposed to King Baldwin II of Jerusalem that a monastic order be founded to protect pilgrims from the bandits who preyed on them. With the support of the powerful Bernard of Clairvaux, reformer of the Cistercian order of monks, the Knights Templar were given a headquarters near the supposed site of the Temple of Solomon in Jerusalem, from which they took their name. They started with only nine knights, vowed to poverty, but with Bernard's backing they became an official order, endorsed by the Church, and a favourite charity. All over Europe people began to donate or bequeath money and land to the Knights Templar, and they became an extremely important financial force.

Bernard and Hugues devised the Rule for the Knights Templar, one which was largely based on the oldest monastic rule, that of the Benedictines. The Order was to adopt individual poverty – no man was allowed to have a lockable purse in which he could keep private wealth – and chastity. Clause 71 declared:

> We believe it to be a dangerous thing for any religious to look too much upon the face of woman. For this reason none of you may presume to kiss a woman, be it widow, young girl, mother, sister, aunt or any other; and henceforth the Knighthood of Jesus Christ should avoid at all costs the embraces of women, by which men have perished many times, so that they may remain eternally before the face of God with a pure conscience and sure life.[14]

The Knights Templar had three divisions: the Knights themselves (nobles who joined the order as knights); the Sergeants, who were non-noble and worked in useful trades and the provision of services: smithing, weapon manufacture and logistical support; and the chaplains. Other kinds of labour might be bought in as required, and some knights would elect to serve with the Order on a short-term basis. We might compare the Night's Watch's division into the elite force of the Rangers, the Builders, who maintain the

Wall's infrastructure, and the Stewards, who parallel the Sergeants in providing support services. Maester Aemon takes on the role of chaplain for the men at Castle Black; he understands best the ideology of the Watch and he is sympathetic to both Jon's psychological turmoil and Sam's bookishness. Aemon is over 100 at his death, and Sam speaks a beautiful elegy for him, echoing Beowulf's epitaph after he perishes in killing the dragon. Beowulf was, of all the kings of the world, the 'gentlest of men, kindest and dearest to his people, and most eager for fame'.[15] 'No man was wiser, gentler or kinder,' says Sam. 'He was the blood of the dragon, but now his fire has gone out' (5.7).

There were a good number of other military orders in the medieval period, most usually associated with various kinds of Crusade. The Teutonic Knights originated in a hospital–hostel built in Jerusalem for German pilgrims; the Order thus consisted primarily of German speakers, becoming an official order in 1198. The Teutonic Knights' retreat from the Kingdom of Jerusalem after its fall took them first to present-day Romania and then to the Holy Roman Empire, where, with the support of Emperor Frederick Barbarossa, they undertook the conquest and conversion of the Prussians, who lived to the east. These offered fierce opposition, taking 50 years to overcome; their resistance reminds us of the wildlings' dogged refusal to accept the ideologies of the Seven Kingdoms. The chronicles of the Teutonic Knights detail the savagery of the Prussians, fiercer still than Mance Rayder's hordes, who would 'roast captured brethren alive in their armour, like chestnuts, before the shrine of a local god'.[16] Later the Order campaigned in Poland and Lithuania; their inhabitants resisted conversion in a war that, conducted on a seasonal basis, lasted 200 years. Chaucer's Knight in *The Canterbury Tales* (composed between 1386 and 1400) had obviously served with the Teutonic Knights for he had, Chaucer tells us, often sat at the head of the table, above all other nations in 'Pruce / in Lettow [Latvia] had he reysed, and in Ruce [Russia] / no Cristen man so ofte of his degree'.[17] The verb *reyse*, derived from the German *reisen*, 'to travel', was a technical term among the Teutonic Knights for their summer raiding expeditions into Lithuania, and its use shows how well informed Chaucer was about the political situation in this distant part of Europe. The Order moved their headquarters in 1309 from Venice to the hugely impressive fortress of Marienburg, now Malbork, still to be seen in Poland; given their northern sphere of operations the Teutonic Knights are more similar to the Night's Watch than the Templars. If you've seen the 1938 Eisenstein film *Alexander Nevsky*, with its rousing score composed by Prokofiev, you'll have seen the Teutonic Knights advancing against the forces of the Duke of Novgorod over frozen Lake Peipus and plunging through it to their doom; the spectacle of the almost robotic knights chanting in cod Latin as they advance again the Russian forces is an unforgettable one.

Eisenstein assimilates his Teutonic Knights both to the Nazis and to the German armies of the First World War; his film has nationalist and propagandist intentions and has no sympathy for them. The ideology of the Night's Watch has become rigid, too: they exist, as they now understand themselves, to keep the wildlings out. But their plight, forgotten about by the power centre of the south, under-resourced and underestimated, signals a sense of end of empire. The Roman legions who patrolled Hadrian's Wall gradually abandoned the empire's northern frontier as the centre began to fall apart in civil war and conquest by foreign – so-called barbarian – armies. The will to hold on to the northern border has gone, and, perhaps surprisingly, Stannis turns out to share Jon's vision in settling the Free Folk on the Gift, the tract of fertile farmland south of the Wall. The Gift has traditionally fed and supported the Night's Watch and has often been raided by the Free Folk. The area has become considerably depopulated by the time Stannis comes to address the problems of the northern border, and so the resettlement plan looks promising. Though he is opposed by conservative hardliners within the order such as Bowen Marsh, First Steward of the Night's Watch, Jon has the drive to put the plan into action. Stannis and Jon must find a new strategy to adapt the Night's Watch oath to the geopolitics of the north, redefining the central concept of the 'realms of men' to respect and accommodate the Free Folk. This will be crucial in securing the north against worse threats still: 'we can learn to live with the wildlings or we can add them to the army of the dead' (5.5). The heavily reduced forces of the order need the influx of wildling fighters whom Jon is prepared to admit to its service, but the old guard, it seems, are not ready to come to that conclusion.

BEYOND THE WALL

Osha: 'North of the Wall, things are different. That's where the children went, and the giants and the other old races.' (GT, 66)

As we ride out beyond the Wall into the northern borderlands, we pass through thick pine forests on our way to Craster's Keep. North from there the land grows bleak, treeless and mountainous, with slow-creeping glaciers, stark hillsides and plains of outwash gravel. It's a harsh country where people scratch a living by hunting. A little subsistence agriculture is possible in Craster's domains; but it's also the realm of the uncanny, the land of ice, a place where the old ways prevail, where the stuff of Old Nan's stories is both true and real, and where the customs and beliefs of the rest of Westeros seem to find no purchase.

It's here, north of the Wall, where the wildlings live. These diverse clans and tribes call themselves the Free Folk (a term also used for the Hill Tribes in the Vale of Arryn). The Free Folk both here and in the Vale operate a kind of democracy among themselves. Tyrion observes of his Hill Tribe allies, 'That was the trouble with the clans; they had an absurd notion that every man's voice should be heard in council, so they argued about *everything*, endlessly. Even their women were allowed to speak' (*GT*, 56).

The Free Folk certainly have a more progressive sexual politics than anywhere south of the Wall. Their forces include spearwives: warrior women usually armed with spears, for the spear's shaft length makes it easier for women to wield, though Ygritte is also highly skilled with her bow and arrow. The Free Folk don't have the capacity to forge iron, but over the years they have managed to get weapons through exchange and trade. So too in thirteenth-century Iceland swords became very scarce indeed; small knives, axes and even stones were used as effective weapons in the civil war which raged in the first half of the century.

The tribes of the Free Folk embrace different social practices. Craster lives in a kind of patriarchal fantasy, an extreme version of Walder Frey's habits of multiple marriage and breeding children with little thought to how his offspring might prosper. Craster has an unending supply of young sexual partners in the form of his daughters – nineteen of them when Jeor Mormont leads his Rangers there. In an unusual inversion of what was once common custom – the exposure of female babies and those who fail to thrive or are born with some kind of congenital deformity – Craster retains his daughters and exposes his sons, even the healthy ones. But as we learn, from Jon Snow's horrified point of view, Craster's sons are sacrificed to the White Walkers/Others. What the White Walkers do with them isn't entirely clear; Old Nan thinks that they eat human children. Gilly reckons that the Others are appeased in some way by the gift of the sons, and they leave Craster and his family alone. In the show Craster's last son (except for Gilly's baby) is born months after his father has been killed in the mutiny at Craster's Keep and, at the women's insistence, the child is left out for the White Walkers. At the very end of the episode (4.4), a Walker is seen riding his skeletal horse in the Land of Always Winter. He brings the baby to an altar of ice within a shining circle of icicles, where a group of Walkers have assembled. They wear spiked ice-crowns on their skull-like heads, and as the baby wails, one touches his cheek. To the sound of ice cracking, the infant's eyes turn a depthless blue – the Walkers' eye colour.

Not all the Walkers can be generated from Craster's sons; the traditions of the south suggest that they sleep under the ice during the summers and awaken in winter, or so Old Nan and Osha warn us: 'There's things that sleep in the day and hunt at night,' Osha notes (1.7). They seem to embody the spirit of the ice; their presence freezes water and shatters the strongest metal, and they exist on a very different metaphysical plane from the human. Despite their superhuman strength and invulnerability, as Sam discovers, when he uses one of the cache of dragon-glass weapons he unearths at the Fist of the First Men, dragon-glass blades can destroy the White Walkers. In the books, the Other melts into a puddle on contact with the fossilised fire of the blade; in the show he freezes, cracks and finally shatters. Dragon-glass is a kind of obsidian, volcanic rock formed by fire, and thus the magical antithesis of ice. Sam's study of the books in Castle Black's library gives him superior knowledge about the Others; his brief exchange with Stannis about the value of dragon-glass yields the fact that the rock can be quarried on Dragonstone; information that is bound to come in useful. The unknown metal dragon-steel, mentioned in Sam's books, proves to be Valyrian steel, as Jon discovers at Hardhome. Good to know, but the shortage of Valyrian metal and competent metalworkers suggests that this will be of limited value in the face of large-scale invasion, an intuition confirmed by Jon Snow, for when Sam asks, 'How many Valyrian steel swords are left in the Seven Kingdoms?' Jon replies, 'Not enough' (5.10).

The 'army of the dead', the wights, are more immediately danger-ous than the White Walkers/Others. Reanimated corpses, whose status is marked by eyes which share the icy blueness of the White Walkers, they can lie low, feigning normal death until they spring into murderous action. The wights have supernatural strength, a degree of invulnerability and a single-minded malevolence; they are remotely controlled by the White Walkers. When two dead Rangers are brought back into Castle Black to be examined by Maester Aemon before burial, one, Othor, rises that night, makes his way

æ terra sunecturus sum. Et tur
sum auumdato pelle mea ⁊ in
carne mea. uidebo deum saluato

19. 'The Three Dead', medieval corpses who
remind the living of their fate

to the Lord Commander's quarters and tries to kill Jeor Mormont before Jon and Ghost overcome him. Jon knows instinctively that fire will destroy the wight where weapons don't work, and he is right. Dragon-glass, it later emerges, has no effect on them (so Jon's abandonment of the cache of daggers at Hardhome may not matter so much). The wights can also ride again after death; they have undead skeletal horses which they deploy at the Battle of the Fist of the First Men. The Brothers of the Night's Watch who fall in the battle also become wights, under the command of White Walkers, suggesting that the forces of wintriness are massing for an assault on the south. The Battle of Hardhome (5.8) confirms the existential threat; although the wights are capable of being destroyed by the giant Wun Wun's mighty feet and flaming club, the newly dead immediately rise up to replace them.

The mythic power to resurrect those who have died in battle generates terror in medieval legend; battles are normally resolved by the mounting death toll on the losing side, but if the dead don't stay dead, the battle can continue forever. In Norse myth the princess

Hild (probably a battle-goddess, for that is what her name means) has the power to revive the dead; consequently her father, her suitor and their forces are locked in eternal battle on the Orkney island of Hoy until Ragnarök comes. In the Welsh Second Branch of the *Mabinogi*, Bran, King of North Wales, possesses a supernatural cauldron that regenerates the dead when they are placed inside it. The revivified warriors have lost the capacity to speak. It's all very well having such a wondrous object, but Bran gives it to his brother-in-law, the King of Ireland, and when war comes about between the kingdoms (caused by the Irish king's mistreatment of Branwen, Bran's sister), the Welsh thoroughly regret the wedding gift. Only the self-sacrifice of Efnisien, Bran's half-brother, can destroy the cauldron; he plays dead among the Irish corpses. When placed in the vessel, he stretches out with all his limbs, exploding the cauldron but also bursting his own heart.[18] Even these limited and localised revivifying powers undo the metaphysics of the human world; the illimitable capacity of the White Walkers for regeneration provokes a profound and desperate terror. Only the fact that the army of the dead don't seem to be able to swim – an extension of the strong folkloric belief that running water deters the supernatural – seems to offer any hope for the survival of human life north of the Wall.

In their malevolence and supernatural invincibility the wights recall the undead of Norse tradition, the *draugar*. Often antisocial and unpleasant characters during life, a *draug* continues in a kind of life within his funeral mound. If, as in some sagas, his horse, hound and hawk are buried with him, he feasts on them. When a human hero ventures into the mound, usually to retrieve some of the treasure buried within, he will have to fight the mound-dweller, who can be overcome by decapitation. If the corpse's head is placed between his feet or behind him with the face against the buttocks, he becomes confused and does not revive. These types of *draug* are not especially dangerous unless provoked by interlopers. Another kind, however, does not stay in his burial mound but walks again, attacking cattle, sheep and humans and tearing them limb from limb; they sometimes cause their human victims to become *draugar* in their turn.

The most famous of these monsters in medieval Icelandic tradition is Glam, whose tale is told in *Grettis saga*, probably composed in the early fourteenth century. He was a Swede, a huge, grizzled, unsocial man, happy to take the job of shepherd at a farm high up in a lonely Icelandic valley where some inexplicable disappearances had already occurred. Glam courted disaster by refusing to fast on Christmas Eve or to come to church; rather he headed out into a storm and did not return. Eventually a search party discovered his corpse, blue-black and swollen up as large as a cow. The corpse couldn't be carried down to the churchyard, so he was buried where he was, and soon it became apparent that he was walking again. Men fainted or lost their minds when they caught sight of him, and he started to ride on the farmhouse roof at night. His successor as shepherd was found with a broken neck and 'lamed in every limb'. After a cowman's back was broken, the farm was deserted. Eventually the great hero Grettir, who had already overcome one mound-dweller in Norway, heard of the terror wrought by Glam and he vowed to do battle with him. He waited for Glam in the deserted farmhouse and then wrestled with the monster. Glam succeeded in dragging Grettir outside, but the undead creature fell with Grettir on top of him. At that moment, the clouds drifted away from in front of the moon, and Grettir saw Glam's eyes – the most terrifying thing that he'd ever seen in his life, he said later. Glam prophesied all kinds of bad luck for the hero, and, worst of all, he told Grettir that henceforth whenever it was dark he would always see Glam's eyes before him. Grettir managed to cut off the creature's head, and the body was burned to ashes. That's the end of the undead menace, though Grettir's fortune took a turn for the worse, condemned as he was to outlawry for an act of manslaughter. And he was indeed haunted by Glam's eyes, becoming so afraid of the dark that he couldn't endure to live alone: a fatal flaw in an outlaw.[19]

In other Icelandic stories of *draugar*, even burning the corpse doesn't bring an end to the undead's wickedness. In one tale the nasty old patriarch who refuses to stay in his grave is finally cremated, but some of his ashes are licked up by a cow in calf. The bull calf born from her is preternaturally large, and although the farmer is warned by his foster-mother (who has second sight) that the calf should be slaughtered, he refuses. Eventually the bull runs mad, attacks the farmer, who dies of his injuries, and charges away up into the mountains, where he sinks into a bog and is never seen again. In another saga, the undead creature's ashes are sealed in a lead casket and the casket dropped into the scalding depths of a hot spring; that prevents further hauntings, whether by the *draug* or by his victims. These Icelandic tales of the walking dead share some features with the wights who wander north of the Wall. Even Brothers of the Night's Watch become antagonistic to their former companions once death and uncanny revival has supervened. Glam's terrible eyes, now proverbial in Icelandic, perhaps underlie the blue-eyed sinisterly fixed gaze of the wights, while the idea that beasts can also become possessed by the *draug*'s evil spirit through the ashes ingested by the cow may explain how the White Walkers/Others animate the horses on which they ride.

What *are* the White Walkers – and what do they want? 'Simply put, the White Walkers are the series' vision of war itself: death breeding death breeding death until nothing living is left,' writes one commentator.[20] They're a metaphysical force, a wholly different type of being from the dragons, the Children or any of the humans in the series. Despite the hints about their genesis, a backstory which suggests that the Night's King was once a Commander of the Night's Watch, perhaps even a Stark by blood, they represent something ineluctable and unappeasable. Like death, but a death that's eternally reiterated. That is why they are so terrifying. And their association with the changing climate, the onset of winter, figures perhaps a fate that lies ahead of us all.

GIANTS

The White Walkers/Others are the beings we will be trying hardest to avoid as we venture into the stony wastes beyond the Wall, but they are not the only mythological creatures to be found in the far north. When, among Mance Rayder's army, Jon lays eyes on his first giant, he is astonished; for him giants are the stuff of Old Nan's legends. Ygritte warns him about their sensitivities: she tells him she has seen one hammer a man into the ground like a nail for staring too long at him. Yet giants are somehow to be expected in the world beyond the Wall, for the north is where they belong. In Norse myth giants are of variable size, and the frost-giants, who will attack the gods at Ragnarök, are closely associated with the mountains, with ice-bound and unpromising habitats. Norse giants are not generally particularly stupid, unlike the gullible and easily tricked folklore giants that crop up in English folk tales. They live in handsome halls and have gold at their disposal; they also possess cultural treasures which the gods covet. One Norse poem, the 'Poem of Thrym', tells of a giant as social climber. Thrym steals Thor's mighty hammer Mjollnir and refuses to return it unless he can have the beautiful goddess Freyja as his bride. When Freyja flat-out refuses to head to Giantland, the gods seize upon the suggestion that Thor, with his mighty red beard, could be dressed in female clothes, heavily veiled and sent off to marry Thrym in Freyja's place. Though the imposture threatens to break down when Thor devours almost all the wedding feast single-handedly, the cunning Loki manages to explain 'Freyja's' appetite by claiming that she has not eaten for eight nights in her eagerness to come to her bridegroom. The hammer is placed on the bride's lap to consecrate the relationship, and as soon as Thor's fingers close round its handle, the giant bridegroom and his appalling family are doomed.[21]

The giants of the far north of Westeros are quite tall (about 14 feet); 'fierce things they are too, all hair and teeth, and the wives have beards like their husbands so there's no telling them apart'

(*GT*, 53). Or so says Osha, who claims that her brother killed a ten-foot-tall 'stunted' giant. Big and frightening they may be, but there's no sense of their culture or even why they might want to move southwards with the Free Folk or whether they are also at risk from the White Walkers. Their language is monosyllabic, perhaps tonal like Chinese, and they remain inscrutable to the humans with whom they make common cause. They have an affinity with animals, however; they often ride mammoths, and one is killed at the Battle of Castle Black when his mount runs amok. Like the hairy wild men who are encountered sometimes in medieval forests, the giants use clubs or mauls worked from whole trees. In one medieval French romance, an adventuring knight comes across a giant herdsman in the forest. The giant is extraordinarily ugly, but he converses with Sir Yvain in a civilised enough fashion and directs him to the magical fountain which he seeks. The Herdsman takes care of the wild animals of the forest; they come at his call and fawn at his feet. Though giants normally symbolise the power of nature rather than culture, they work – if only in a rudimentary fashion – to preserve and to protect the wildernesses in which they live. Whether they will successfully settle south of the Wall remains to be seen.

Other Free Folk tribes include the Thenn, who are led by Styr the Magnar. In Norse Styr is a name often borne by violent, anti-social characters: Viga-Styr (Slayer-Styr), who appears in a couple of sagas, is a ferocious fighter and outlaw. His title, Magnar, sounds suitably Norse too, and perhaps it is derived from the popular Scandinavian name Magnus (itself taken from Latin) or from the word *megin* (power), related to 'main' in the English phrase 'might and main'. Styr's co-commander of the Thenn, Jarl, has a name which means 'Earl', and Styr's son Sigorn could be glossed as 'Victory-Eagle'. After doing homage to Stannis, Sigorn marries the heiress of Karhold in a ceremony conducted by Melisandre and he becomes the first head of House Thenn. A good number of the Thenn remain with Sigorn; others break away after Mance's defeat and return to their ancestral valley. The tribal name Thenn echoes the Norse and Old English 'thegn', or nobleman, and thus it's not too much of a surprise that Styr's people assimilate to life south of the Wall, adopting the social structures of the Seven Kingdoms in founding a House, swearing loyalty to Stannis, and converting to the religion of the Lord of Light. In the books the Thenns are the most culturally advanced of the Free Folk. They retain knowledge of how to work metal and they possess a reasonably good supply of metal weapons: 'They mine tin and copper for bronze, forge their own arms and armor instead of stealing it. A proud folk and brave' (*DD*, 49). Their home valley lies in a volcanic area where the underground heat sources have made their microclimate warmer and the ground more fertile than elsewhere north of the Wall.

The ice-river clans, by contrast, are cannibals who practise scarification: scarring their faces in order to terrify their enemies. The ice-river folk hunt the Inuit-like men of the Frozen Shore who have sleds and dogs and live on what they catch from the sea: mammals and fish. They have names like 'The Great Walrus', or so we learn when one is given as a hostage to Jon Snow when the Free Folk settle south of the Wall (*DD*, 58). In the show, the Thenn retain their cultural superiority – the idea that the warmer the climate the more civilised people are will come under pressure in following chapters – but they have also been given the traits of scarification and cannibalism, borrowed from the books' ice-river clans. Loboda, the leader of the Thenns at Hardhome, wields a very impressive double-headed axe, though it does not avail him against the White Walker who finally runs him through. They are more intransigent than other Free Folk, as Tormund and Karsi both have cause to observe ('I fucking hate Thenns'). It will be interesting to see whether the show-Thenn will adapt to the social conditions south of the Wall, jettison their cannibalism and indeed convert to belief in R'hllor, or whether they will succeed in retaining their striking cultural identity as they adjust to life in the Seven Kingdoms.

THE THREE-EYED RAVEN/CROW

The mystical figure, the Three-Eyed Raven in the show, is in the books the Three-Eyed Crow. The Crow/Raven summons Bran to him for purposes which have yet to be clearly revealed. In Irish mythology, crows are representatives of the goddess of battle, the Morrígan, who can manifest herself in three different female forms. In Old English and Old Norse the raven is one of the beasts of battle (along with the eagle, also a carrion-eater, and the wolf) who presage slaughter. I noted above that war-leaders can be praised in Norse skaldic poetry as men 'who give the wolf breakfast'; they were said to be equally generous in providing food for ravens. This raven/crow comparison springs to Jaime Lannister's mind as he is standing vigil over the rapidly decaying corpse of his father:

> There were crows circling the seven towers and great dome of Baelor's Sept even now, Jaime suspected […] 'Every crow in the Seven Kingdoms should pay homage to you, Father. From Castamere to the Blackwater, you fed them well.' (FC, 8)

And Tywin's corpse, horrifically, seems to grin at this unspoken praise from his son.

In some forms of Hindu ascetic practice the interior third eye gives access to arcane knowledge of different kinds. The Three-Eyed Raven/Crow, when encountered in human form, is a frightening figure who sits in a cave far north of the Wall: 'a pale lord in ebon finery sat dreaming in a tangled nest of roots, a woven weirwood throne that embraced his withered limbs as a mother does a child' (DD, 13). His body is twined about with the roots of a weirwood tree, and through them he seems to be connected with the weir-woods of Westeros; through the rhizomic tangle he is able to see all that transpires in the sacred places of the north. And he is seen by Melisandre too, in her flames, though she is not sure who he is: '*A wooden face, corpse white.* Was this the enemy? A thousand red eyes floated in the rising flames' (*DD*, 31). As the Crow, he reveals himself to be Brynden Rivers, also known as Lord Bloodraven, a one-time Lord Commander of the Night's Watch who vanished when out on patrol. His crow form, then, perhaps refers to the nickname the Free Folk give to members of the Night's Watch, and suggests the dark magic that he practised while properly alive; the Raven identity chimes with his knowledge-gathering capacity.

Brynden's one-eyed status, his connection with ravens and crows, and the tree system into which he seems to be physically incorporated link him suggestively with Odin. The god is a master of magic and of wisdom. He knows spells and charms and the wisdom of giants and men, which he has gained through his wandering. And by hanging himself on the world-tree Yggdrasil as a sacrifice, 'himself to himself' as the Norse poem 'Sayings of the High One' tells us, suffering for nine days and nine nights with neither food nor drink, he wins the runes.[22] These are not just a writing system, allowing the preservation and communication of knowledge; they also have magical properties over the material world. Odin knows much of the past, the present and of the future too. He and the other gods will perish at Ragnarök, but he also knows the secret that his dead son Baldr will, it seems, return in the new world to come. The First Men used runes as a writing system, Sam, who has studied the history of Westeros, reports, and he offers an important perspective on what passes for ancient history in the Seven Kingdoms:

> The oldest histories we have were written after the Andals came to Westeros. The First Men only left us runes on rocks, so everything we think we know about the Age of Heroes and the Dawn Age and the Long Night comes from accounts set down by septons thousands of years later. (*FC*, 7)

Odin can see into 'all the worlds' from his high-seat, Hlidskjalf, a lofty vantage point which finds a counterpart in the Three-Eyed Crow's vision of all that transpires in the north through his connections to the trees. Like Hugin and Munin, the Three-Eyed Crow flies across the Known World to gather intelligence for its master. And it has called Bran to become an initiate into the knowledge of the north's ancient powers. What Brynden will teach Bran, deep in the cave in the Haunted Forest, and how far Osha, Meera and even Hodor can mitigate his transformation into the not-quite-human, is an intriguing and open question.

THE OLD GODS

In some mystical way, Brynden has enmeshed himself into the weirwood complexes which grow near the castles and holdfasts of the north. Here the old gods may be invoked, in groves of trees with stark white trunks and startling red leaves. It's possible to see faces in the striations of the bark encasing these trees, and sometimes a tear of scarlet sap will trickle down the trunk. When Tyrion hears that Winterfell has fallen to Theon Greyjoy he remembers the godswood from his visit to the alien north: 'the tall sentinels armored in their grey-green needles, the great oaks, the hawthorn and ash and soldier pines, and at the center the heart tree standing like some pale giant frozen in time' (*CK*, 45). The religion of the Old Gods, followed by the First Men and their northern descendants, is an animist veneration of the powers of the natural world. In this respect it seems rather like the religion being practised in Britain before the arrival of Christianity, both by the British, as described by Roman historians, and by the Anglo-Saxons. For the British Celts trees, particularly oak trees, seem to have been important in druidic rituals, and rites were performed outdoors. We have only slightly better evidence of Anglo-Saxon religion: the Anglo-Saxon historian Bede records around 730 CE how, when Saints Augustine and Paulinus came to England to convert the pagan Germanic immigrants, the Pope, Gregory the Great, warned Augustine not immediately to pull down the temples where the people worshipped, but rather to destroy the idols and to reconsecrate the buildings to the Christian god.[23] Evidence from place names suggests that there were both temples and small shrines, and larger outdoor complexes in Anglo-Saxon paganism: the place-name element *hearh*, which we find in modern English *Harrow*, seems to designate just such a sacred grove located on a hilltop under the open sky.

The old gods then are a collective, chiming with the designation of the Germanic gods as a group, sometime called *bönd* (the ones bound together). And 'beyond the Wall they are the only gods', Osha tells Bran (*GT*, 53). Some of the Celtic goddesses too, such as the *Matronae*, or mothers, function collectively. As against the religion of the Seven, with its specialised functions for different aspects of the divinity, the old gods are undemanding: they have no priests, no institutions and very little by way of dogmas or creeds. 'It's your gods with all the rules' (1.1), says Ned to Catelyn, who follows the southern religion of the Seven. We don't know much about the religions of the Thenn and other more exotic Free Folk, while Craster has developed a different kind of cult which entails the sacrifice of his male offspring to the Others. The quid pro quo seems to be immunity from attack for him and his daughters.

The Children of the Forest are closely associated with the old gods; they are the aboriginal inhabitants of Westeros, predating its invasion by the First Men, and subsequently by the Andals. The Children are not, however, human; they have retreated from inter-action with humans in the face of successive waves of invasion and they cling on in little enclaves beyond the Wall, in particular in the vast caverns that lie beneath the Haunted Forest. Their priests are greenseers, possessed of prophetic powers, and they have a powerful affinity with nature and with the old gods. The legends of Westeros ascribe magic, musicality and shape-shifting to them. The Children seem to have an interest in bringing Bran to Brynden, in recruiting him to the caste of greenseers, and they help the little party – Bran, Hodor and the two Reeds – when they are attacked by wights just before they reach Brynden's cave. Martin insists that the Children are not elves, and they are clearly not the kind of Tolkien elf who represents an immortal, highly cultured and rather melancholy past civilisation. Nor are they tall and beautiful with pointed ears and a distinctly superior attitude to the humans they encounter. Rather, they are defensive and anxious, small and brown, dressed in leaves and barkskin; in the books they have four fingers with claws rather than nails, and golden eyes with slit-shaped pupils, like cats or snakes. The show's Children are more human-like, but are clearly different from the human races of the Known World.

Despite Martin's determination to distinguish his non-human beings from the elves of high fantasy, the Children do have an affinity with the Icelandic *huldufólk*, or 'hidden people'. Christian legend recounts the origin of the *huldufólk* among the children of Adam and Eve, just like humans. God came to visit the couple and their offspring after they had left Eden, and the children were paraded for his inspection. 'Are these *all* your children?', God asked, and Eve hesitated, because there was a group of little ones whom she hadn't managed to wash before the divine visit and whom she was keeping out of sight. 'Yes,' she told God untruthfully, and God, who knows all things, pronounced, 'Let those who are now hidden, stay hidden.' Ever since, the 'hidden folk' have lived in fairy mounds and elf-hills, barely visible to their human cousins. Sometimes they intervene in human affairs, particularly if their dwellings are under threat, but mostly they keep themselves to themselves.

WINTER IS COMING

Qhorin Halfhand: 'We're at war, we've always been at war and it's never going to end because we're not fighting an enemy, we're fighting the North and it's not going anywhere.' (2.6)

Winter is always already here north of the Wall. The empty whiteness of the winter north provokes a kind of *horror vacui*, a fear of emptiness. The eyes perceive shadows and shapes lurking among the dark trees. Against the snow the White Walkers can be hard to see; only the icy-blue gleam of their eyes and the icicle-cracking sounds of their speech reveal their movements before they are already upon their victims. No wonder the southerners fear winter's icy conditions prevailing in their own homelands, even if they refuse to take the White Walkers seriously. Winters last for years in Westeros, evoking the horror of the Old Norse *Fimbulvetr*, the Mighty Winter, a precursor of Ragnarök. The thirteenth-century Icelandic politician and writer Snorri Sturluson describes the *Fimbulvetr* like this:

> The first sign is that the winter called *fimbulvetr* comes. Then snow drives from all directions. There are many frosts and keen winds. The sun has no effect. Three such winters run together with no summer in between. And before another three such winters pass all the world falls to fighting.[24]

And so when the white raven comes from the Citadel declaring the onset of winter, it portends the difficulties to come. The folk north of the Wall, the wildlings in their skins and furs with their knowledge of how to survive the cold would be well placed to come through the winter, were it not for the awakening of the White Walkers, but the terror of these spectral figures and the wights that follow in their wake drives the Free Folk south. Climate change leading to massive and violent population shifts: it's a timely reminder of what effects global warming could have on our world. The people of Winterfell with their winter gardens and steaming hot springs might have endured through the winter too, had the castle not been sacked, the glasshouses smashed to smithereens and the godswood left bereft. Further south, members of the Small Council are undismayed when a raven comes from the Wall bearing news of the stirrings beyond. 'Cold winds are rising and the dead rise with them,' is Mormont's report, begging for resources and reinforcement. Pycelle dismisses the call: 'the Northerners are a superstitious people.' Tyrion is more sympathetic, for he knows that 'the Night's Watch is the only thing that separates us from what lies beyond the Wall' (2.2). Cersei, however, sniffs at the idea of 'snarks and grumkins', and the Night's Watch's plea goes unheard.

Even discounting the White Walkers, winter is going to bring hardship, but the Seven Kingdoms' strategists are not planning to make adequate provision for the smallfolk against the privations to come. 'We have enough wheat for a five-year winter. If it lasts any longer,' shrugs Lord Baelish, 'fewer peasants' (2.1). But this was before the Riverlands were laid waste in the War of the Five Kings; food has to be imported to King's Landing through the good offices of the Tyrells and somehow paid for too. Trouble lies ahead for the southern kingdoms: profound social unrest manifests itself in religious zealotry, the ordinary people of King's Landing turn against their rulers (though Margaery knows how to handle them through conspicuous do-gooding), the Lannisters' gold is running out and Stannis is taking hold of the north. The lands in the west of the Known World, south of the Neck, are where we shall head next, riding down the kingsroad, hoping not to attract attention from the roving bands of brigands and mercenaries. Our course is set for King's Landing, for Dragonstone, sunny Dorne and the lands of the Reach, where a very different climate – for the moment – prevails.

20. *Jaime – Uncut*

CHAPTER 3

THE WEST

Ned to Catelyn: 'I'm a Northman, I belong up here with
you, not in that rat's nest they call the capital.' (1.1)

I t's time now for us to take the kingsroad south from Winterfell,
through the squelching bogs of the Neck, and to ride down
into the lush, green Riverlands, the fertile foodbasket of
the Seven Kingdoms. We're on our way to the capital, King's
Landing, where the complex politics of late medieval kingship
operate, where the court and the Small Council are central, and
where chivalry is a key part of aristocratic ideology. The Faith
of the Seven holds sway here, a religion which has a great deal
in common with medieval Catholicism. We'll also meet some
of the more important figures in the series, and see how their
social status affects their behaviour: in particular Varys, Master
of Whisperers; Cersei, queen, queen regent, and dowager queen
in quick succession; the Machiavellian Lord Petyr Baelish, with
his endless plotting; and Tyrion, the brilliantly sardonic dwarf.
Many of the cultural features which we discussed in Chapter
One find their epitome in the society of southern Westeros, for
the capital and the lands immediately surrounding it define the
'normal' in Westeros. While we're here in the centre of the Known
World (in Westerosi thinking, at any rate), we should be able to
get a much clearer picture of what motivates the most powerful
figures in the Seven Kingdoms.

The Iron Throne and ideals of kingship

Our journeys through the south start from the very centre of it all: the Iron Throne, forged from the thousand swords of the enemies of Aegon I Targaryen, which sits in the middle of the Great Hall at the heart of the Red Keep.

It's horribly uncomfortable, impossible to lean back in (for a king should never rest easy, Aegon thought), and prone to slicing those who don't occupy it with dignity. Joffrey cuts his hand quite badly when he leaps excitedly out of it. The throne's uncomfortableness and dangerousness is symbolically significant. 'I swear to you, sitting a throne is a thousand times harder than winning one,' as Robert Baratheon says to Ned Stark in Season One. The throne makes physical and visible the difficulties of kingship, for holding and ruling the kingdom justly is a very different matter from winning the throne through conquest. Kings and heroes need different qualities; medieval epics often contrast the strength of the hero with the wisdom of the king. And there's a kind of irony in the fact that the object desired so powerfully by the five kings – and many others – should be so unlovely. Yet it vividly figures the violence that accompanies the transfer of power, and the force necessary to retain it.

Kingship has its own romance; a myth which Joffrey believes in unequivocally: 'I am the king,' he foams during the Riot of King's Landing, unable to believe that the citizens should dare to throw cowpats at him (2.6). What Joffrey does not understand, though his mother has some inkling of the situation, is the precarious hold that the members of the Baratheon dynasty have on the throne. For they are pretenders, an interruption to the centuries of Targaryen rule, and their situation is by definition unstable. While primogeniture works to assure Joffrey's right to inherit, the questions about his legitimacy, widely published by Stannis, and his youth call into question his capacity to hold on to the throne which he occupies. 'Woe to the land where a child is king' was a common medieval

21. The Tower of London, Traitor's Gate

saying. Uncles, great lords, the powerful of various hues compete to advise a young king, to exercise influence over him, and once he achieves his majority and wishes to take full control of his realm he can face opposition. England was relatively fortunate in the council that ruled the land during the long minority of Henry VI, for example, who inherited the throne at nine months old. But once Henry assumed his full powers, his rule was quickly perceived as indecisive and unfocused.

In a sense, Robert (who prefers 'whoring and hunting and drinking' to policy making in Tywin's phrase (4.3)), Joffrey and even Tommen might all regard themselves as well served by delegating major decisions to the Hand of the King and the Small Council. Even with much power residing in the Wardens of the North and West and the other quasi-autonomous lords of Dorne, the Vale, the Iron Islands and the Riverlands, the complexity of ruling the

Seven Kingdoms requires the growth of government in King's Landing, creating a bureaucracy that is largely hidden from view but which underpins the work of the Master of Coin, the Master of Whisperers, Grand Maester Pycelle and the Hand himself. The Seven Kingdoms are in this respect much like late medieval England, ruled from Westminster. Nevertheless, justice seems to be dispensed by direct petition to the king, or his deputy, the Hand, rather than making law through parliamentary procedure or administering it through independent law courts.

The difference between royal rule and lordship is nicely summed up by Ned's belief that if you are to execute a man, you should strike off his head yourself. This is a principle he imparts to his children and which is strongly pointed up by his own death at the hands of the sinister, silent headsman, Ilyn Payne, with his punning name. Robb labours the point when he declares himself King in the North: 'Neither Joffrey nor any of his men shall set foot in my lands again; if he disregards this command, he shall suffer the same fate as my father. Only, I don't need a servant to do my beheading for me' (2.1). Robb talks warmly to Talisa about his father's vision of lordship as paternal: that the Lord of Winterfell should be a father to his soldiers, 'to the charwoman scrubbing the floors' (2.8). Renly too has the warmth, the common touch which makes a man a good king and a good leader, asking 'How's your foot?' to a soldier as he strolls among his host (2.3). Like Shakespeare's version of Henry V, Renly can bring a 'little touch of Harry in the night' to the men who serve him. Renly, I think, was probably right when he opined that he would be a better king than the humourless and fanatical Stannis. Without the Red Woman, it's hard to see how Stannis could muster the charisma a king needs to lead successfully – and yet Davos loves him. As Salladhor Saan remarks, 'you Westerosi are funny people. He chops off your fingers and you fall in love with him!' (2.2). In the show, Stannis's rigour extends to a zeal for good grammar when a member of the Night's Watch declares that the death of large numbers of wildlings means less enemies for them. 'Fewer,' mutters

Stannis under his breath (5.5), a pedantic insistence on correct usage that he's already failed to impress upon Davos in an earlier season.

THE COURT

The court at King's Landing is where all the major players display a public face while pursuing their private agendas. Although we tend to associate the challenges of playing the courtier with later English monarchs, in particular Henry VIII and Elizabeth I, it was in medieval courts that the understanding first arose that the role of courtier was becoming a specialised and unnatural way of being. 'I travelled through the Free Cities with a group of actors. They taught me that each man has a role to play. The same is true at court,' says Varys to Ned (1.9), and he is absolutely right. The courtier must humour, advise, protect and encourage the king; he must put aside his feelings in order to fulfil that role, even though he will also be working for his own personal advancement. Medieval moralists were often concerned about the doubleness that successful court life demanded, as inviting hypocrisy and flattery as the primary ways of interacting with the monarch. They worried too that the luxury of court life, the cushions, the fancy sauces, musicians and the chatter of women would diminish the capacity of the king and his nobles to withstand the hardships of military campaigning, or to think through the cleverest strategies for diplomacy or defence. Saxo Grammaticus, a monk who wrote his history of Denmark around the year 1200, puts his criticism of court manners into the mouth of a disgruntled old hero called Starkad when offered a golden hairband by his lord's civilised German queen:

> It is grotesque for a man of battle
> to bind his locks with twining gold.
> That style better suits a bunch
> of soft effeminates.

Give the present to your spouse,
who loves debauchery and lusts as his fingers turn
the rump of a capon toasted brown
to pick its guts.

Valiant men eat raw rations.
No need of a sumptuous spread, I think,
for stout-hearted bosoms which meditate
the practice of war.[1]

Starkad's stance, and the vehemence with which he expresses it, is
exceptional, but his views are not so far from those of Ned Stark,
who has no desire to participate in the tournament arranged to
celebrate his appointment as Hand. Indeed he is, as we shall see
below, horrified when he discovers how much it will cost, and how
much the kingdom is in debt.

The court of King's Landing is a varied one, with its comple-
ment of knights and ladies, Kingsguards, jesters and entertainers,
but only a handful of players really count. Grand Maester Pycelle
is apparently an old dodderer, though he is still capable of amusing
himself with Baelish's prostitutes. He is quite useless when it comes
to formulating strategy for the Battle of the Blackwater; his only
contribution is to hand Cersei the essence of nightshade which
she comes very close to administering to Tommen in the battle's
aftermath. Lord Varys, the Master of Whisperers, is a much more
important figure, a conduit for intelligence gathered from across
the Known World. Thus he knows when he and Tyrion take stock
before the battle that Daenerys has survived her ordeal in the Red
Waste and has found a kind of sanctuary in Qarth, though it's not
clear how his information travels so quickly across the distances of
Essos. Varys is one of my favourite characters; his skirmishes with
Petyr Baelish (whom he does not like) and with Tyrion (whom he
does like) tell us much about his priorities. Asked by Ned, 'Tell me,
Varys, who do you truly serve?', he replies smoothly, 'The realm,

my lord, someone must' (1.8). And indeed, with no family, no hope
of descendants, no House and no land to maintain, Varys is free to
use his intellect and talents for higher ends. The later revelation that
he is working for a Targaryen restoration (and his sabotage of the
positive effects of Kevan Lannister's regency) call into question the
disinterestedness to which he laid claim in his conversation with
Ned. In the show, Varys left King's Landing with Tyrion, bound for
the Free Cities, and it's possible that his story is going to develop
somewhat differently.

Varys too is alone among the great figures at court in appre-
ciating Tyrion's strategic intelligence. 'You're quite good at being
Hand, you know. Jon Arryn and Ned Stark, they were good men,
honourable men, but they disdained the game and those who
play it. You enjoy the game [...] and you play it well' (2.8). Tyrion
searches through stout volumes for advice about sieges, and he
listens attentively to Bronn's views on the advisability of round-
ing up known thieves before the city begins to starve. His plan to
conceal the enormous quantities of wildfire, manufactured by the
Guild of Pyromancers, within the Crownlands' ships at mooring is
a well-kept secret and a highly effective defensive response. Tyrion,
we sense, regrets the terrible loss of life on both sides; Stannis, in
contrast, when warned that hundreds will die if he disembarks
and attacks the walls of the capital, retorts, 'Thousands!' Stannis's
will to power is innate; he acts as ruthlessly – even suicidally,
pitching foot soldiers against cavalry at the Battle of Winterfell –
when deprived of Melisandre's counsel as he does when she is
prompting him.

Tyrion has a special status as a dwarf and yet – problematically
for Tywin and Cersei – he is a Lannister. He functions as joker, as
truth-teller, as a tortured soul in a complex relationship with his
family. In medieval belief dwarfs were often considered as malig-
nant; they have a particular role in medieval romance as conduits
of information, but in that function they are often churlish. A
dwarf actually strikes one of Queen Guinevere's maidens across

the face with his whip, refusing to give his master's name when the
queen enquires it. In Norse tradition dwarfs are craftsmen, skilled
in metalwork in particular; though cunning, they can be grateful
when well treated. In one story a dwarf manages to reattach the
severed feet of a maimed hero, a favour he grants because the man
had been kind to his daughter. Tyrion shares the dwarf-smith's
imaginative capacity: he cleverly modifies his saddle design to help
Bran and he shows remarkable strategic leadership in the Battle of
the Blackwater. His lustfulness is typical of the dwarf too; in another
Norse tale, four dwarfs craft the most splendid of necklaces, the
legendary Brisingamen. The beautiful goddess Freyja longs for it,
and does not baulk at the price demanded: she willingly spends a
night with each of the four craftsmen.[2]

22. Freyja encounters the dwarfs forging the Brisingamen necklace

Yet one of Tyrion's particular strengths in the show is precisely to subvert the stereotype of the dwarf in medieval and folkloric traditions. He deploys many one-liners, but he's not a comic character, as Tolkien's dwarfs often are. Nor is he treasure-obsessed and avaricious as folkloric dwarfs can be; the Lannister gold has provided all his wants so far, and he resists sailing with Shae to Pentos because he fears to lose that valued status as a member of a Great House. Tyrion's intelligence is far removed from low dwarfish cunning; he's much smarter than Rumpelstiltskin, and he also lacks that folk-tale dwarf's spitefulness. He made, as Varys observed above, a pretty good acting Hand, and if he takes on that role for Daenerys, she will truly reap the benefits of his clear-sightedness and ethical cast of mind. Tyrion probes searchingly into the queen's vision of rulership, explaining that he wants to find out if she's 'the right kind of terrible'. 'What kind is that?' 'The kind that prevents your kingdom from being even more so,' Tyrion responds (5.8). It's unusual for any Westerosi nobles to think holistically about the responsibilities of power, but Tyrion's outsider status, his struggle for acceptance, has given him extraordinary insight. As Martin observes:

> [I]f you look at the books, my heroes and viewpoint characters are all misfits. They're outliers. They don't fit the roles society has for them. They're 'cripples, bastards, and broken things' – a dwarf, a fat guy who can't fight, a bastard, and women who don't fit comfortably into the roles society has for them.[3]

Both show and books have foregrounded Tyrion's (metaphorical) growth into a bigger and better human being since we first met him in the brothel outside Winterfell. His marginalisation has enabled that learning process, but he also draws much of his effectiveness as a character from his subversion of what we – and most of the rest of the Known World – expect a dwarf to be.

THE QUEEN

Among the great movers in the court, we finally come to Cersei. Cersei is essentially a short-term strategist, reacting to events rather than shaping them. At first, her main motivation is to keep secret the incestuous relationship with Jaime and her children's true parentage. After Joffrey's succession, she soon realises that he will be impossible to control – not least in his impetuous decision to behead Ned Stark; 'that bit of theatre will haunt our family for a generation,' as Tyrion points out (2.1). Cersei continues to spar with Tyrion over the conduct of the kingdom while he is acting as Hand, and tries to have him killed during the Battle of the Blackwater. Tyrion's furious threat when he fears that Cersei will avenge his strategic dispatch of Myrcella to Dorne – 'I will hurt you for this. A day will come when you think you are safe and happy […] and your joy will turn to ashes in your mouth, and you'll know the debt is paid' (2.8) – seals his fate after the Purple Wedding.

The roles of queen, queen mother (which Cersei assumes after Robert's death) and queen regent (while Tommen is in his minority) were regarded in medieval Europe as both dangerous and influential. Councillors worried about the queen's access to the king; her capacity to persuade him in private to particular courses of action, often to use her influence in favour of her own kinsmen, was one recurrent anxiety. In Anglo-Saxon England, the wives of the kings of Wessex were no longer consecrated as queens, after an infamous scandal. Eadburh, daughter of King Offa of Mercia, was Beorhtric of Wessex's extremely unpopular queen, or so Asser, Alfred the Great's biographer, tells us:

> as soon as she had won the king's friendship she began to behave like a tyrant after the manner of her father – to loathe every man whom Beorhtric liked, to do all things hateful to God and men, to denounce all those whom she could before the king, and thus by trickery to deprive them of either life or

power; and if she could not achieve that end with the king's
compliance, she killed them with poison.[4]

In 802, according to Asser, Eadburh tried to poison her husband's
favourite, but the king accidentally drank the poison first, followed by the hated young man, and both died. Eadburh fled to the
court of the Emperor Charlemagne at Aachen, with a great deal of
treasure stolen from Wessex. Charlemagne asked the young widow
whether she would rather marry him or his son; without thinking
strategically, Eadburh opted for the son, 'since he's younger than
you', and the offended Emperor then refused to let her marry either
of them, making her abbess of a convent instead. This new career
did not last long, for Eadburh was discovered in a sexual liaison
with an Englishman and thrown onto the streets. She finally died
a beggar in Pavia, Italy.

After this, Asser says, kings' wives were made to occupy very
restricted roles in that kingdom. It wasn't until Charlemagne's successor, Charles the Bald, insisted his daughter Judith be crowned
queen as a condition of her marriage in 856 to Æthelwulf, Alfred's
elder brother, that the queenship was restored. The behaviour of
which Eadburh is accused might well remind us of Cersei. Setting
up a court within a court, creating a faction loyal to her rather
than to the king, seeking to undermine his own trusted followers
and finally poisoning her husband: all these actions confirmed
medieval historians' worst fears about queens. Yet marry a king
must, if he is to have children, and thereby he entrusts his safety to
a woman who may not love him, and who may have very different
loyalties from him.

Once the queen was widowed, her influence depended on her
being the mother of the next king. If he were very young, it was
likely that a council of advisers would be appointed to oversee the
realm, quite often the young king's uncles. This could cause further
difficulties: if the uncles were his father's brothers, it's clear that the
death of the royal heir would open up the possibility of an uncle

inheriting. The fate of the Princes in the Tower at the hands of their paternal uncle Richard III is only one example of the danger facing the young king. The maternal uncles have less of an interest in the throne, which they can't inherit, and so both Jaime (father as well as uncle to Joffrey and his siblings) and Tyrion work to maintain their nephews' position. The queen mother's influence once again is unofficial, but it's clear that Cersei wields a great deal of authority. In a powerful scene where Cersei is sparring with the smirking Baelish about the incest rumours and his own self-made status, Baelish insinuatingly remarks that knowledge is power. Cersei orders her men to seize him and threatens to have them cut his throat. Baelish is, for once, terrified. 'Power is power,' Cersei retorts (2.1). But she also knows that she needs Baelish, particularly when she has to work with a Small Council that's low on brains and talent in Season Five, after her uncle Kevan Lannister has refused to serve as Hand as long as his niece intends to remain the power behind the throne.

Power is highly precarious when a woman wields it. The queen mother faces being supplanted by her son's queen, and the competition between Cersei and Margaery Tyrell ('that smirking whore from Highgarden', as the queen memorably calls her daughter-in-law (5.2)) for influence over the increasingly erratic Joffrey, over Tommen and over the people of King's Landing, plays out along familiar lines. A well-loved medieval tale is that of the Calumniated Wife: a king marries a beautiful woman who arrives in his kingdom, often having been set adrift in a boat. The queen becomes pregnant, and her husband is unavoidably away when the child is born. Seizing her opportunity, his mother sends him a message that his wife has given birth to a monstrous baby. Although the husband responds humanely, saying that he will wait to see the child for himself, his mother forges a response, commanding that mother and baby be cast out to sea in the boat in which she arrived. Through divine providence, mother and child are preserved, the truth is discovered, the loving husband is reunited with his family – and the jealous mother-in-law is put to death. The story – a version of which is told by Chaucer in *The Canterbury Tales* – illustrates in an extreme form the tensions which arise when a son marries, magnified by the struggle for unofficial power in the politics of the court.[5]

Cersei makes many enemies, then; after her father's death she systematically alienates Jaime, the powerful Tyrells, and even the Iron Bank of Braavos. Her decision to rebuild the navy, to avoid dependence on Highgarden's sea power, looks strategic, but it's motivated primarily by her jealousy of Margaery. And her decision (in the books) to make a deal with the Faith – to whom the Crown also owes a vast amount of money – to have the debt cancelled in return for the agreement to permit them to rearm, will be the catalyst for disaster. Cersei's aunt Genna observes to Jaime:

> Cersei has put some bastard on the council too, and a Kettle in the Kingsguard. She has the Faith arming and the Braavosi calling in loans all over Westeros. None of which would be happening if she'd had the simple sense to make your uncle the King's Hand. (*FC*, 33)

Genna is right. In the books Cersei's battle with Margaery culminates in the extraordinarily ill-judged accusation that her son's wife has committed adultery. The Blue Bard is tortured into admitting to his own and others' liaisons with her. In this, Margaery's plight resembles that of Queen Anne Boleyn, accused of a sexual relationship with the musician Mark Smeaton. Smeaton gave evidence against her under pressure and most likely torture, implicating five more men, including Anne's own brother George, as her sexual partners. All, apart from the poet Sir Thomas Wyatt, and Richard Page, were executed the day before Anne's death. The High Sparrow offers Cersei his assurance about Margaery's trial; it will be conducted by an ecclesiastical court: 'Who is truly fit to judge a queen, save the Seven Above and the godsworn below? A sacred court of seven judges shall sit upon this case' (*FC*, 43). In the show it's Loras's sexual orientation and Margaery's perjury on his behalf that brings them into the ambit of the Faith's judicial power. But the Faith's reach does not stop there. 'What will we find when we strip away your finery?' the High Sparrow asks Cersei. 'A young man came to us [...] and he has much to say about you' (5.7). And as Lancel's testimony reveals, Cersei is at least twice as guilty as Margaery, vulnerable to charges of perjury and treason (with regard to Robert's death) as well as fornication.

Cersei's imprisonment reveals to her how far the apparatus of terror, formerly the prerogative of the Crown, has now become an instrument of the Faith. To win bail from the dungeons under the Great Sept, she is forced to confess to her guilt in respect of one of the charges: her adultery with Lancel. The High Sparrow decrees that she must perform the 'walk of atonement', to walk stark naked through the streets of King's Landing from the Great Sept to the Red Keep, pelted with filth and reviled by the crowd, accompanied by a septa ringing a handbell and chanting, 'Shame! Shame!' (5.10). Cersei's long, golden hair is shorn, and she has no protection from the stares and jeers of the crowd. The scandal of such enforced public nudity, particularly visited upon a woman, would normally have been unthinkable in medieval religious practice; the sight of the female body was considered highly conducive to sexual temptation. There is some evidence, however, that adulterous lovers, if actually caught in the act by the local judge and two council members, could be hounded through the streets, bound together in a state of nakedness. This legal condition prevailed in the province of Agen in the south of France, though, as with a good number of other provisions in medieval law, it's very hard to know how often, if ever, it was enforced: the judge would certainly have to have good local information.

The nearest parallel in English history to Cersei's plight is that of Elizabeth Shore (also known as Jane), a mistress of Edward IV. After his death in 1483, King Richard III constrained her to do public penance. The charge was supposedly her promiscuity, but in the hurly-burly of the late stages of the Wars of the Roses, it seems much more likely that Richard had a political motive: Jane had been associating since Edward's death with the Marquess of Dorset, who had rebelled against Richard. Jane was made to walk from Paul's Cross to Ludgate prison one Sunday. She was clad only in her underclothes and carried a lighted taper, and attracted a great deal of attention. No less an authority than Sir Thomas More, writing some 50 years later, yet while Jane was – so he claimed – still alive, described her ordeal: 'in which she went in countenance & pace demure so womanly, & albeit she were out of al array save her kyrtle only: yet went she so fair & lovely [...] that her great shame wan her much praise'.[6]

In a well-known medieval tale, retold by the Italians Petrarch and Boccaccio, and also by Chaucer, the blameless peasant-born Griselda is experimented on by her sadistic husband to see what

23. Griselda removes her rich clothes and returns to her father's house

kind of ill treatment might drive her to protest. Finally, having failed to break her will, he proposes to send her home to her father, despoiled of all the clothing that he has given her. In Chaucer's version of this story ('The Clerk's Tale'), Griselda requests that she be at least allowed to wear her smock, to cover the womb which bore her husband's children: 'Lat me nat lyk a worm go by the weye,' she pleads.

The cruel Walter gives her permission to wear it. Griselda's walk is greeted sympathetically by the populace, who weep for her and curse her ill fortune; Griselda herself is dry-eyed and silent. Both Griselda and Jane Shore got off lightly in comparison to Cersei; it seems hard to imagine how she can ever live down the terrible shame associated with the public display of her naked body.[7]

Cersei did indeed share her bed with Lancel, and thus made herself vulnerable to accusations of unchastity; she has kept back the admission of her incestuous bond with Jaime. That the queen should be brought so low by a charge of fornication, when she is a widow, ostensibly in charge of her own body, indicates the changing mores that the Sparrow cult has brought about (see below for more on the Sparrows). Women with power, whether or not they misuse it as Cersei does, are always vulnerable to attack through their sexuality; men, in contrast, can behave as they wish. Robert's illegitimate offspring were scattered across King's Landing before Joffrey massacred them. Both Cersei and Margaery face trial. 'Your trial will separate the truths from the falsehoods,' the High Sparrow warns (5.10). Cersei opts for trial by combat, Margaery for an ecclesiastical court hearing. How the cases will be resolved remains to be seen, but that hulking new recruit to the Kingsguard whom Qyburn permits to carry Cersei to her quarters after the walk of atonement looks to be a more than adequate replacement for the Mountain as her champion.

Southern warfare

Our journey southwards from Winterfell took us through a country devastated by the War of the Five Kings. The Riverlands, the breadbasket of the Seven Kingdoms, has been put to fire and sword by roving bands of soldiers. King's Landing has escaped serious damage from Stannis's attack, though its harbour is clogged with the wrecks of the Baratheon fleet. Harrenhal, the mightiest castle in all the Seven Kingdoms, is still ruined from the aerial dragon-attack of 300 years ago. War brings anguish to the great and the smallfolk alike, but the smallfolk have little stake and usually little interest in its outcomes. At a local level, it does not much matter whether it's Lannister men or Ser Gregor Clegane pretending to be a Tully who burns a man's home and crops, rapes his wife and slaughters his children. 'It comforts me to think that even in war's darkest days, in most places in the world absolutely nothing is happening,' says the Blackfish to Catelyn (3.3), but that's not how it feels to the kind farmer who takes in Arya and the Hound and who is robbed and beaten for his pains, or to the war's many other victims.

The lack of political unity in the Seven Kingdoms means that there is no standing army. 'Why should every lord command his own men? It's primitive,' complains Joffrey (1.3). The north adheres to a military system rather like Anglo-Saxon England's: the lord has a group of close warrior comrades, called *heorthgeneatas*, or 'hearth-companions', in Old English. He also has subordinates who are pledged to his aid, the bannermen who bring men to fight on his behalf. The tie between lord and bannerman depends on loyalty and oath-swearing, not on payment. Like the Anglo-Saxon militia, the *fyrd*, these men are not necessarily trained fighters or especially well armed, but they probably have axes, shields and short swords. Talisa remarks about one casualty among Robb's poor bloody infantry that 'he's a fisherman's son – probably never held a spear until three months back' (2.4). Later medieval kings also relied on calling up lords to wage warfare for them, and their men were better trained than these hapless peasants. The great magnates of late medieval England maintained and paid their own fighters, who wore their distinctive livery. These men, trained to kill, in effect constituted small armies; they enforced law and order across the lord's lands, but could also visit violence on their lord's enemies. The Lannisters have their own such system of maintenance: thousands of Lannister men apparently ready to do their will. 'Now we've got as many armies as there are men with gold in their purse,' complains Robert (1.5). Jaime is able to bring 30,000 men in an instant response to challenge Robb's advance into the Riverlands. This is by no means all the Lannister forces, for Tywin has an equal number. Robb has managed to muster 18–20,000, though 2,000 are sacrificed in his feint to draw out Jaime's forces in the Battle of Oxcross, where Jaime is captured. Such standing armies are expensive to maintain; the gold of Casterly Rock is not enough in the longer term to sustain the numbers which the Lannisters throw into their struggle for power.

Until the War of the Five Kings breaks out, catalysed by Joffrey's petulant execution of Ned Stark, the realm has appeared relatively secure. The various threats around the Wall are largely discounted by the southerners, and it's assumed that the underfunded Night's Watch, 'ill-disciplined boys and tired old men' (1.3), will keep the Free Folk under control. The Narrow Sea, like the English Channel, keeps other enemies at bay. The logistical difficulties of getting a mounted horde onto a fleet of ships are probably insurmountable, despite Khal Drogo's boasts to the contrary. Seaborne enemies are to be feared; though there are not enough Iron-Islanders to do much more than raid along the coastline and seize Moat Cailin, the Stormlanders under Stannis – with the support of Salladhor Saan – have a much more formidable fleet. Their ships, built like medieval Mediterranean galleys, with rowers below decks and sails above, can carry a large number of men, and are reasonably manoeuvrable. They are equipped with naval rams at the prow, and it is the use of these against the King's Landing ships at anchor which proves so catastrophic in the Battle of the Blackwater.

Davos senses that something is amiss when there's no sign of a naval defence, but his old smuggler's instinctive suspicion is explained away by his son, Matthos: Stannis's night attack has simply taken Joffrey's forces by surprise. But Davos knows, as we do, that Varys already knows what Matthos had for breakfast, and that something else must be afoot. In the show, the huge number of barrels of wildfire hidden within the Crownlands fleet constitute Tyrion's secret weapon, as Davos realises in horror: 'A flash of green caught his eye, ahead and off to port, and a nest of writhing emerald serpents rose burning and hissing from the stern of *Queen Alysanne*' (*CK*, 58). The long shots of the battle in 'Blackwater' (2.9), with the hellishly lurid leaping green flames of wildfire meeting the yellow of the ordinary fire, set by the King's Landing archers, resemble Hieronymus Bosch's vision of hell.

The defence plan of the books depends primarily on wildfire, but also on the submerged iron chain which Tyrion has installed across the harbour mouth. Once this is raised, the ships in the Baratheon fleet cannot retreat but rather are forced to remain corralled in the raging green inferno until they are utterly consumed. The men under Stannis's direct command, already landed on the other side of the river, cannot now cross in force to reach King's Landing; that they have ships left safely outside the harbour explains how Stannis manages to escape.

Wildfire, that deadly secret of the Pyromancers' Guild, is a version of Greek fire, an extremely effective substance developed around 672 CE by the chemists of Byzantium, an equivalent of the Guild of Pyromancers, and immediately used to great effect against the Muslim fleets which had already taken control of Syria, Palestine and Egypt. Greek fire continued to be deployed right up to the thirteenth century; European Crusaders in the Middle East reported on its effectiveness. What the ingredients of Greek fire

24. Greek fire being used in a naval battle

were still remain unclear. The recipe was a closely guarded secret which, once lost, was never recovered.

Modern scholarship suggests that it was petroleum-based (there were plenty of oil wells near the Black Sea), mixed with resin for adhesion, and that its deadliness was enhanced by being launched by catapult or a kind of grenade launcher from specially adapted ships. It was the forerunner of napalm, the mixture of petroleum-based acids, with a gelling agent to provide the essential stickiness, that was widely used in the Vietnam War. The thirteenth-century French chronicler Jean de Joinville memorably describes the terrifying experience of facing Greek fire during an attack on a Crusader encampment at the mouth of the Nile in 1249:

> This Greek fire was such that seen from the front as it darted towards us it appeared as large as a barrel of verjuice, and the tail of fire that streamed behind it was as long as the shaft of a great lance. The noise it made in coming was like that of a thunderbolt falling from the skies; it seemed like a dragon flying through the air. The light this huge, flaming mass shed all around it was so bright that you could see right through the camp as clearly as if it were day.[8]

Tyrion's ruse with the chain, which (in the books) he raises after Stannis's fleet has sailed into the mouth of the Blackwater River, thus entrapping the ships once they've rammed the wildfire-laden vessels and are themselves aflame, may be adapted from the famous chain that the Byzantines deployed to close off the Golden Horn in the face of enemy naval attack. Made of huge wooden links riveted together, the chain could be dragged by ship across one side of the Golden Horn to the other. The bold Viking king of Norway, King Harald Hardrada, who met his end at the Battle of Stamford Bridge in 1066, found a way of getting round the chain. Earlier in his career, around 1042, he found himself in jail in Constantinople. He broke out of prison and abducted the beautiful Maria, a young woman related to the Empress Zoë; then Harald and his Scandinavians, the famous Varangian guard, seized two galleys in the Golden Horn and sailed towards the chain lying across the entrance. Harald's plan was at least partly successful. While the oarsmen rowed at full tilt, the other crew members ran with all their gear to the back of the ship, tilting the prow in the air, so that the galley had sufficient impetus to leap up onto the chain. At Harald's command, the oarsmen ceased rowing and the crew ran forwards, tilting the ship over the chain and into clear water. And thus the ingenious Viking sailed off into the Black Sea, dropping off young Maria to be safely escorted back to the Byzantine court. The second galley was not so fortunate; that ship foundered and many men were lost.[9] If only Davos Seaworth had managed to think up such a manoeuvre!

CHIVALRY

Chivalry is integral to the culture of the southern parts of the Seven Kingdoms, though, as we saw in the last chapter, the north too is a strongly militarised society. In Westeros, as in medieval Europe, aristocratic men's main social role is to fight: to maintain their personal honour, to defend their lands or to fight for the king against external enemies. Or go on the attack: to raid the lands of rivals, or – as has happened more than once in Westeros's history – to invade and conquer another territory. The fundamental requirement for noblemen to bear arms and know how to use them poses important and recurrent questions. Whom are the nobility to fight, when the land is not under threat of invasion? How can they be prevented from conducting endless petty civil wars? The answer to the second question is that the keeping of internal peace depends very much on the authority of the king. Whatever Robert Baratheon's character failings, he and his Small Council successfully kept the Seven Kingdoms at peace after he assumed the throne. In medieval England, the energies of the aristocracy could – as in the Hundred Years War – be focused on annual campaigns in France. The quantity of territory which changed hands in any one year was not normally very impressive, but fortunes could be made and lost through capturing, then ransoming, important enemies. Geoffrey Chaucer, the fourteenth-century poet, was himself captured when quite young during a French campaign of 1360. He was speedily ransomed by King Edward III for the sum of £16. More dramatically, King Jean II of France was captured by the English after the Battle of Poitiers in 1356. He was taken to England where he remained until 1360; his son Louis then replaced him as hostage while Jean went back to France to try to arrange for the payment of an enormous ransom. But when Louis escaped and fled from London, Jean felt honour-bound to return to England in his son's place, and there he died of illness shortly afterwards.

Being a hostage was not too grim a business if you were highborn. Like Theon, raised as an equal to the Stark children, the well-born hostage could expect to be treated like other nobility. Jean wasn't chained up in a dismal dungeon; since he had given his word of honour not to escape, he lived in John of Gaunt's brand-new palace at the Savoy. Jean's household accounts show expenditure on horses, dogs, falcons, a chess set, a clock (new technology at the time), and various musical instruments; his presence added style and panache to Edward III's already splendid court. No medieval monarch would have treated Jaime as Catelyn and Robb Stark do, caging him in public within the camp; by contemporary standards, treating a noble prisoner well but refusing ransom for him was already rather poor behaviour.

While England and France were engaged in whittling away at one another's territorial holdings, relative peace – apart as always from the depredations of the Scots – obtained at home. Once the Hundred Years War was over, however, the fifteenth century saw recurrent civil war: the Wars of the Roses, discussed in the Introduction. With no common enemy to unite them, the magnates fell to feuding among themselves. Perennially conducting foreign wars was not a pragmatic or affordable policy for European monarchs, and in the intervals of peace it was important to hone fighting skills and divert the nobility. Chivalry as cultural institution, associated with mounted noble fighters, developed from the twelfth century onwards for a number of reasons. Not the least of these was the need perceived by the clergy, who worked as secretaries, tutors and chaplains to the aristocracy, to school their violence and touchiness about honour and face, and to introduce them to courtesy (the ultimate courtly virtue), good manners, thinking logically and treating women with respect. Christian behaviours like defending the weak, fighting against the wicked, deference to women, telling the truth and offering a fair fight to the opponent became incorporated into the romances composed by the clerics and consumed – both read and listened to – in vast numbers by the knightly classes. And thus, over the course of three centuries, the barbarian warriors of early epic turned themselves into knights and began to behave more like the romance heroes – Lancelot, Tristan, Arthur himself – whose exploits entertained them in the evenings.

In Westeros, chivalry is partly a marker of social distinction and breeding – the Hound always growls when addressed as *ser* – and partly a set of behaviours. Knightly identity distinguishes those who belong to named Houses from mere smallfolk. A knight must have a horse and a sword as a bare minimum, and most knights are affiliated to a particular lord. Hedge knights are lordless; often very poor and given to roaming the land, sleeping under hedges and making a living by fighting in tournaments (and perhaps with a little banditry on the side), they have few claims to status. Like Don Quixote, they try to do their best in the face of poverty. Most knights, though, are affiliated to a House and wear its sigil. They have a strong sense of honour, and claim to treat women with gallantry. It's this romantic world, of knights and ladies, of true love and heroic achievement, as in the old songs about Jonquil and her knight-fool Florian, that bewitches Sansa and makes her believe herself to be in love with Joffrey. A more pragmatic and critical view of chivalry is robustly offered by the Hound:

> A knight's a sword with a horse. The rest, the vows and the sacred oils and the lady's favors, they're silk ribbons tied round the sword. Maybe the sword's prettier with ribbons hanging off it, but it will kill you just as dead. Well, bugger your ribbons, and shove your swords up your arses. (SS, 34)

Medieval knighthood had a religious dimension. Even those knights who weren't explicitly members of religious military orders (like the Knights Templar discussed in the previous chapter) would keep vigil in church the night before they were dubbed; watching over Tywin's body, Jaime remembers how he knelt all night on bleeding knees before the altar of the Warrior. When dawn came, Ser Barristan Selmy struck him on the shoulder with his sword, making him bleed afresh but also converting the boy into a knight.

While peace reigns, the knights of the Seven Kingdoms keep their skills sharp by competing in tournaments. Jousting – two knights tilting against each other on horseback, each trying to knock the other from his mount; hand-to-hand combat on foot, using swords and shields; and the mêlée, a general free-for-all

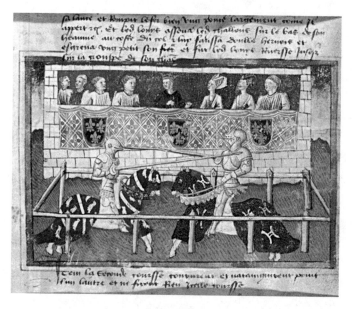

25. Two knights joust, watched by noblemen and ladies

involving a large number of knights, all offered useful training in handling horses, individual combat and manoeuvring in a group. Tournaments in the real world could be terribly dangerous affairs; although efforts were made to civilise the custom by using special padded tournament armour and blunted weapons, and by having referees to judge whether the codified rules were being broken, there were many casualties. And of course, in the days before antibiotics, even a small wound could become infected and turn into gangrene. Pouring boiling wine – the Hound's method of self-disinfection – into the injury may have had some effect, but it wasn't to be relied on. During the first half of the thirteenth century many of the greatest names among the English nobility – the Earl of Essex, the Count of Holland, his son, who inherited his title, and that second Count's brother – all died from tournament injuries. In 1279 the King of France's brother sustained such dreadful head injuries in his very first tournament that he was incapacitated for the rest of his days. In 1241 in Germany, 80 knights died in a single tournament – many, it seems, from heatstroke caused by their heavy armour.[10] Clearly there are more dangerous aspects to tourneying than having to face the Mountain.

Nevertheless, tournaments had their uses; they were not just keeping the nobility battle-fit and occupied. A good tourneyer might make his fortune, catch the king's eye and be granted his favour. When war was looming a smart king might go to a big tournament and recruit as many promising fighters as he could. In Westeros, the tournament fulfils similar functions. 'They give the great a chance of glory and the lowly a respite from their woes' (1.4), says Varys when Ned Stark challenges him about the wastefulness of the tourney held to celebrate Ned's appointment as the Hand. The entertainment value of the Tourney of the Hand is high; most memorably, Loras Tyrell's mare is on heat and distracts the Mountain's stallion so that he loses the joust. The mêlée is won by Thoros of Myr, whose flaming sword gives him a considerable advantage against mounted opponents. The spectacle of the tourney epitomises the glamour and the glory of medieval chivalric culture:

> The splendor of it all took Sansa's breath away; the shining armor, the great chargers caparisoned in silver and gold, the shouts of the crowd, the banners snapping in the wind ... and the knights themselves, the knights most of all.
>
> 'It's better than the songs,' she whispered. (GT, 29)

There's a considerable history of tournaments in the Westerosi past. Ser Arthur Dayne (the Sword of the Morning, Rhaegar Targaryen's best friend) had an extraordinary record in the lists: winner of the tourney that celebrated Viserys's birth and runner-up to Rhaegar at the tourneys of Storm's End and Harrenhal. It was at Harrenhal that Rhaegar chose Lyanna Stark as the 'queen of love and beauty' over his own wife Elia Martell: a choice which led to Rhaegar's abduction of Lyanna, Robert Baratheon's betrothed, and ultimately to Robert's Rebellion. Jaime holds Ser Arthur up as the epitome of knighthood to the lesser members of the Kingsguard after he returns to King's Landing: 'I learned from Ser Arthur Dayne, the Sword of the Morning, who could have slain all five of you with his left hand while he was taking a piss with the right.' (SS, 67).

Medieval romance originates the custom of knights fighting ostensibly for their ladies; in Chrétien de Troyes's late twelfth-century romance *Erec et Enide*, Erec meets Enide, the daughter of a poor knight, when he is searching for a knight whose dwarf has insulted the queen by striking her damsel (see above, p. 105). He learns that the annual Tournament of the Sparrow-Hawk will be held the next day; the discourteous knight Yder usually wins this and presents the prize to his lady. Erec vows to take part in the tournament, fighting on behalf of the lovely Enide, for he sees through her tattered silk dress to the beauty that lies beneath. Defying Yder, who assumes that no one will be brave enough to challenge his claim that his lady is the loveliest present, Erec overcomes him in fair fight, causing him quite a serious head injury. Once he has surrendered, Erec dispatches him to Camelot to apologise for his dwarf's discourtesy. Meanwhile, the sparrowhawk is presented to Enide, and Erec asks her father for her hand in marriage. 'That day she had won much honour, joy and dignity. Her heart was full of gladness for her bird and for her lord: her joy could not have been greater.' Erec is a king's son, and he speedily makes arrangements to instal his parents-in-law in his own land, granting them two stout strongholds and a great deal of gold and silver with which to maintain them. Enide will be taken in her old dress to Arthur's court, where Guinevere will personally see to her new wardrobe. And everyone is happy – except for Yder's damsel, who weeps at the loss of her sparrowhawk and her pre-eminent status.[11]

That the beauty and nobility of women effectively operates as a pretext for fighting between men, in formal contests intended to regulate their standing in the honour hierarchy, points to an important function for women in medieval societies. Without their presence at tourneys, the customs of knighthood, the brotherhood between men, especially the important relationships of affection and loyalty which obtain between them, could appear dangerously male-centred, shading even into a masculine erotic. The woman, by contrast, guarantees her knight's heterosexuality: it is she whom he loves, she for whom he fights. The preoccupation of chivalry with men – with their bodies, their vulnerability, their rivalry over status – is obscured by the rhetoric of romantic love and the claim that knightly competition is really all about service to their demanding ladies.

For, as Sansa soon discovers, the knights of King's Landing only pay lip service to the idea that ladies should be cherished. In the show Ser Meryn Trant obeys Joffrey's orders to beat Sansa on more than one occasion: when she is made to view her father's head and again after Robb's victory at the Battle of Oxcross. Trant's shockingly unchivalrous behaviour draws criticism from Tyrion: 'What kind of knight beats a helpless girl?' 'The kind who serves his king, Imp!' retorts Ser Meryn (2.4). During the Battle of the Blackwater, it's probably Stannis's foot soldiers who Cersei fears will rape the women if the city falls, but there's no sense that Stannis's knights would offer them any protection. Chivalry towards women is honoured more in the breach than in the observance – the better characters call out lack of chivalry when they see it, but those they criticise are rarely abashed. Some knights of course do adhere, at least in public, to the tenets of chivalry. Jaime does not kill Ned in their fight outside Littlefinger's brothel because 'it would not be clean' (1.5), and he is furious with the Lannister man who maims Ned mid-fight with the Kingslayer. And it's Jaime, too, whose unease about what Vargo Hoat/Roose Bolton and his men might be doing to Brienne at Harrenhal impels him to return and rescue her from the bear pit.

Contrasting with the chivalric ideal is the sellsword, or mercenary. Although such men are despised they can make an enormous strategic difference, both as individuals and en masse. Certainly

Tyrion owes his life to the roving sellsword Bronn, not only for championing him in the trial by combat before Lysa Arryn, but also for protection on other occasions. Sellswords operate largely on their own account in Westeros; in Essos, by contrast, they form into mercenary companies, where they make a reasonable living. We'll see more of them in the next chapter, but here it suffices to note that the problem with sellswords is that their loyalty is for sale. Tyrion gambles that his reputation will make Bronn risk his life to defend him in the Eyrie, and Bronn's no-holds-barred tactics work very well as the luckless Vardis Egen hurtles downwards through the Moon Door. 'You don't fight with honour!' gasps Lysa Arryn. 'No … he did,' grins Bronn (1.6). The proverbial saying 'A Lannister always pays his debts' is sufficient to keep Bronn on Tyrion's side and he even grows rather fond of his lord, but when Tyrion asks Bronn to fight again in the trial by combat occasioned by Joffrey's death, Bronn declines. Cersei's bribe, elevating Bronn to a lordship by marrying him to the mentally impaired Lollys Stokeworth, the putative heiress of Castle Stokeworth, has had the desired effect.

GOLD AND THE ECONOMICS OF WESTEROS

The economy of the Seven Kingdoms is in a parlous state. As Master of the King's Coin, Petyr Baelish does his best to disguise the state of affairs, pretending insouciance when Ned arrives in King's Landing and attends his first Small Council meeting. 'The Master of Coin finds the money, the King – and the Hand – spend it' (1.3), he smirks as Ned protests at the cost of the tourney staged to celebrate his appointment. In fact, as Tyrion discovers when he becomes Master of Coin in his turn, Littlefinger has been borrowing from the Lannisters, compounding the realm's dependence on Lord Tywin. In a painful interview with his father, Tyrion seeks to rein in the extravagant spending on Joffrey's wedding: 'Yes, the incomes are considerable, but they are barely sufficient to cover the usury on Littlefinger's loans. Will you forgive the throne's debt to House Lannister?' 'Don't be absurd.' 'Then perhaps seven courses would suffice.' (SS, 32). Although 'for all the gold under Casterly Rock' is a proverbial Westerosi expression, the mines which provide the Lannisters' fortune are running out of gold. Years of war have brought ruin to some of the most fertile parts of the Seven Kingdoms and the smallfolk are feeling the pinch. And winter is coming.

One enduring question about the finances of the Westerosi polity is quite how Petyr Baelish, with his thriving brothel business, comes to be entrusted with financial responsibility. The answer lies in the past: Littlefinger embodies the kind of rising man who could take advantage of new opportunities for social mobility. In this respect (if not in most others) he's reminiscent of Geoffrey Chaucer. Chaucer's father and grandfather were both London wine merchants, while at her marriage his mother owned 24 shops in the city. The well-connected bourgeois family were able to place their son Geoffrey as a page in the household of the Countess of Ulster, married to the king's second eldest son. Thus his royal connections began; soon he was travelling to Europe with his noble masters, journeying as far as Italy and Spain on the king's business and marrying one of the queen's ladies-in-waiting. Chaucer was appointed Comptroller or Master of the Customs at the Port of London, serving in that capacity for 12 years. In 1389, he was appointed Clerk of the King's Works, travelling far afield to oversee the king's building programmes. The bourgeois young man ended his career in major, if not stellar, royal offices (these would have been reserved for the nobility). But Chaucer's son Thomas served as Chief Butler of England for almost 30 years, as a High Sheriff, Knight of the Shire of Oxfordshire, and five times Speaker of the House of Commons. And Thomas's daughter Alice married William de la Pole, first Duke of Suffolk. Alice was the richest woman in England after the queen in her day, and her son married Elizabeth, sister of Edward IV and Richard III; we met her in Chapter One as Margaret of Anjou's custodian. Alice's wonderfully rich tomb, featuring her effigy above and her mouldering cadaver below, can be seen in the church of St Mary at Ewelme in Oxfordshire, in one of the best-preserved fifteenth-century building complexes in the country. From vintner to duchess in two generations is an impressive testament to the social mobility opened up in fourteenth- and fifteenth-century England through the effects of the Black Death, the expansion of the king's civil service and a change of dynasty on the throne.

Littlefinger is no Chaucer (as far as we know, at least – we don't see him working on his poetry in his private moments). Nevertheless, from relatively humble origins in the Fingers, a depressingly poor patch of land to the north of the Vale, from a House that can't even attract its own maester, he has done extraordinarily well. Like the Chaucers, Littlefinger's fortunes thrive on social unrest:

> Chaos isn't a pit. Chaos is a ladder. Many who try to climb it fail and never get to try again. The fall breaks them. And some are given a chance to climb; they cling to the realm or the gods or love. Only the ladder is real. The climb is all there is. (3.6)

This conversation between Varys and Littlefinger in the episode entitled 'The Climb' counterpoints the desperate efforts of the wildlings, led by Jarl and the Magnar of Thenn, to scale the Wall. Baelish's life has been less dramatic than that, but he has climbed much higher than the Wall's 700 feet. Fostered at Riverrun with the more powerful and better-born Tullys, Petyr exploited Lysa Arryn's romantic obsession with him. Jon Arryn made him Master of Customs at Gulltown, the principal port of the Vale, where his acumen increased income to the Vale ten times over. This began his social ascent; through Lysa and Jon Arryn's patronage he was

called to King's Landing, presumably started up the brothel business
which he runs with unsentimental efficiency, and was promoted
to Master of Coin. Varys reads him shrewdly: 'He would see this
country burn if he could be king of the ashes' (3.4). Once he has been
created Lord of Harrenhal (however empty a title that might be) in
the wake of the Battle of the Blackwater, Littlefinger is happy to cede
his office to Tyrion, demoted from the role of the Hand, and to put
his new schemes into action. He regards Sansa, both as the heiress
to Winterfell and as the image of her beloved mother, as key to his
greater ambitions; for his tenure of the Lordship of the Vale cannot
be the limit of his achievements. We've known from the famous
'sexposition' scene of the first season that Littlefinger wants it all:

> Baelish: 'You know what I learnt losing that duel? I learnt that
>   I'll never win. Not that way. That's their game, their rules.
>   I'm not going to fight them: I'm going to fuck them. That's
>   what I know, that's what I am, and only by admitting what
>   we are can we get what we want.'
> Ros: 'And what do you want?'
> Baelish: 'Oh, everything, my dear. Everything there is.' (1.7)

Petyr Baelish's timely demitting of the office of Master of Coin
has saved him from direct association with the disastrous state of
the realm's finances, revealed when Tyrion takes over the books:
'Littlefinger's gold is made from thin air, with a snap from his finger,'
the dwarf realises (3.3); there's no substance behind the opulence
of the court. The Crown was 6 million dragons in debt when Ned
took over as Hand; half of this sum was owed to the Lannisters.
The cost of the war has only intensified matters; Tyrion has little
time to improve the realm's position, in particular to prevent the
ridiculously extravagant 77 courses of Joffrey's wedding feast, before
he himself is arraigned.

The Crown is also heavily in debt to the Iron Bank of Braavos
(see Chapter Four). The only recourse for Cersei, facing bankruptcy

as the Lannister gold fails, is to refuse to repay the loans made by the Iron Bank, and thus she recruits them to the side of the rebels. In the show Stannis, with Davos's help, is enabled to recoup his forces after the Blackwater Bay disaster with a loan from the Bank; the argument that the current regime of the Seven Kingdoms is a poor risk, especially if Tywin were to die, wins the day. While Jon and Stannis enter into negotiation with the Iron Bank, Cersei is hoping that other banks, in Myr and Pentos, may be prepared to extend credit to Tommen's government; the consequences of the Crown's debt to the Faith is discussed below.

The finances of the Baratheon dynasty, then, are not dissimilar to those of later medieval England. The Crown was constantly in search of ways to augment its income via taxes of various sorts in order to finance the war with France in the fourteenth and early fifteenth centuries. The economy had taken an enormous hit with the Black Death; the population reduction of between a third and half damaged productivity, raised the wages demanded by the survivors and contributed to the falling into abeyance of various kinds of forced labour levies. In effect, if a lord wanted his harvest bringing in, he now had to pay someone to do it. Trying to raise money through direct taxation, such as the poll tax which led to the 1381 Peasants' Revolt, proved both highly unpopular and difficult to collect. Indirect taxes, such as the duties collected by Chaucer at the Port of London, became crucial in underpinning the economy. The aristocracy too were land-rich but cash-poor: their estates were often entailed, meaning that land could not simply be sold off. Crack lawyers were employed to find ways of raising the entail so that money for equipping expeditions to fight in France (for the king could not afford to bankroll the armies), for ransoming prisoners, or for spending on the growing quantities of luxury goods and staples on sale in the markets of London and the other cities, could be generated from land.

Other parts of Westeros have evolved beyond the main raiding/tribute/gold-giving/slaving patterns which seem still to inhere among the Dothraki (see Chapter Five); slaving is regarded as beyond the pale for the Westerosi and causes Jorah Mormont's exile. And, for the most part, the Crown's problems with its money supply have little effect on the rest of the kingdoms. These depend on an agricultural subsistence economy, making use of small coins as units of exchange in market transactions. However, with the coming of winter and further restriction of the food supply, the dependence of those in the capital on the resources of the Reach, the most temperate and fertile part of the Seven Kingdoms, is likely to tilt the balance of power even further in favour of the Tyrells of Highgarden, the Reach's capital. For neither rich nor poor can eat the gold under Casterly Rock, and the rising prices of food in the capital signal yet further urban unrest and political trouble for Cersei and her Small Council.

THE FAITH OF THE SEVEN

The worship of the Seven is the distinctive religion of southern Westeros, though it is coming under threat from the cult of the Red God, R'hllor, whom we'll meet in Chapter Four. The Seven correspond to important archetypes of medieval thinking: the Father, Mother, Maiden, Crone, Warrior, Smith and Stranger. There are three male and three female figures; the Stranger has no gender and is not generally worshipped. The three female figures clearly intersect with modern goddess-worship, and very likely with Mediterranean and ancient Near Eastern beliefs about the female divinities honoured before the adoption of Christianity. The Father occupies the position in the divine hierarchy usually held by the king of the gods (the All-Father, as Odin is called, or Jupiter, whose name is derived from 'Zeus-Pater', Zeus the father). The Warrior, perhaps like Thor or Mars, is honoured explicitly by Jaime; the Smith is patron of craftsmen, while the Stranger is to be feared. Seven is an auspicious number in Christian thought – not quite as much as the Three of the Trinity – but the seven virtues, deadly sins and gifts of the Holy Spirit, among others, confirm its godliness.

In some ways the Faith of the Seven is very much like medieval Catholicism. Its priests (septons and septas) are vowed to celibacy and they worship within church-like buildings, or indeed the cathedral-scale edifice of the Great Sept of Baelor in King's Landing. Prayers are offered and hymns sung within the septs, and people often swear by 'the old gods and the new', or exclaim 'Gods be good!' Yet the Faith seems to have little impact on people's lives beyond marriages, funerals and of course coronations. The sept comes into its own on the morning of the Battle of the Blackwater, when Sansa ducks into the one in the Red Keep:

> Sansa had never seen the sept so crowded, nor so brightly lit; great shafts of rainbow-colored sunlight slanted down through the crystal in the high windows [...] the air was hot and heavy, smelling of incense and sweat, crystal-kissed and candle-bright. (*CK*, 57)

Sansa sings the hymns and prays along with the folk in the sept, but when the septon leads the congregation in prayer for Joffrey, invoking the Smith, the Warrior and the Father, she's had enough, and shoulders her way out of the building.

There's little sense of ethical teaching as promulgated by the Faith, and people are prone (like Catelyn and Sam) to saying that praying to the Seven has failed to yield results: 'The Seven have never answered my prayers. Perhaps the old gods will,' says Sam, electing to swear his vows in the godswood (1.7). Although Ned remarks to Catelyn, 'it's your religion which has all the rules,' it's quite hard to distinguish between the different mores produced by class, gender or ethnic differences and those derived from the Faith's religious teachings. Septons and septas in general don't garner much respect: the Stark girls take little notice of Septa

Mordane, and most of the other septons whom we meet in the southern lands are ineffectual, socially conservative, timorous or drunken and criminal. The paedophile Septon Utt, hanged for his crimes by the Brotherhood without Banners, the smallfolk outlaw group of Thoros of Myr and Beric Dondarrion, is simply the worst of a fairly unimpressive group of men and women; one notable exception is Septon Meribald, whom Brienne meets in *A Feast for Crows*. Yet, even Meribald walks barefoot to atone for the lechery of his youth. In this, the Faith resembles the corrupt late medieval Church as seen through the eyes of satirists such as Chaucer. In the 'General Prologue' to *The Canterbury Tales*, Chaucer gives us a fat monk, overly fond of hunting and feasting; a friar who is a frequenter of taverns and arch-seducer of women; a prioress who apes the manners of great ladies and cares more about her little dogs than the hungry; and the Pardoner and Summoner, two different types of ecclesiastical official, who are venal, ignorant, hypocritical and corrupt in different ways.[12] The Faith has been deliberately excluded from the political processes of the realm; there's no place for the High Septon on the Small Council, no communal prayers within the palace, no regular attendance at the equivalent of mass for the nobility or the knightly classes. It's the women and the old men who crowd into the sept before the Battle of the Blackwater to beg protection from the deities, not the fighting men.

Why (up until the great renewal of popular religion in the wake of the War of the Five Kings) is the Faith so ineffectual? I suspect it's because the Faith isn't associated with learning, with the vital technologies of reading and writing. The preservation of knowledge and the teaching of future generations are the province of the maesters, who may profess any faith they like and who are expressly apolitical; thus the Faith has lost purchase in the Kingdoms' politics. This has not come about by accident; a law passed in Maegor's time had forbidden septons to carry arms, disbanding the Faith Militant, the religious military orders which had fought against

Maegor's legal innovations. 'Even Aegon tr[o]d lightly where the Faith was concerned […] it was his son Maegor who broke their power, but even then the Faith came back under kings like Baelor the Blessed,' Martin has commented.[13]

The struggle between the Faith and the Crown, renewed through Cersei's capitulation to the Sparrows' demands that the Faith Militant be allowed to arm again, echoes one of the most significant political conflicts of the earlier medieval period. At stake was the establishment of the relative rights of the Church and of the king. In England, the issues included both who had the right to make clerical appointments and, crucially, the relationship of ecclesiastical and civil courts to one another. Ought the Church be able to drag lay-folk into ecclesiastical courts and fine them for their sins – a useful source of income? Could the Church insist that priests be tried for murder in their own courts, not regarded as subject to the same laws as ordinary men and women – a practice known as 'claiming benefit of clergy', and widely misused? And ought priests be able to appeal to the papal Curia instead of accepting the decisions of English courts? Such debates were central to the estrangement between Henry II and Thomas Becket; a struggle that ended in the archbishop's murder in 1170 and the king's excommunication – at least temporarily.

'The Pope! How many divisions has he got?' Stalin is reported to have said in 1935. Luckily for him, perhaps, the Pope had no army he could call up against the enemies of Christianity. The medieval Church had the possibility of excommunicating errant monarchs and placing under interdict countries whose kings displeased the papacy; this meant that no sacraments could be performed – no baptisms, absolution or giving of the last rites – and was an effective way of bringing the recalcitrant to heel. But in a realm where the aristocracy seem only to pay lip service to the Faith, it's not surprising that respect for the sanctity of septs and the personal safety of septons and septas has vanished during the ravages of the war. And it's also not surprising that the smallfolk should rise up to defend their religion, and to call for the rearming of the Faith if the security of its buildings and its clergy can be assured in no other way. Brienne encounters the first signs of the revival of popular piety as she rides to Maidenpool in search of Sansa: a party who are travelling with the bones of murdered septons and septas to King's Landing, in order to seek justice.

> 'These are the bones of holy men, murdered for their faith. They served the Seven even unto death. Some starved, some were tortured. Septs have been despoiled, maidens and mother raped by godless men and demon worshipers' […] The septon lifted one of the traces of the wayn upon his shoulder and began to pull. The begging brothers took up the chant once more. (*FC*, 4)

The Sparrows (perhaps a reference to Luke 12:6: 'Are not five sparrows sold for two farthings? and not one of them is forgotten before God') are on the rise. The barefoot septon whom Brienne meets in this company explains, 'the sparrow is the humblest and most common of birds, as we are the humblest and most common of men' (*FC*, 4). The Sparrows have massed in order to protect the religious (through violence), and they demand justice and respect for the Faith. Later they will mutate into the Order of Poor Fellows, a revived military order, and the Begging Brothers, a version of the mendicant orders of the high medieval period. Like the mendicant order of the Franciscans, whose brown robes they share, they reject materialism, preferring to wander from place to place, begging for alms and, presumably, preaching to those they meet. Cersei's assassination of the High Septon, appointed by Tyrion to replace the prelate murdered during the Riot of King's Landing, results in the appointment of a Sparrow as High Septon. And, as we've seen, it's not long before the new order is instigating a moral crackdown and employing the practices of the Inquisition: isolation, threats, torture and public confession. 'Belief is so often the death of reason,' Qyburn observes to Cersei (5.8); who defines what reason is – by which Qyburn and Cersei mean realpolitik – has become the prerogative of zealots.

And perhaps revolution is in the air. The High Sparrow tells Olenna Tyrell, 'You are the few; we are the many – and when the many stop fearing the few...' (5.7). He leaves the threat hanging there, but it's not long before we see indeed that the Sparrows are no respecters of social rank. As Tyrion drily observes when he hears of developments in King's Landing: 'Give me priests who are fat and corrupt and cynical [...] the sort who like to sit on soft satin cushions, nibble sweetmeats, and diddle little boys. It's the ones who believe in gods who make the trouble' (*DD*, 22).

THE REACH

Time now, with such dangerous popular movements taking hold among the smallfolk, to head out of King's Landing. Even the nobility have perceived that charitable giving and ostentatious piety are the new aristocratic style. We'll ride westwards to the Reach, the garden of the Seven Kingdoms, famous for its vines and the wine they produce, in particular the warm golden wine that comes from the Arbor, an island off the coast of the Reach. Mace Tyrell boasts to Tycho Nestoris, the supremo of the Iron Bank of Braavos, that 'the vintners say this might be the best year for red grapes in half a century' (5.9); although Mace promises to send him a cask of this autumnal vintage, the ascetic and scrupulous Tycho replies: 'I'm afraid I don't partake.' The Reach is a land of rolling hills and terraced vineyards; the huge river Mander runs through it, watering its fertile fields and nurturing the fruit for which the region is renowned. The Reach is ruled by the Tyrells, whose sigil is the rose, for flowers grow here in abundance. The people of the Reach are accomplished and noble practitioners of chivalry, which originated there. Ser Arys Oakheart epitomises the men of the Reach: brave, gallant, susceptible to the charms of women and instinctively distrustful of the Dornish among whom he finds himself. For there is an ancient rivalry between the Reach, the original home of the Faith of the Seven in Westeros, and the land of Dorne: Ser Arys remembers the tapestries in his ancestral home as depicting 'Lord Edgerran the Open-Handed, seated in splendor with the heads of a hundred Dornishmen piled round his feet' and 'The Three Leaves in the Prince's Pass, pierced by Dornish spears, Alester sounding his warhorn with his last breath. Ser Olyvar the Green Oak all in white, dying at the side of the Young Dragon' (*FC*, 13). These are very old legends, allusively told, but the reference to Alester and Olyvar recalls the story of the sworn brothers Roland and Oliver, heroes who fought for Charlemagne, Roland's uncle (and father in some traditions). The two friends perished at the pass of Roncesvalles in the Pyrenees, a battle which took place in 778 CE. They were betrayed by the traitor Ganelon and slain by Saracens attacking the kingdom of the Franks from Moorish Spain (a culture with strong similarities to Dorne). Roland had refused to blow his mighty olifaunt, or war-horn, until the very last minute, confident that the Frankish rearguard could hold off the enemy, while the wiser Oliver remonstrated with him, urging him to call for aid. The *Chanson de Roland* is the earliest poem preserved in French, probably dating from the mid-eleventh century, and it wonderfully encapsulates the epic heroism which helped form the new traditions of chivalry, a cultural institution which originated in France.[14] No wonder that this legend has been incorporated into the Reach's history, the land which takes the practice of chivalry more seriously and enthusiastically than the men of the Crownlands, and very much more seriously than the fierce fighters of the north.

The Faith arrived first in the Reach as it was the first region colonised by the Andals. The Starry Sept in Oldtown was the principal place of worship before the Great Sept of Baelor was raised in the new capital of King's Landing. And it's in Oldtown too that the maesters are trained at the Citadel, and are sent out across the Seven Kingdoms. Although they specialise in different kinds of expertise,

gaining a different kind of metal link to their chains for every quali-
fication, the maesters who serve in the castles and strongholds of the
realm are general healers, teachers, facilitators of communication
(in their control of the ravens) and advisers. The maester must be
male: as in medieval Europe, it's often a calling for noble younger
sons who won't inherit from their fathers, and they relinquish their
family names on appointment to a castle. The maesters are ideologically opposed to the practice of magic, though its study is possible;
a link of Valyrian steel is granted to those who master it.

Oldtown itself is a gracious old city; there's no slum like Flea
Bottom among its stone mansions and stately guildhalls. It's 'a
veritable labyrinth of a city, all wynds and crisscrossing alleys and
narrow crookback streets' (FC, Prologue). Like other university
cities, there are student haunts where the trainee maesters let off
steam, and where the young novice Pate waits to meet the Alchemist
to whom he surrenders the Archmaester's stolen iron key. To me,
Oldtown sounds rather like medieval Oxford, except that it's also
a major port; ships come from all over the Seven Kingdoms, the
Free Cities and the Summer Islands, bringing knowledge as well as
merchandise. It's a place of learning and literacy: Scribe's Hearth is
'where Oldtowners came in search of acolytes to write their wills
and read their letters. Half a dozen bored scribes sat in open stalls,
waiting for some custom. At another stall, books were being bought
and sold' (FC, 45).

DORNE

> Tywin: 'We are not the Seven Kingdoms until
> Dorne returns to the Fold.' (4.3)

From the Reach we must travel over the Prince's Pass with its
tragic history, down into Dorne, that searingly hot, mountainous
desert land, where fresh water is scarce. The heat of the extreme

south is countered with massy architecture, cool, tiled courtyards and formally laid-out water gardens with gushing fountains and trickling water. The Dornish are ethnically distinct from the other Westerosi. Dark-haired, olive-skinned, hot-blooded and passionate, they are a stylish and flamboyant people:

> The lords wore silk and satin robes with jeweled belts and flowing sleeves. Their armor was heavily enameled and inlaid with burnished copper, shining silver, and soft red gold. They came astride red horses and golden ones and a few as pale as snow, all slim and swift with long necks and narrow beautiful heads. (*SS*, 38)

They retain some of the customs of the Rhoynish people who migrated to Dorne from the mighty river Rhoyne over in Essos: tolerance of homosexuality and sexual liberty for women, and equal inheritance rights for women, mark them as different from the more patriarchal people of Westeros. For 'Dorne is different', as Arys Oakheart thinks to himself (*FC*, 13). Under Dornish law, Myrcella would inherit the Iron Throne ahead of Tommen; the political ramifications of that possibility are the preoccupation of the Sand Snakes, the daughters of Prince Oberyn, who seek vengeance for their father's death. Their attempts to persuade their uncle, Doran Martell, Dorne's ruler, to seek revenge, parallel the whetting undertaken by women in the Icelandic sagas. Here mothers, sisters and wives take it upon themselves to urge their menfolk to vengeance for slain kindred, displaying the victim's bloodstained clothing or railing at their sons until they are roused to action.

Just so, Tyene tries to needle her uncle into taking revenge:

> Tyene unfolded the piece she'd been embroidering. It showed her father, Prince Oberyn, mounted on a sand steed and armored all in red, smiling. 'When I finish, it is yours, to help you remember him.'

'I am not like to forget your father.'

'That is good to know. Many have wondered.' (*FC*, 2)

As Doran considers Tyene's plan – of declaring Myrcella the rightful queen – Tyene pushes him further: 'Some men *think* because they are afraid to *do*.' Most Icelandic men would have leapt into action once their honour had been called into question by a woman. Doran is a martyr to gout – 'No wonder you can't stand. You have no spine,' hisses Ellaria Sand (5.9) – but he is also too wise to succumb to the Sand Snakes' rhetoric. Dorne is holding back its strength for the moment, for the upheavals in King's Landing represent a considerable opportunity for Dorne to seize back some of its independence.

DRAGONSTONE

One more stop before we leave Westeros behind: Dragonstone, from where it's not so far across the Narrow Sea. This island at the entrance to Blackwater Bay is the original Targaryen seat in Westeros; built of forbidding black stone, its towers carved by Valyrian masons into the shape of dragons, it's a forbidding and gloomy place, 'a godforsaken rock' in Stannis's words (*SS*, 36). Stannis resents the fact that Robert gave him this bleak rocky fortress rather than Storm's End, the heir to the Iron Throne's traditional castle, awarded to Renly. We'll talk more about Dragonstone's role as the centre of the R'hllor cult in Westeros in the next chapter. For now, we'll consider that its princess, Shireen, was one of the few known survivors of greyscale. She caught this horribly contagious disease as a child, infected by a doll brought to the island by a Dornish trader. No one knew that his goods harboured greyscale, Stannis recalls: 'Everyone advised me to send you to the ruins of Valyria, to live out your short life with the Stone Men' (5.4). But Stannis scoured the world for maesters who could offer a cure, and Shireen was saved, though disfigured. Greyscale is endemic beyond the Wall, and children usually die of it. It was in northern Europe, predominantly Norway, Iceland and parts of England, where leprosy, greyscale's real-world parallel, lingered well into the nineteenth century.

The Stone Men are outcasts; their greyscale has caused their skins to calcify so that they literally appear to be made of stone. They have lost all feeling in their limbs, and when the greyscale affects their brains it engenders a murderous madness. Traditionally the Stone Men are exiled to Essos: to the Sorrows on the River Rhoyne in the books, to Valyria in the show, and it is there that Tyrion encounters them. The mere touch of a Stone Man can infect a victim with the disease, and Tyrion, unlike his companion, is lucky to escape. Just as the Stone Men are exiled from civilisation, so medieval lepers were cast out of society for fear both of infection and of the sinfulness that was believed to have caused the disease. Leper hospitals were established where they might be nursed away from the community; the early thirteenth-century historian Matthew Paris estimated that there were 19,000

26. A leper with his clapper and beggar's staff

leprosaria across Europe, though it's hard to know where he got his figures from. Medieval literature depicts lepers as roaming the countryside begging for their livelihoods, ringing a bell or carrying a clapper to warn people to leave out gifts of food for them and then to retreat.

In a twelfth-century version of the French romance of *Tristan*, that of Béroul, the unfaithful Queen Yseut is threatened with being handed over to a community of lepers. She will become their sexual plaything as a punishment for her infidelity, for leprosy was widely thought to be contracted through sexual intercourse. Tristan disguises himself as a leper and rescues his beloved; his disguise points to a moral contamination in loving his uncle's wife.[15] In a fifteenth-century Scots poem by Robert Henryson, Cresseid, the heroine of Chaucer's earlier great poem *Troilus and Criseyde*, contracts leprosy as a divine punishment after she has cursed the gods. Cresseid is taken in by a kindly group of lepers who teach her how to live in her new condition, and she dies with a new understanding of the wrongs she has done.[16]

Baldwin IV, known as the Leper King, was King of Jerusalem in the twelfth century. His tutor, William of Tyre, discovered he had leprosy when he saw him among a group of boys, playing at digging their fingernails into one another's arms; Baldwin did not feel any pain. The full development of the disease only became apparent a few years later, at puberty; Baldwin was not expected to live long, but in fact his reign lasted for 11 years and he died at the age of 24. His right arm and hand were badly affected by the disease, so he is said to have learnt, like Jaime, to fight with his left hand. The Shrouded Lord, in the books the leader of the Stone Men, may owe something to Baldwin. The Shrouded Lord is partly the stuff of legend, for he has lived far longer than seems consonant with the illness; as Tyrion suspects, his may well be a title held by a succession of greyscale victims.

In the books there's a faster-acting, highly virulent version, greyplague, which behaves like the Black Death. The parallel is

27. A boys' game of hitting one another enables
William of Tyre to discover Baldwin's leprosy

upheld by an episode from the history of Oldtown, way back in the
youth of Grand Maester Pycelle. Greyplague came to the city and
three quarters of the population died. Lord Quenton Hightower
ordered the city to be quarantined; all the shipping in the harbour
was burned and no one was allowed to enter or leave the city. The
Reach was saved from the outbreak developing into an epidemic,
though Lord Quenton was murdered by the survivors (*FC*, 8). Just
so, the little village of Eyam in Derbyshire contained an outbreak
of bubonic plague in 1665, accidentally imported (like Shireen's
doll) in a flea-ridden roll of cloth sent from London. Eyam's rector
and the Puritan minister took charge in the ensuing outbreak,
isolating the village for fourteen months while the disease ran

its course. 'Plague stones' were designated to mark the boundary which should not be crossed, and outsiders would leave food and other vital commodities on the 'Coolstone' in exchange for coins doused in disinfecting vinegar.

It's perhaps unfair to say farewell to Westeros from one of its gloomiest and least-loved corners; we should at least pause to take in the intricacy and craftsmanship of its castle and reflect on the feelings of the first Targaryens to live there, who'd left behind their 'city of a thousand years' in response to a prophecy of doom. But that's a story for Chapter Five. For from here we journey over the Narrow Sea, to the dramatic city of Braavos.

28. *Arya, Star of Winterfell*

CHAPTER 4

ACROSS THE NARROW SEA

Tyrion: 'There's more to the world than Westeros, after all.' (5.8)

BRAAVOS

Time to take ship now across the Narrow Sea, setting out from Dragonstone and hoping for a strong breeze to drive us briskly over these difficult, often stormy waters to make landfall on Essos. Our voyage along the eastern shores of the Narrow Sea will start with the northernmost port on the coastline. Just as in the opening sequence of 'The House of Black and White' (5.2) our ship brings us – like Arya – through the legs of the mighty Titan of Braavos, as we sail into the harbour of this important sea-city. Braavos has many affinities with medieval and early modern Venice, with its networks of dark canals and elegantly arching bridges.

Decaying palazzos, busy markets, lively brothels and wine-soaked taverns jostle against one another in this crowded townscape, and the streets are thronged with high-born ladies in strange headdresses, merchants hurrying to make their next deal, servants scurrying on errands in the fish and fruit markets and traders crying out their wares. By night, Braavos is a dimly lit and dangerous place; swaggering bravos in velvet and brocade roam from piazza

29. A view of the Piazza San Marco, Venice, by Canaletto

to piazza, picking fights for the sake of honour and reputation, and the taverns and pleasure-houses come into their own. Courtesans in their pleasure-barges glide along the canals, and the mummers, the itinerant acting troupes who put on their shows in playhouses, taverns or anywhere there's space, keep the city entertained. That Braavos contains the cry 'bravo' – the acclamation of the opera house – and 'bravura' in its name sums up the place: it's assured, dangerous and enticing, all at once. Syrio Forel, Arya's much-loved 'dancing master' and former First Sword of Braavos, was a typical Braavosi in his confidence and panache. For Braavos pre-eminently has style: its bravos fence elegantly and deftly, a technique known as the Water Dance; the courtesans, like Japanese geisha, are cultivated, skilled in various arts, refined in their conversations and appearance, and well-known about the city, drawing flocks of young men as their admirers, even those without hope of being able to afford intimacy with them. Like the Venetian carnival, the annual Uncloaking festival, which celebrates the city's decision to reveal its whereabouts – to launch itself on the Known World as a major trading and banking power – is ten days of revelry and licence. The citizens take to the streets in masks, drinking, flirting, dancing and fighting, all in celebration of their remarkable history.

For Braavos was founded by runaway Valyrian slaves and for a long time kept its existence secret. Slavery is not tolerated in the city, nor do its traders deal in human traffic (though they will ship almost everything else); Braavos's alliance with Pentos is predicated on the outlawing of slavery in that city also, though it's clear from Illyrio Mopatis's household with his bodyguards of out-of-condition Unsullied that the southern city operates a 'don't ask, don't tell' policy in this regard.

Like Venice, Braavos has its arsenal, not so much a storage building for weapons but rather a shipyard:

> a knob of rock that pushed up from the water like a spiked fist, its stony battlements bristling with scorpions, spitfires, and trebuchets. 'The Arsenal of Braavos,' Denyo named it, as proud as if he'd built it. 'They can build a war galley there in a day.' (*FC*, 6)

The city is the transport hub of the Narrow Sea. Gilly and Sam change ships for Oldtown there, and its pleasures lure the Night's Watch brother Dareon from his oath and his duty. An excellent singer, Dareon prefers to frequent the whores of the Happy Port brothel and the taverns, and he's making a decent living when he runs foul of Arya. In one of the many guises she takes on in her training in the House of Black and White, Arya is selling oysters on a little cart as 'Cat of the Canals'; she kills Dareon for his desertion and tosses his body in a canal. It seems odd that Arya should still hold to the laws of Westeros and feel empowered to execute its justice in a city founded by rebel slaves, but perhaps it's her residual loyalty to Jon Snow that makes her angry when she finds a deserter from the Watch.

Braavos is a proud city, then, with an unusual history. Ruled by a Sealord, like the Venetian Doge, its fortune is founded on trade – it has the Known World's largest merchant fleet – and on banking. It is not a military or naval power, preferring soft, economic power over the hard power exercised by the lost civilisations of Ghis or Valyria. Here Braavos diverges from the Venetian Republic; travelling in the eastern Mediterranean reveals that every significant city has its Venetian-built fort, from Crete to Cyprus, from Dubrovnik (a central show location) to Negroponte (modern Chalchis on the eastern Greek coast). Venetian galleys plied along the Hellespont up into the Black Sea, via Constantinople. Tunis and Alexandria were important emporia for obtaining African goods, brought down the Nile or by camel caravan across the Sahara; Tyre, Tripoli in Lebanon and Antioch were their ports in the Near East. Venice didn't just control the trading routes of the eastern Mediterranean; it profited too by shipping military forces over to the Holy Land in the successive Crusades of the High Middle Ages. And when the kingdom of Outremer had collapsed and the Crusaders had been ousted from Palestine (as discussed in Chapter Five), there was the lucrative business of pilgrim transport. Margery Kempe of Lynn, the fifteenth-century Englishwoman whom we met in Chapter One, tells us a little about waiting for some months in Venice before taking ship to Jerusalem, passing her time with regular visits to a convent. Margery was travelling with a group of other pilgrims, with whom she had an extraordinarily fractious relationship, for she abstained from meat-eating and wished always to be talking about the Gospel at communal mealtimes. The rest of the group regarded themselves as being on holiday and wanted to enjoy themselves; although they deliberately left Margery behind at one point during the journey across Western Europe, pilgrim groups converged in Venice and so she caught up with them.

Margery describes how the pilgrims had to arrange their own passage on a Jerusalem-bound galley, purchasing bedding for themselves and making sure that they had plenty of containers

30. A woman's head in a fifteenth-century headdress
on a pew end in King's Lynn Minster

full of wine (not as excessive as it sounds, for water was scarce
and often undrinkable). Margery intended to take the same ship,
but then had a divine premonition that she should choose another
vessel. However much her fellow passengers disliked her, they
quickly thought better of travelling on a galley about which Jesus
himself had reservations and they transferred to her ship, where
they bullied her unmercifully all the way to the Holy Land. There's
no space here to describe Margery's adventures in Jerusalem and at
the River Jordan; suffice it to say that her fellow pilgrims continued
to be horrible to her while the various Muslims ('Sarazyns') that
she encountered were kindness itself. God commanded Margery
to return via Rome, so she took ship for Venice once more; this
time the voyage was clearly rougher, for most of her companions
were extremely sick and very afraid. It's a shame that Margery
doesn't tell us more about Venice – after all, she gives quite vivid

accounts of her stays in Rome and Jerusalem.[1] Like the Venetians, the Braavosi profit indirectly from their pre-eminence in maritime transport. More important than passenger services to the port of Braavos is the merchant shipping industry. This has given rise to a rather modern financial infrastructure: insurance brokers and credit and foreign-exchange facilities. In other words, the Iron Bank of Braavos.

THE IRON BANK

Situated at the head of the Adriatic, with her mighty navy and merchant shipping, Venice was the obvious place for the foundation of the first medieval merchant bank in 1157. Although Jewish money-lenders, many fleeing from persecution in Spain and untrammelled by the Christian prohibition of usury, had already started to offer credit and insurance services across the Mediterranean seaports, they were often not allowed to buy property within Christian cities. Instead they would bring a bench (*banco*) to the piazza and trade from there, hence the word for bank in most European languages echoes its origin in 'bench'. Similarly, the Thin Man deals in insurance from his stall near the Braavos waterfront; his reneging on his obligation to pay out in case of loss has attracted a contract on him with the Faceless Men, though Arya's distraction by Ser Meryn Trant's arrival means that he lives to swindle his customers another day.

The huge wash of funds for the financing of successive Crusades and the need to borrow money for the republic's expansion into the eastern Mediterranean led to the establishment of the Bank of Venice. It's no coincidence that Shakespeare's exploration of the theme of international finance is called *The Merchant of Venice*, for its plot reflects exactly the meshing together of finance (in particular shipping insurance and credit for cargo futures) that made the city so rich and so powerful. Over time, Italians had managed to find a justification for lending at interest that did not contradict the

Church's teachings on the subject: loans might not carry interest, but a mandatory insurance premium would be demanded in case of repayment default. Or, it was argued, it was wrong to extract interest for loaning consumables – food, grain, fuel – but permissible for non-consumables, including, of course, money. Banking grew up in other areas of Italy, in particular Lombardy. Italian bankers from Florence and Lucca worked with the English Crown under kings Edward I, II and III to provide, in effect, current account and overdraft facilities to finance the kingdom's wars on various fronts: against the Scots, the Welsh and of course France. Just so, the Iron Bank finances (and makes a decent profit on) the wars of Westeros. Mace Tyrell reminds Tycho Nestoris that 'some consider usury distasteful, dishonourable', and he flatters the Iron Bank's chief official by praising the Bank's willingness to deal, indeed to gamble, for the promise of reward. 'We are not gamblers here at the Iron Bank, Lord Tyrell,' responds Tycho, blandly. But Mace ripostes, 'You are the world's best gamblers, and all the bets you won built this' (5.9). With 'this', Mace gestures towards the huge edifice of the Iron Bank, but more broadly he means Braavos and its fortunes.

Chaucer's *The Canterbury Tales* describes financial wheeler-dealing among merchants in London, Paris and Bruges. The Merchant, resplendent in a Flemish beaver hat, bores the other pilgrims by always talking about his profits: involved in foreign-exchange dealing in the Low Countries to finance his import–export business, he manages his affairs so well that 'wiste no wight [no one knew] that he was in dette'. This, with typical Chaucerian slipperiness, could mean that no one knew that the Merchant was in debt because he wasn't, or more likely that the Merchant was well aware of the role that reputation played in maintaining a positive credit rating.[2] Foreign-exchange dealing was one way of getting round the usury prohibition; clearly an English merchant needed Low Country currency (*scheeldes*) for the English wool trade with Bruges, Antwerp and Ghent, and a percentage could be skimmed off when the exchange was made.

31. *The Moneylender and his Wife*

In 'The Shipman's Tale', the protagonist journeys from St Denis, near Paris, on a business trip to Bruges to buy some merchandise on credit. He notes that for merchants, 'ye knowe it well ynogh / Of chapmen, that hire moneie is hire plogh / we may creance whil we have a name' (As you know well, for merchants, their money is their plough; we can speculate while we have a [good] name). The merchant's trip to Flanders goes well, but the cost of the goods is more than he expected: he gives a promissory note to a lender in Bruges and subsequently must raise enough francs to buy the foreign exchange to redeem his note. The note amounts to 20,000 *scheeldes*; he discharges the debt, 'payd eek in Parys / to certeyn Lumbardes redy in hir hond / the somme of gold / and gat [got] of hem [them] his bond'. He goes home cheerful, having calculated that he has made a good thousand francs' profit, in part on his goods and in part because of the more favourable exchange rate he can get in Paris in comparison with Flanders. The Lombards act as the Flanders merchant's agents, remitting the payment to him.[3] Chaucer, as Comptroller of Customs in the Port of London, was well versed in the practices of merchants in the import–export business, and he talks about *creaunce* and *chevyssaunce* (offering or using credit for profit) with some expertise. Foreign-exchange dealing was certainly regarded, even by the Church, as exempt from the prohibition on usury, for international trade was impossible without some such provision.

The functionaries of the Iron Bank of Braavos lack the dash of Venetians; instead they share the austere canniness of the money-men of the Low Countries. Braavos, we should remember, is on the same latitude as the Eyrie, and the mists that creep along the canals of a morning are distinctly chill in their clamminess: 'Braavos was a city made for secrets, a city of fogs and masks and whispers' (*FC*, 34). The dark clothing and lack of showiness displayed by Tycho Nestoris, the bank's most prominent representative, suggests rectitude; he recalls the prudent officials we see in the paintings of Rembrandt, such as the 1662 'Syndics of the Drapers' Guild' (*De Staalmeesters*) in the Rijksmuseum, Amsterdam. The Iron Bank's prosperity is founded on the city's political stability. It's stayed aloof from the various wars between the other Free Cities which still rage from time to time, and since it has few natural resources, none of its neighbours have bothered to attack it. Stability is crucial for a banking system: no one will invest in a business which may be sequestered or sacked with a change in the political climate, and thus the Iron Bank has the edge on the banks in the other Free Cities. The Iron Bank is relentless in claiming repayment from those who owe it money; 'the Iron Bank will have its due' is almost proverbial. When Tyrion, the newly appointed Master of Coin, finally gets a chance to examine Lord Baelish's books he is horrified at what he discovers. 'He's stealing it?' asks Bronn.

'Worse, he's borrowing it. The Crown owes millions to my father,' Tyrion explains. But: 'It's not my father I'm worried about, it's the Iron Bank of Braavos […] If we fail to repay these, the bank will fund our enemies.' Lord Tywin too recognises the Bank's hidden political clout: 'You can't run from them, you can't cheat them, you can't sway them with excuses. If you owe them money and you don't want to crumble yourself, you pay it back' (3.3). And that reputation, indeed, seems to be the basis of the Iron Bank's success. When the Iron Throne defaults on its payments, the Bank decides to back Stannis's claim, subjecting Stannis and Davos, his Hand, to a humiliating interview (4.7). Stannis, so Tycho Nestoris reckons, is not a good risk, but Davos persuades the board that, nevertheless, the Baratheon forces represent the best chance the Bank has of recovering the millions on which the Iron Throne has now defaulted, and the financing is secured.

In the books, the Iron Bank itself takes the initiative in deciding to back Stannis; Tycho Nestoris arrives at the Wall in search of him and is directed by Jon Snow to Stannis's expedition to retake Winterfell. Nestoris has a rather ponderous bankerly manner: 'The banker pressed his fingers together. "It would not be proper for me to discuss Lord Stannis's indebtedness or lack of same,"' but he goes on to assert that Robert's debts 'belong to the Iron Throne […] and whosoever sits on that chair must pay them' (DD, 44). The Bank retaliates against Cersei's cessation of repayments; Westerosi enterprises are finding it hard to get credit, not just from the Iron Bank but from the other Free City banks as well, compounding the economic problems caused by the wars. The default was driven, as we saw in Chapter Three, by Cersei's decision to concentrate on rebuilding the navy so that she need not depend on the Tyrells for sea defence, now that the Iron Throne's ships lie rotting beneath Blackwater Bay. 'We need our own bank, Cersei decided, the Golden Bank of Lannisport. Perhaps when Tommen's throne was secure she could make that happen' (FC, 36). Given that Cersei knows that the gold mines of the Westerlands are exhausted and the Lannisters will soon be hard-pressed to pay any of their own debts, this rumination shows just how little she understands about finance. For, 'when princes failed to repay the Iron Bank, new princes sprang up from nowhere and took their thrones' (*DD*, 44).

VALAR MORGHULIS

The other business of interest in Braavos is the strange trade plied by the inhabitants of the House of Black and White, the massive windowless building to which Arya is admitted on her arrival in the city. The House is the temple of the God of Death, the Many-Faced God, where people can come and seek euthanasia at the acolytes' hands. It is also the headquarters of the Faceless Men, a guild of assassins. We've met Jaqen H'ghar in Westeros, where he and Arya struck up a strange friendship. On parting he gave her the coin that assures her passage to Braavos and her admission to training in the House; he teaches her the High Valyrian phrase *valar morghulis* (all men must die). Jaqen H'ghar has proved capable of killing without detection, but he has also made it clear that he kills on his own terms, and he acts entirely dispassionately. When Arya meets him he has the face and manner of a man from Lorath, which partly explains his idiosyncratic way of speaking: 'A man is thirsty', 'A girl may have three deaths', and so on. But he can also change his face when he needs to, a gift which is underwritten by the faces which hang in the storeroom in the deepest level of the House. Why Jaqen H'ghar was operating undercover in Westeros is unclear; was his initial encounter with Arya, being transported from the Black Cells below the Red Keep to the Wall, sheer coincidence, or was his intention always to recruit her? In the books he appears subsequently to have infiltrated the Order of Maesters (*FC*, Prologue) as 'the Alchemist', with a motive that has yet to emerge.

Arya is now training to become a Faceless Man, an assassin like Jaqen H'ghar, and must abnegate her own personality in order to

become 'No One', the only identity to which the fully fledged assassin will admit. This is hard for Arya with her strong and stubborn
individuality, and it's not clear that she will necessarily be accepted
into the Guild, though she is certainly learning some useful skills
in her apprenticeship to the God of Death. The greatest obstacle
for her, perhaps, is the arcane philosophical system that underpins
the beliefs of the Faceless Men and their demand for dispassionate
dealing. The Guild is effective, but extremely expensive to employ,
and since they are not particularly interested in profit they whimsi-
cally refuse commissions or impose conditions which demand that
the commissioner reconsider how much he really wants to take
his enemy's life, arriving perhaps at a truer calibration of its cost.

The medieval period too had its secret society of assassins: the
Nizari Ismailis, an Islamic sect formed in the late eleventh century
in Persia and Syria. The Nizaris opposed the Sunni Seljuq dynasty
that held sway in Persia and successfully seized several mountain
forts; this gave rise to the nickname given to their leader, Hassan-i
Sabbah: 'The Old Man of the Mountains'. The headquarters of the
fidai, as the men trained in espionage and assassination were called,
was one of these forts: Alamut, in what's now north-western Iran.
These men were young, vigorous, though obviously expendable,
and were remarkable in that they had no animus against ordinary
citizens and, like the Faceless Men, tried to avoid collateral casualties when carrying out their assignments. The task of infiltrating
the victim's retinue, speaking the right language and blending in
with his servants and advisers called for particular skills and intelligence. The selective elimination of enemies through killings often
carried out in public places struck fear into the Nizaris' enemies and
increased their political leverage. Daggers were the usual weapon,
often dipped in poison, though a dagger pinning a threatening note
to a pillow could often be just as effective in bringing enemies to
heel. The main sect of assassins was finally put out of business when
the Mongols destroyed its Alamut headquarters in 1256 as part of
the campaign of Hulagu, the khan undertaking the invasion of Syria

and Palestine (discussed in Chapter Five). The Syrian branch of the assassins survived into the fourteenth century, working for the Mamluks of Egypt; at that time Ibn Battuta, the great Moroccan traveller, mentions their distinction of being willing to kill for a fixed sum of money and describes them as 'The Sultan's Arrows':

> when he desires to send one of them to assassinate some foe of his, he pays him his blood money. If he escapes after carrying out the deed, the money is his, but if he is caught it goes to his children. They have poisoned knives with which they strike their victims but sometimes they fail and are themselves killed.[4]

The historical facts about the Assassins are nowhere near as excit-ing as the legends which spread about them in the medieval world. John Mandeville knew of them and relates how their leader, the Old Man of the Mountain, trained them in his mountain fortress. Named Catolonabes by Mandeville, he had a walled garden built here, a veritable paradise of flowers and trees, sweetly singing birds and wonderful beasts, where beautiful virgins and handsome young men were to be found wandering its pathways and drink-ing from its jewel-adorned wells. Whenever a knight came there, so Sir John tells us, the Old Man would 'maken hem to drynken of a certeyn drynk', which intoxicated him and greatly enhanced his pleasure in his surroundings. Then the Old Man would spring his offer: if the knight would go and kill a certain man 'that was his enemy or contrarious to his list [opposed his desires]', and if he died in the attempt, Catolonabes would make sure that after death he found himself in a paradise that was a hundred times lovelier than the mountain fortress, full of willing maidens with whom he might freely have sex and who would yet remain virgin. This policy, Mandeville reports, was very successful, and the Old Man had killed numerous enemies through his 'sotylle deceytes and false cawteles [guiles]'. But not long ago, Mandeville relates, the castle was destroyed and Catolonabes' sway over his disciples destroyed.[5] And indeed only about 100 years had elapsed since the destruction of Alamut and less than that since the 1273 defeat of the sect's Syrian branch. Mandeville's account garbles Hassan i-Sabbah's name almost unrecognisably; he also mentions an intoxicant, which in Marco Polo's equally unreliable account is identified as a drug, assumed to be hashish. There seems to be no truth at all in the legend of the Paradise-like garden (rather difficult to cultivate on a rocky mountain outcrop) nor in that of the narcotic haze in which the young men signed up for service, but the word *assassin* migrated quickly into European languages for a hired and secretive killer: it appears, in a slightly different form more closely related to Arabic, in English as early as 1340. The assassins – with their fictional link to hashish – continued to haunt the imaginations of the west as epitomising the subtle, covert Oriental killer.

We'll take ship out of Braavos now, sailing back under the legs of the Titan with its echoes of the Colossus of Rhodes, one of the Seven Wonders of the Ancient World. Our course lies southwards past the other Free Cities, and as we sail we'll consider their history and the Disputed Lands that lie between the Narrow Sea coastline and the mighty city of Volantis, our final destination. We'll be chary about disembarking in Pentos, Myr or Tyrosh, for these cities seem to be locked in perpetual skirmishes with one another, much like the city states of medieval Italy. And, as in Italy, their battles are often fought by proxy, through mercenary or sellsword companies that roam through western Essos, bringing death and plunder in their wake.

THE MERCENARY COMPANIES

We've seen sellswords operating singly in Westeros, itinerant fighters who'll follow any lord who pays them, like Bronn. Such men are useful enough; though, fond as Bronn is of Tyrion, he's not inclined to act as the dwarf's champion for a second trial by combat against the Mountain. The contrast between men who are sworn to their lord, as the bannermen are, obliged to fight when called upon, and paid standing armies, as retained by the Lannisters, was discussed in Chapter Three; contemporary medieval moralists deplored the breakdown (as they saw it) in human relationships caused by the replacement of bonds of love and sworn service by salaries and paid hire. The mercenary companies did not operate in England, but they were well known and much feared in

32. Sir John Hawkwood's funerary monument in Florence

France and particularly in Italy, where one of the most notorious bands was led by an Englishman, Sir John Hawkwood. His wonderful funerary monument, commissioned in 1436 and sculpted by Paolo Uccello, is one of the masterpieces in the Church of Santa Maria del Fiore in Florence.

Little is known about Hawkwood's early life; he was born in Sible Hedingham in Essex, where his father held a small amount of land. He seems to have fought in his youth in the Hundred Years War, perhaps at the battles of Crécy or Poitiers. After the 1360 Treaty of Brétigny brought (temporary) peace between England and France, Hawkwood moved east into Burgundy and joined a mercenary company. These 'great companies' would plunder and ravage the countryside, much like the Lannister troops in the Riverlands; it did not particularly matter to them whose territories they were attacking. Hawkwood eventually rose to command the so-called

'White Company', a huge band operating in northern Italy. Like the sellsword companies of Essos, the White Company fought for whoever would pay it: in 1364 it fought for Pisa against Florence, though the following summer Hawkwood and his closest officers swapped sides and fought for Florence instead. Thereafter the White Company saw many campaigns in Italy, fighting for the Viscontis of Milan against a Florentine alliance, then for the Pope in the kingdom of Naples. In the last years of his life – and hence the memorial – Sir John gave his services exclusively to Florence, serving as commander-in-chief of the city's armies until his death in 1394.

Hawkwood's success in the later years of his career depended on two factors. One was managing to retain a small corps of skilled and loyal officers. The second was his successful amalgamation of the roving English bands of mercenaries into a single company, mostly fighting with lances and bows and arrows, and keeping that force together. Many of the English were from Essex, indeed hailing from close to Hawkwood's family manor – in effect his bannermen. They were particularly good at fighting on foot and riding at night; they found the relatively mild Italian winters no hardship. Hawkwood became wealthy. Gifts of land and money were lavished on him by a grateful Florence in virtue of his service against his former employers, the Viscontis. Villages and small towns would pay the White Company to leave their district; ransoms and booty also swelled his coffers. Hawkwood paid his men well, assuring their loyalty, and he prospered in Italy. He planned to retire to England and Essex, buying property in London and near the family manor through the kinds of middlemen discussed above. He was in the process of realising his Italian assets in preparation for return to England when he died. The grateful Florentines planned a splendid grave, but in the event his bones were sent home to Essex at the request of King Richard II; this occasioned the long delay in completing the commission in Santa Maria del Fiore.

The sellsword companies who operate in Essos seem generally less effective than the White Company; this may well be a question of leadership. The habit of such companies as the Second Sons of changing sides for money cannot help their reputation. When they are hired to defend Yunkai, the Second Sons are commanded by Mero, the so-called Titan's Bastard, whose brutal reputation has made them unemployable in the Free Cities. After Daenerys's forces rout them while they are busy getting drunk, Mero flees and Brown Ben Plumm takes over. The company fights for Daenerys for a while, then, predictably enough, defects back to Yunkai, and it is thus that Tyrion, Penny and Jorah end up on their books. The Second Sons' name reflects the position of many medieval younger sons; with no hope of inheriting under primogeniture, they left home to make their fortunes by their sword. Tyrion jokes that, as a second son himself, joining the company was his destiny. Other companies include the Stormcrows (who leave Stannis in the lurch in the Winterfell campaign), the Windblown (led by the Tattered Prince), the Company of the Cat and a good few others, little distinguished from one another except by their reputations for keeping or breaking their contracts.

The Golden Company (clearly superior even to Hawkwood's White Company) are a cut above the other rabble. They were founded by a bastard son of House Targaryen, known as Bittersteel, who was exiled at the end of the First Blackfyre Rebellion, in order to employ the various nobles who had also been exiled. Tyrion reflects:

> From that day to this, the men of the Golden Company had lived and died in the Disputed Lands, fighting for Lys or Myr or Tyrosh in their pointless little wars and dreaming of the land their fathers had lost. They were exiles and sons of exiles, dispossessed and unforgiven … yet formidable fighters still. (*DD*, 5)

The Company has a strong reputation for keeping its word and its contracts, for discipline and effectiveness, though recently they broke their contract with Myr, an aberration which has caused comment even in Westeros, and made their way to Volantis. It emerges that they have been suborned by Illyrio Mopatis to put their 10,000 men – highly experienced archers – and many more horses and elephants at Daenerys's service and they expect to rendezvous with her there in order to mount the long-awaited invasion of Westeros, an invasion which will, finally, bring these exiles home. But when they learn that Dany is detained in Meereen, they throw in their lot with Jon Connington and his ward, and set sail for the Stormlands. They are going home, fulfilling John Hawkwood's long-cherished dream to see the county where he was born once again.

The other Free Cities

Our voyage southwards takes us past more of the Free Cities: Pentos, Tyrosh, Myr, Lys. There's no time to stop and explore them, but as they glide by on the port side of our swift Braavosi ship, tales are told of these strange societies. In Pentos, we learn from no less an authority than Illyrio Mopatis, they have a sacral kingship: the fertility of the land and of the king are one, and if the crops fail he must die:

> In Pentos we have a prince, my friend. He presides at balls and feasts and rides about the city in a palanquin of ivory and gold. Three heralds go before him with the golden scales of trade, the iron sword of war, and the silver scourge of justice. On the first day of each new year he must deflower the maid of the fields and the maid of the seas […] Yet should a crop fail or a war be lost, we cut his throat to appease the gods. (*DD*, 1)

The idea of the king who embodies the luck of his people and who guarantees the fertility of the land was made popular in the early twentieth century by the great anthropologist Sir James Frazer, in *The Golden Bough* (1922). Frazer drew his examples from Greek and ancient Near Eastern myth, and there's some controversy as to whether such sacrifice was part of European religion. There's a much-debated tale of one of the earliest Swedish kings, recorded in the thirteenth-century Icelander Snorri Sturluson's great work *Heimskringla* (Circle of the World), relating just such a custom. One year the harvest failed completely in Sweden, and so many oxen were sacrificed to the gods at the great temple in Uppsala. The next year the harvest was just as bad, and they took to sacrificing men, to no better effect. In the third year, therefore, the chieftains met together and decided that the famine was King Domaldi's fault. So they seized him, killed him, and reddened the sacrificial ring with his blood. Whether this fixed the harvest immediately or not isn't clear, but his son took the throne after him, and the harvests were always good during his reign. There's a wonderful picture over the central staircase of the National Museum in Stockholm, painted by the artist Carl Larsson in 1915. It's called *Midvinterblot* (Midwinter Sacrifice), and it vividly depicts Domaldi's death for his people. Although it was commissioned exactly to fill that space, it was rejected by the museum board; only in 1997 did the museum finally buy it from the collector who had acquired it and hang it in its rightful place. Whether Snorri's medieval account, which drew on a ninth-century Old Norse poem, was correct about this prehistoric Swedish custom is debatable, but Pentos, with its Greek-sounding name, clearly adheres to the sacral-kingship model. The Pentoshi also rely on more pragmatic ways of safeguarding their city: highly vulnerable to Dothraki raids, they make a point of staying on good terms with the horselords, paying them off and feasting them lavishly when they come to the city. It's no coincidence that Illyrio Mopatis, one of the leading Pentos traders, brokers and hosts the marriage of Daenerys to Drogo. He may be a 'cheese-monger', as Tyrion derisively terms him (cheese is a major Pentos export), but he has the contacts to obtain the dragon eggs that are Daenerys's wedding present.

As Pentos sinks behind us, Myr and the islands of Tyrosh and Lys lie ahead. Myr, renowned for its lace, has been at war on and off with Lys for 300 years, so we won't put in there. Tyrosh, with its pear brandy, its gaudily dressed people with their penchant for dying their hair green or purple, epitomised by the swaggering Daario Naharis, is more attractive as a destination. But the folk are greedy and quarrelsome, always hoping to chance their arms on seizing the Stepstones and making claim on the Disputed Lands (for what they are worth). Their wealth is derived from their exploitation of a certain kind of sea snail; these provide the dyes which they use to such striking effect. Tyrosh suggests 'Tyrian purple', the hugely expensive dye manufactured from the murex sea snail, originally by the ancient Phoenicians. The Romans too prized the dye for its colour fastness and its rarity, using it to colour the borders of the togas worn by certain classes; in some cases the whole garment might be dyed purple. How exactly it was made is not entirely clear; Aristotle describes part of the process, including the hideous smell that arose from the large vats of decomposing sea snails which were the raw material for the dye. And this stench may be reason enough not to drop anchor in the harbour of Tyrosh, however colourful its citizens.

As for Lys, it's the home of Salladhor Saan, the jolliest of pirates and Davos Seaworth's good friend, but it's also notorious for its alchemists who brew up such poisons as the 'tears of Lys': 'A rare and costly thing, clear and sweet as water, and it leaves no trace,' Varys tells Ned (*GT*, 30). Varys was born in Lys, so he should know. Another uninviting port, so we'll set our course beyond it for Volantis. Nor will we journey upriver to Qohor, Norvos or Lorath, braving the Sorrows and the Stone Men who lurk there. The people of Lorath sometimes become sellswords, but otherwise

stay put on their chilly islands in the Shivering Sea. Qohor has the
character of a northern city, surrounded by forests. It is defended
by an army of Unsullied, and its people worship the Black Goat, a
deity who demands daily blood sacrifice. Furs and pelts and timber
from the dense forests of northern Essos are the basis for Qohorik
prosperity, along with their renowned skill in metalworking, for its
smiths still retain some knowledge of working Valyrian steel. Tobho
Mott, the best metalworker in King's Landing, and the master to
whom Gendry was apprenticed, is Qohorik. So too is the savage
Vargo Hoat, leader of the Bloody Mummers, the man who maims
Jaime and devises the fight between Brienne and the bear (in the
show this is Locke, a quite different character). When Vargo tries
to rape Brienne, she bites his ear so savagely that the wound turns
septic and disables him. Thus he is able neither to escape nor to
defend himself when the Mountain retakes Harrenhal. His fate, to
be serially dismembered, has a baroque horror to it which seems
to require more imagination than we'd normally attribute to the
Hound's hulking brother. Vargo Hoat's limbs are cooked and fed
as 'roast goat' – a pun on his name and on the Qohorik god – to
the northern prisoners in Harrenhal. Hoat's fate is reminiscent
of that of Jormunrekk, the emperor of the Goths, in the Norse
poem 'The Lay of Hamdir'. Jormunrekk had ordered his son to be
hanged and his wife to be trampled to death by horses because his
evil councillor had told him untruthfully that they were having
an affair. Jormunrekk laughs triumphantly when he hears that his
wife's half-brothers have come to avenge her, but they are wearing armour which makes them invulnerable and they seize their
brother-in-law:

> Then said Hamdir the strong-minded:
> 'You were longing, Jormunrekk, for our arrival,
> brothers born of the same mother, within your citadel.
> You see your own feet, you see your own hands,
> Jormunrekk, hurled into the hot fire.'

But Hamdir and his brother had earlier made the fatal mistake of slaying their own despised half-brother when he offered, in riddling terms, to help them, and now they lack someone to cut off Jormunrekk's head. This gives Jormunrekk time to shout to his men to stone the brothers, since weapons cannot hurt them; the two young men die defiantly, having achieved a notable vengeance, even though they were the last of their line. Vargo Hoat's cannibalised fate chimes too with the legend of the Rat Cook, a tale Old Nan told Bran about the Nightfort on the Wall. The cook killed the king's son and served him up in a pie; the gods were horrified at this impiety, for the king was a guest under the Nightfort's roof and the killing was an offence against guest-right. Thus they turned the cook into a giant white rat, doomed always to feed upon his own children. Medieval story knows of Philomela and her sister Procne, who fed Procne's son to his own father in revenge for the king's rape of Philomela. And indeed Gudrun, mother of Hamdir and his brother, had, in an earlier marriage, slaughtered her sons and served them to her husband (no less a figure than Attila the Hun) in vengeance for his murder of her brothers.[6] Kin-cannibalism is worse of course than ordinary cannibalism, for incorporating one's own flesh and blood into *one's* flesh-and-blood is a huge breach in the natural order. Maybe it's just as well that the prisoners never knew exactly what the Mountain was feeding them on.

VOLANTIS

'Rich, ripe and rotted, Volantis covered the mouth
of the Rhoyne like a warm wet kiss.' (DD, 6)

And now at last we make landfall at Volantis, the huge port city at the mouth of the Rhoyne, the oldest and proudest of the daughter-cities of Valyria. Just as Greece and Rome established colonies around the Mediterranean, so Valyria expanded its power along the seaboard by founding new settlements at strategic port locations. After the fall of Valyria, we're told that Volantis regarded herself as the heir to Valyrian power and tried to impress her authority on the other cities; Lys and Myr were temporarily subjugated, but, with the aid both of Aegon the Conqueror on the back of his dragon Balerion the Black Dread, and of Braavos, they successfully rebelled. The damage done by this war, which devastated the Disputed Lands to the west of the city, along with the stranglehold that the inland, upriver cities of Norvos and Qohor could exercise on trade along the Rhoyne, saw off the Volantene bid to found a new Freehold.

That Volantis's name chimes with 'volatile' seems no coincidence; the governance of the city is divided between two parties: the tigers (in modern parlance, 'hawks'), the party of the military and the aristocracy, the Old Blood of Valyria; and the elephants (the 'doves', or perhaps the multinationals), who represent the interests of trade – merchants and moneylenders. Volantis has evolved a triarch system, in which three men rule the city, with one standing for re-election each year. Unlike the short-lived Roman triumvirates, the triarchy seems to have been a highly effective mode of governance: the involvement of three people mitigates conflict and rivalry between any two members. The fact that the elephants have been in the ascendancy for the last 300 years has checked Volantis's militaristic aspirations and been foundational for the city's prosperity. Moreover, the annual elections – ten days of drinking, debauchery, mingling of social classes and topsy-turviness – seem, like medieval carnival traditions, to have the important function of dampening social unrest, channelling the aspirations of the underclasses into licensed and strictly delimited self-indulgences. 'The whole city had seemed drunk. Sailors and soldiers and tinkers had been observed dancing in the streets with nobles and fat merchants, and in every inn and winesink cups were being raised to the new triarchs' (*DD*, 56). For all the craziness and boundary-breaking involved in such popular festivals, they function – ironically – as a means of perpetuating the same old unequal

power relations; that Volantis's carnival ends with the election of
the new triarch, drawn from a highly limited and undemocratic
pool, simply underscores the general oppression. Like the bread-
and-circus tournaments of Westeros which Varys saw as distracting
the poor of King's Landing from their day-to-day misery, the riot
and revelry that accompanies the elections acts as a kind of safety
valve for those excluded from the political process, those who
cannot prove their descent from Old Valyria.

There's much wisdom in this custom; Volantis is a city which has
five slaves to every free man or woman, 'slaves with their bent backs
and tattooed faces who scurried everywhere like cockroaches' (*DD*,
27). Talisa Maegyr, Robb Stark's beloved in the show, was a nobly
born Volantis girl, destined for a life of 'playing the harp, dancing
the latest steps, reciting poetry in Valyrian'. She left the city when
her eyes were opened to the slave trade's pernicious nature (2.8).
Her brother had drowned in the river Rhoyne on a hot day, playing with other children. He was resuscitated by a slave who knew
how to restart his heart; on that day Talisa vowed that she would
abandon the pointless pursuits of the noblewoman's life, 'dances
and masquerades', and she would train, like the slave, in healing.
Having resolved when she was old enough to leave home, that she
would never live in a slave-city again, she had come to Westeros,
where slavery is outlawed. But now the tensions among the slave
population are rising. In part this unrest is stoked by the religion
of the Lord of Light, R'hllor, discussed below, in part by the news,
percolating back from Slaver's Bay, about Daenerys's freeing of the
slaves there. The Red Priest Benerro preaches in Volantis every
evening about the equality of all people within the cult of R'hllor,
listened to by a large audience of slaves and the dispossessed. Tyrion
and Varys are making their way over the huge thronged, shop-lined
bridge – like medieval London Bridge or the Rialto in Venice – with
criss-crossing covered walkways and mellow-toned overlapping
roofs in search of the nearest brothel (5.3). Tyrion stops to listen to
a red preacher, an Asian-looking woman, who is addressing a rapt

crowd of slaves, invoking Dany as their saviour. The Red God, she declaims, 'hears the king as he hears the slave. He hears the Stone Men in their misery.' 'Good luck stopping the spread of greyscale with prayer,' scoffs Tyrion, and Varys hurries him away.

The widow of the waterfront, a former slave but now an influential commercial power within the city and someone with her finger on the popular pulse, perceives that Volantis would be vulnerable if Daenerys chose to extend her campaign of slave liberation to that city. 'Tell her we are waiting, tell her to come soon' (*DD*, 27), says the widow, whose scarred face recalls where her slave tattoos were excised when she won her freedom. Slave revolts occurred from time to time in late Republican Rome; these are known as the First, Second and Third Servile Wars. The first two revolts were quickly put down, but in the case of the Third Servile War, which began in 73 BCE and involved the well-known slave-leader Spartacus, the revolt started among the gladiators, who had ready access to weapons. At first the rebels had considerable success, raiding in the countryside to the south of Rome; under Spartacus's leadership they defeated the military forces sent against them. By the end of the year 70,000 men had flocked to join Spartacus's army; it seems likely that some of them aimed to escape from Roman jurisdiction over the Alps while others were content to remain in southern Italy raiding at will. But in 71 BCE the renowned general Crassus defeated the slave forces in the far south of Italy. Spartacus probably died on the battlefield, while 6,000 captured slaves were crucified, the crosses erected at intervals along the Appian Way leading back to the city of Rome. The power of crucifixion – as a shocking and horrific mode of execution and as a public warning of the fate awaiting those who sought to challenge the institution of slavery – is apparent both to the Astapori and the Great Masters of Meereen; both cities make use of it to discipline their slave populations and to defy Daenerys.

Why tigers and elephants? They are suitably exotic creatures from a Westerosi perspective; medieval people knew little about tigers, though the first mention of one in English is recorded in the year 1000, where they are said, rightly, to be fierce beasts. More relevant perhaps is the famous male African elephant which King Henry III of England was given by his brother-in-law, King Louis IX of France, in 1255. This beast had been presented to the crusading king by the emirs of Egypt, and it may well be that Louis was glad to pass the animal on to his fellow monarch. The elephant was presented to Henry in France; thus he had the problem of getting the creature home to England – or rather the Sheriff of Kent did. The elephant's passage from Wissant near Calais, across the Channel and upriver to London cost £6, 17s and 5d, according to Exchequer documents. The elephant was accommodated in the Tower of London's menagerie, in a specially constructed cage, and here a huge number of people came to visit him. These included the chronicler Matthew Paris, who not only sketched the elephant but also described him as ten years old and ten feet high, greyish-black, without fur, but with a very hard and rough hide. Ponderous and robust, the elephant used its trunk to obtain

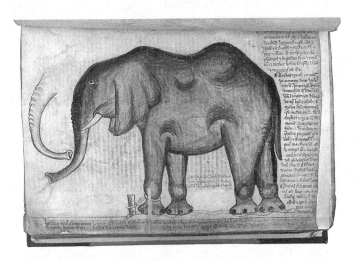

33. Matthew Paris's sketch of King Henry III's elephant

food and water, and had, Matthew noted, small eyes near the top of its head.[7]

The elephant, which proved rather expensive to maintain, died in February 1257; its bones, interestingly enough, were acquired by Westminster Abbey with the king's permission. Whether the canons of the abbey simply wanted the ivory of the elephant's tusks or whether they had some other use for the bones is a matter of speculation. Volantis makes considerable use of elephants as draught animals, and it also employs them in war: a number of them are shipped to Slaver's Bay for the attack on Meereen, though how easy it would have been to control shiploads of elephants in the storms experienced by Victarion Greyjoy's fleet as he sailed eastwards is an open question.

Before we leave Volantis, we should note that the ubiquitous board game of Essos, cyvasse, originated here. Cyvasse is a game modelled on battle strategies, apparently a Known World version of chess. Cyvasse may be simpler than chess, though a game seems to take just as long. It has ten kinds of piece: as in the earliest forms of chess there's a king and an elephant, but also, and importantly for the game's metaphorical function in the narrative, a dragon, two forms of cavalry (light and heavy horse), the trebuchet (a counter-weighted catapult) and the catapult (a term which includes both trebuchets and mangonels), crossbowmen and spearmen (both of whom can slay from a distance) and the rabble – presumably the equivalent of pawns. The dragon is the most powerful piece on the board, but it can be removed by a catapult or trebuchet; dragons can remove elephants. And, as in chess, the goal is to 'kill' the king, the equivalent of 'checkmate'. Tyrion's skill in cyvasse, which only emerges once he is in Essos, is hugely valuable: it disposes Brown Ben Plumm to take him on and it symbolises his tactical intelligence in the 'Game of Thrones'. Arianne Martell, by contrast, is left with a cyvasse set when she is imprisoned on her father's orders, but she never bothers to engage with the game. When she finally has an interview with her father, Doran, significantly, is studying a cyvasse board, and it's no coincidence that in the resulting conversation Doran's long-term strategic vision for Dorne's role in the 'Game' is finally revealed.

Cyvasse has spread from Essos into Westeros: 'Cyvasse, the game was called. It had come to the Planky Town on a trading galley from Volantis, and the orphans had spread it up and down the Greenblood. The Dornish court was mad for it,' observes Ser Arys Oakheart, who has no enthusiasm for the game (*FC*, 13). His failure to think strategically, a skill which cyvasse would have honed, will prove fatal. Cyvasse is a courtly recreation – Margaery and her cousins are keen on it – and it's no great surprise that Tyrion should be so good at it; he must have learnt it, like his High Valyrian, as a boy, as part of the aristocratic education that he received in Casterly Rock.

Chess seems to have originated in Afghanistan and western India in the fourth and fifth centuries CE, and spread rapidly into Persia. This earliest form of the game, known as *chaturanga*, divided the pieces into four groups: infantry, cavalry, elephantry and chariotry. These would evolve into the modern pawn, knight, bishop and rook respectively – the word *rook* in fact preserves the Persian word for a chariot, while *chess*, *check* and *checkmate* derive from *shah*, the Persian word for a king and 'Shah mat! [the king is helpless!]'. *Fers*, a now obsolete term for the queen, is related to the Persian word *vizier*, a councillor or minister, for in the earlier version of the game this powerful piece was the king's right-hand man rather than his spouse. After the Muslim invasion of Persia, the game spread rapidly through the Muslim world and thence into Europe via the Moorish civilisation of Spain, up the Volga river to Russia and Scandinavia, and via the Normans into England. Though the pieces in the Muslim game were blocks of different colours and sizes, in line with the Islamic prohibition against depicting living creatures, they soon took on representa-tive forms: the elephant (*al-fil* in Arabic) became known as the count, the dog, the counsellor or the fool, before it finally settled into the bishop in the twelfth and thirteenth centuries. Chess soon became a much-loved pastime. Moralists condemned the game; the churchman Peter Damian rebuked the bishop of Florence in 1061 for his hobby. The bishop should have been aware of its evil effects, the saint argued, and indeed chess, like any other game, offered occasions for gambling and provoked violence if the outcome displeased. Yet – and this was the bishop's counterargument – it is a game of skill and promotes logic, patience and strategic thinking. In his *Disciplina clericalis*, written in the twelfth century, the Spanish Petrus Alfonsi noted that chess was one of the seven key skills that knights should possess. Petrus was born Jewish in the town of Huesca in Muslim Andalusia, and it's clear from his writing that chess was already well established as a pastime. It wasn't just the intellectual component of chess that made it a useful skill for the well-born man; chess also gives occasion for two people to spend long hours with their heads bent over a board. Men and women could play together without scandal, allowing intimacy to develop; thus the game began to take on romantic connotations. In Chaucer's memorial poem for Blanche, the wife of John of Gaunt, the 'Book of the Duchess', the poet describes how he fell asleep and in his dream met a man dressed all in black. The dreamer learns how this man had long loved and finally won the heart of the 'faire White'. The man in black describes how 'false Fortune' played chess with him, and 'with hir false draughtes dyvers / She staal [stole] on me, and tok my fers [queen]' with cries of 'Chek' and 'Mate'. The poet delicately mediates Blanche's death as the culmination of a chess game; both love and life could be figured through chess-derived metaphors.[8]

When men played chess with one another, then, long, private conversations could take place, conversations that didn't cause remark as withdrawing into a private chamber might have done. So Tyrion gains a great deal of intelligence about what's going on in Essos from his cyvasse game with the Volantene customs official Qavo Nogarys (*DD*, 22). So popular was chess that texts addressing chess problems, like the chess columns we find in modern newspapers, began to appear in the thirteenth century. Margaret of Anjou, Henry VI's queen, had red and green chess sets made of crystal and jasper; the famous twelfth-century Lewis chessmen, carved out of walrus ivory and whales' teeth and discovered in the Western Isles, testify to the game's popularity among the Scandinavian aristocracy. And just as the *al-fil* could metamorphose into the dog, the fool or the bishop, so the rook in the Lewis sets is shown as a berserker, the infamous warrior who, in Icelandic saga, would work himself into a foaming rage and gnash on his shield with his teeth before battle.

THE CULT OF R'HLLOR

Whereabouts in Essos the religion of the Lord of Light originated is mysterious, but it's clearly a very important cult in Volantis, for the Temple of R'hllor there is even bigger than the Great Sept of Baelor in King's Landing. Benerro is termed the High Priest; is he the patriarch of the whole religion, or is he merely the High Priest of the Volantis temple? The religion is fairly widespread in Essos, in the Free Cities at least; although in Braavos, as also in Oldtown and likely in Dorne, the temples serve the adherents of the religion who are passing through rather than suggesting that there's a substantial local following. The first time we encounter the Lord of Light's followers is at Dragonstone, where Melisandre of Asshai, the Red Woman, has successfully converted Stannis and at least some of his retinue to the new religion. Efforts to introduce R'hllor-worship more widely in Westeros don't seem to have been particularly successful. Thoros of Myr had the mission of attempting to convert Aerys, the Mad King; surprisingly, given Aerys's obsession with fire, Thoros got nowhere. However, his own faith was wavering at this point in his career; it's only when the dragons are hatched and the red comet is seen in the sky – a moment which coincides with our first sight of Melisandre and her proselytising – that Thoros experiences a surge of renewed faith and power. He forms the Brotherhood without Banners and successfully revives Beric Dondarrion from death several times. Thoros's spiritual journey suggests that there is a cosmic interconnectedness between the dragons and the power of the Lord of Light, for Melisandre too senses an escalation in her own powers. Stannis has his doubts from time to time:

> 'Melisandre swears that she has seen me in her flames, facing the dark with Lightbringer raised on high. *Lightbringer!*' Stannis gave a derisive snort. 'It glimmers prettily, I'll grant you, but on the Blackwater this magic sword served me no better than any common steel.' (*SS*, 54)

The religion of R'hllor worships a single all-powerful deity immanent in fire who is opposed by the Great Other, a principle of cosmic evil. The religion could then be described as Manichean: believing that there are two balanced and near-equal powers at work in the world (in contrast to, say, the all-powerful Christian or Jewish God who suffers evil in the world for reasons which cannot be understood by limited human minds). The religious thought of R'hllor's followers, insofar as its dogma is made clear, seems to be comparable with the beliefs of medieval Cathars and similar heretical sects, who regarded this world as irredeemably fallen and thought that salvation could only come in the next world. Human souls belonged in the world of light, in heaven, but many had been captured by the Evil God, robed in flesh and placed in this world in order to suffer. The Cathars, who lived in Languedoc in southern France, believed that life was so worthless that there was no point in procreative sex, for it just produced more unhappy inhabitants of this corrupt world. Reincarnation also formed part of Cathar belief; leading a good life might break the cycle of reincarnation and allow the soul to remain in the world of light forever. Men and women were regarded as equal within Catharism; while ordinary folk avoided meat and refused to participate in Catholic religious practices, the elite *perfecti* (the sect's spiritual leaders) led lives of great asceticism: eschewing sex and alcohol, and fasting frequently. They might not kill any living creature nor take oaths. Ordinary Cathars would receive a sacrament known as the *consolamentum* just before their deaths when such sustained renunciation was not hard to maintain, but the *perfecti* practised this challenging asceticism for decades.

The Cathars were regarded as representing a threat to medieval Catholicism, both in terms of belief and their unwillingness to participate in Catholic Church ritual. Their refusal to swear oaths brought them into conflict with feudalism's hierarchical organisation; they were critical of the corruption of the Church at the highest and lowest levels. Thus Cathar difference was taken as a thoroughgoing critique of the established Church, and it responded with violence. Arnaud Amaury, the Abbot of Cîteaux, tried to preach orthodox Catholicism to the Cathars – to no effect: the Crusade against them was formally declared by Pope Innocent III in 1208. Arnaud Amaury was appointed the Crusade's military leader, along with the Earl of Leicester, Simon de Montfort. Horrendous persecution ensued. It was Arnaud who is said to have uttered the infamous words before the great massacre at Béziers in 1209 in which as many as 20,000 people were slaughtered, 'kill them all; God will know his own.' The Albigensian Crusade (as the campaign against the Cathars was known) and the Inquisition were largely successful in eradicating Catharism from Languedoc; the great ruined Cathar castles can still be seen, perched on the top of hills or limestone outcrops across the province and, in cities such as Albi, Béziers with its ruined castle, and Carcassonne, there's a strong sense of the turmoil of the persecution.

Cathars who did not recant were burned at the stake after being interrogated by the Inquisition; it's from the Inquisitors' documents that we know much of what has been recorded about them.

34. Cathars being expelled from Carcassonne in 1209

The cult of R'hllor has also been compared with Zoroastrianism, a dualistic religion originating in Persia. It holds that Ahura Mazda, the creator, is all good, but is no longer immanent in the world. Good proceeds from him, while forces of evil try to destroy his creation. In the world Ahura Mazda's goodness is in conflict with evil, embodied by Ahriman; such influences can be countered by righteous living. Fire is central in Zoroastrianism as an element of ritual purity; in the religion's earlier forms sacred fires were made on hilltops, and only later did they move indoors into fire-temples. Sacred fires are kept burning eternally (in practice the oldest fires are around 250 years old), and unbelievers may not be admitted where they burn.

Three factors distinguish the worship of the Lord of Light from either Catharism or Zoroastrianism: first, the enthusiastic proselytising for the religion by Melisandre and, to some extent, the other priests of R'hllor whom we encounter. Second, the shocking sacrifice of humans to the god, whether as criminals or as victims. Third, neither of the real-world religions has a concept of a messiah figure. Melisandre's missionary activities have already proved highly successful by the time we meet her at Dragonstone, so we can only conjecture how she persuaded Stannis and Selyse of the superiority of the religion of the Lord of Light over the Faith of the Seven. In that crucial opening scene (at the beginning of 'The North Remembers', 2.1), we see the folk of Dragonstone gathered on the beach, burning their treasured statues of the Seven. The conflagration reminds me of the cult film *The Wicker Man* – except that, for once, no humans are being incinerated. Cressen, the Maester of Dragonstone, runs among the worshippers, pleading with them to reconsider what they are doing: abandoning the faith of their ancestors for this newfangled cult. Stannis and Melisandre also insist that the Free Folk convert, at least nominally, to the worship of the Lord of Light, in order to pass through the Wall. 'R'hllor was a jealous deity, ever hungry. So the new god devoured the corpse of the old, and cast gigantic shadows of Stannis and Melisandre upon the Wall, black against the ruddy red reflections on the ice' (*DD*, 10).[9]

Among the Anglo-Saxons, the Frisians and the Irish in the fourth to seventh century, an argument much like Cressen's was raised against the introduction of Christianity. Christian sources depict the pagans as extremely anxious about the loss of continuity and connection with their forebears. Their anxiety was compounded by the Christian insistence that the unbaptised were inevitably hell-bound, even if they had never had the chance to hear the Gospel preached. As recounted in a late folk tale collected in the nineteenth century, the Irish hero Oisín returned from a 300-year sojourn in the Other World to find an Ireland he no longer recognised. His father Finn, the leader of the *Fianna*, a band of outlaw-heroes, and all his friends and kinsmen were dead. There was recompense (of a sort). Oisín had lived long enough to meet St Patrick, now proselytising in Ireland, and could be baptised, if

he so wished, thus attaining salvation. Though other Irish legendary heroes would leap at the chance of baptism when offered by
Celtic saints, Oisín stoutly refused; what was good enough for his
father and kinsmen was good enough for him, and he preferred to
pass eternity where they were, even in hell. Dismounting from his
horse, Oisín immediately shouldered the burden of his true age,
withered, crumbled and died.[10]

For those converting to Christianity from the polytheistic
religions of Scandinavia, the Germanic tribes and the Celts, the
new faith offered some answers to important metaphysical questions. The Christian historian Bede, writing in the early eighth
century, depicts the reaction of one of King Edwin of Northumbria's
councillors to the Gospel, preached to the court by St Paulinus
around 614:

> The present life of man upon earth, O king, seems to me, in
> comparison with that time which is unknown to us, like the
> swift flight of a sparrow through the house in which you sit at
> supper in winter, with your ealdormen [noblemen] and thegns
> [warrior-lords], while the fire blazes in the midst, and the hall
> is made warm, but the wintry storms of rain or snow are raging
> abroad. The sparrow, flying in at one door and immediately out
> at another, whilst he is within, is safe from the wintry tempest;
> but after a short space of fair weather, he immediately vanishes
> out of your sight, passing from winter into winter again. So this
> life of man appears for a little while, but of what is to follow
> or what went before we know nothing at all. If, therefore, this
> new doctrine tells us something more certain, it seems justly
> to deserve to be followed.[11]

The king's high priest Coifi is so enthusiastic about the new doctrine
that he immediately calls for the destruction of the old religion's
idols and temples. Borrowing a spear from the king (for priests
were forbidden to carry arms) and mounted on a stallion (for

they might not ride any horse except a mare), Coifi rides to the temple and casts a spear inside it. Thus the temple is desecrated, the idols are overturned, and the whole precinct is set ablaze. We have, of course, to treat Bede's account with caution: he writes as a convinced Christian who can see no good in the pagan past and who suppresses details about its customs and philosophy. Nevertheless, the missionaries who came to Anglo-Saxon England met with surprisingly little opposition. St Augustine of Canterbury first landed in Kent in 597; here the king was easily persuaded into baptism for his queen, Bertha, a Frank, was already Christian. The missionary endeavour spread from court to court, concentrating on winning over the king, the queen and the nobility, and enjoying much success. The Pope, Gregory the Great, advised a softly-softly approach, building churches on the same sites as temples, gradually erasing the old ways rather than putting them to fire and sword. And the assurance of heaven, a glorious afterlife open to every-one who believed and was baptised, has its attractions. Though the Ironborn believe in a kind of watery Valhalla, feasting in the halls of the Drowned God, it's not clear that women, children and those who die in bed rather than with a sword in their hands will also fetch up there, any more than they were thought to merit an eternity of feasting and fighting in Valhalla itself.

R'hllor promises protection from the 'night which is dark and full of terrors', a struggle that will only end when Azor Ahai, with his magical sword Lightbringer (a nod to Lucifer, the Star of the Morning, but also the rebel angel who becomes Satan in Christian tradition) comes again. Lightbringer was forged with great difficulty; as in other medieval traditions, including the forg-ing of the sword Gram, the weapon of Sigurd the Dragon Slayer in Norse, the sword is forged twice and shatters twice before the final forging creates a weapon that can cut through anything.[12] In the legend of Azor Ahai the final tempering of the sword was brought about by the hero plunging the sword into the breast of his beloved wife Nissa Nissa. Her soul was thus infused into the

metal and endowed it with its supernatural powers, enabling Azor
Ahai to slay monsters, perhaps even dragons: 'When he thrust his
sword into the belly of the beast its blood began to boil. Smoke
and steam poured from its mouth, its eyes melted and dribbled
down its cheeks, and its body burst into flames'; so Jon relates to
Clydas the Steward (*DD*, 10).

Human sacrifice is thus integral to the origin story of the messiah's most potent symbol, and it's scarcely surprising that sacrifice
is emphasised in Melisandre's version of the cult. The mass burn-
ings of those who will not bow the knee to the Lord of Light or to
Stannis recall the excesses of medieval Catholicism rather than the
rituals of any other world religions. The very Cathars whose teachings are partly reflected in R'hllor's cult died in their multitudes
on the pyres of the Inquisition; death by burning, a surefire way
of eliminating enemies without risking that their graves become
a site of pilgrimage and veneration, was regarded as an effective
way of chastening the faithful.

Whether Azor Ahai and the 'Prince that was Promised' (a
messiah who appears in Old Valyrian prophetic sources) are one
and the same remains to be seen. The prophecy of the Prince is
well known to Maester Aemon and is important to the Targaryen
idea of themselves, yet it's not at all clear that the followers of
R'hllor would imagine Azor Ahai as arising among the descendants of Valyria.

The Red Priests Benerro and Moqorro both think that the rise
of Daenerys and the return of the dragons are significant, and
Moqorro sets sail to Meereen to investigate whether Daenerys
could be Azor Ahai reborn:

> From smoke and salt was she born to make the world anew.
> She is Azor Ahai returned … and her triumph over darkness
> will bring a summer that will never end … death itself will
> bend its knee, and all those who die fighting in her cause shall
> be reborn'. (*DD*, 22)

The myth of the Prince and his sword as the one who can vanquish the Great Other (and perhaps, by extension, the Others) may be crucial in the eschatology of the Known World, but no one much, apart from Melisandre, seems to be relying on it, either as a solution to the threat posed by the White Walkers/Others as winter approaches, or as an apotheosis which would change the Known World forever.

As we've observed with the Faith of the Seven and the cult of the Old Gods, it's not clear that any religions in the Known World have an absolute transcendent validity, that their gods do in fact exist outside the minds of the faithful. We might be tempted to align ourselves with Euron Greyjoy's cynical listing of 'Horse gods and fire gods, gods made of gold with gemstone eyes, gods carved of cedar wood, gods chiseled into mountains, gods of empty air ... I know them all' (*FC*, 19). Yet something mystical is clearly at work with the Three-Eyed Crow/Raven, and Thoros has succeeded in reviving both Beric Dondarrion and Lady Stoneheart through R'hllor's powers. Jon Snow's only hope may lie in Melisandre harnessing the same revivifying powers. Does the Red God only work for those who believe unequivocally in him? It looks as if, like the powers of the Warlocks of Qarth, the rebirth of the dragons has galvanised the energies which R'hllor's cult harnesses. For indeed the snow preventing his advance on Winterfell does melt after Stannis sacrifices his daughter, Shireen, whom he loves most of all, to R'hllor. However, satisfying the bloodthirsty god is of little use, given the unpredictability of human factors: the horror of Stannis's sellswords at his action, their defection with his horses to the Boltons, and above all the response of Selyse, combine in ways which anyone who wasn't a fanatic could have predicted.

We might do well to exercise some scepticism about Stannis and the Red God. Stannis isn't my (nor indeed his own) idea of a mythic hero who can vanquish the powers of Darkness: only Melisandre seems convinced of this, and when she leaves his camp before battle to ride away to Castle Black she may already have revised her views. How far she truly believes and how far she is content to manipulate Stannis, Selyse and the other Westerosi adherents to the cult is an open question; her sleeves and pockets are, after all, stuffed with powders and potions which interact with the flames of her night-fires, 'a trick to make them see the truth', as she says to Selyse (4.7), and her prophecies have a habit of going astray. It's one thing to see images in the flames – just as with the dream-interpretations we'll discuss in the next chapter – and quite another to understand what they signify, as Melisandre discovers more than once. We would do well to keep Tyrion's rumination in mind: 'Prophecy is like a half-trained mule. It looks as though it might be useful, but the moment you trust in it, it kicks you in the head' (DD, 40).

Volantis is a city in flux, then; with an election underway, the growing discontent of the vast slave population, the incendiary news that has percolated westwards of Daenerys's doctrine of slave liberation, the threat this poses to the vested interests of this great merchant city, and the new fervour with which the religion of the Red God is being preached in its squares and piazzas: all these are coming together to prophesy – despite Tyrion's doubts – trouble ahead. There's a strange smell here in the city: 'it hung in the hot, humid air, rich, rank, pervasive. *There's fish in it, and flowers, and some elephant dung as well. Something sweet and something earthy and something dead and rotten*' (DD, 27). It's high time to get out of town, to leave the storm-tossed ocean of the southern Essos coastline, and to take horse across a different sea: the grassy plains of the Dothraki.

35. *Daenerys Stormborn*

CHAPTER 5

THE EAST

Ser Jorah Mormont: 'The Dothraki have two things
in abundance, grass and horses.' (1.2)

Avoiding the mayhem of the Volantis election season, we turn eastwards to the Dothraki Sea, that great inland steppe of grassland where the different *khalasars* of the Dothraki people roam. Good horses, a flexibility about what we're prepared to eat and a supply of precious objects to keep our hosts happy – these are going to be crucial to the success of our travels among the horselords.

THE DOTHRAKI

'I think they have more horses and mares
than all the world besides.'

JOHANNES DE PIANO CARPINI (1254)[1]

The dark-haired, copper-skinned riders, organised in bands of male warriors called *khalasars*, each with a *khal* at their head, lead a nomadic existence. They live in yurts and eat mostly meat: duck, goat and dog are offered to Daenerys in the early stages of pregnancy when she's grown tired of horse. The Dothraki are of course impressive horsemen; armed with a curved sword and lightly armoured in leather jerkins, they rely on their speed, their numbers and the quality of their mounts for lightning raids. 'For a man on horseback a curved blade [*arakh*] is a good thing, easier to handle,' but it's no good against steel plate, Ser Jorah tells us (3.3). Their fighting skills are second to none in Essos; the Dothraki Sea is ringed with ruined cities ravaged by the horselords, and their reputations terrify those in their path.

'The Dothraki don't believe in money; most of their slaves were given to them as gifts' (3.3), Jorah tells Daenerys, though his definition of 'gift' is rather imprecise. The economy of the horselords is simple, based on raiding and tribute – or, more properly, the payment of protection money: 'The horselords come, we give them gifts, the horselords go,' explains the Volantene customs officer Qavo Nogarys (*DD*, 22). There is a large market in Vaes Dothrak, for the city lies on the caravan route across the Dothraki Sea, one taken by those who prefer not to sail past the ruins of Valyria or to pay the extortionate customs duties charged in Qarth. The trading that takes place there is between merchants from east and west; the Dothraki might come to seek novelties in exchange for their plunder, but they are not traders, except for their involvement with the slave trade. In this, their usual prey are the peaceful Lhazareen, or Lamb-men, who tend their flocks to the east of the steppes and whom the Dothraki sell on to the cities of Slaver's Bay or through Volantis. The Dothraki despise this humble pastoral folk: 'Does the horse mate with the lamb?', asks Mago (1.8), when Daenerys is horrified by the human cost of a slave-raid on the Lhazareen. Her well-meant intervention, to save the *maegi* (healer or magic-worker) Mirri Maz Duur from further rape, rebounds horrifically upon her; the quarrel among the *khalasar* about Drogo's apparent indulgence of Daenerys's humane sentiments leads indirectly to his death and the dissolution of the *khalasar*.

Much of what we know about the Dothraki is imparted by Jorah Mormont, who has lived among them for a long time and speaks

fluent Dothraki. When we first encounter them in Pentos, at the
wedding of Drogo and Daenerys, they seem to be the epitome of
savagery, particularly in contrast with the urbane ways of Illyrio
Mopatis. Excessive drinking, feasting on roasted meats, public sex,
ululation, howling rather than music, and loud and blatant boasting: these are the hallmarks of Dothraki celebration. 'A Dothraki
wedding without at least three deaths is considered a dull affair,'
observes Jorah (1.1). And indeed, the boasting about bravery in
battle leads to challenge, one-to-one combat and death for the loser.
Drink and the public reckoning of relative honour are prone to
causing violence in warrior cultures; the Old English poem called
by editors *The Fortunes of Men*, dating from the late tenth century,
imagines just such a fight in the mead-hall:

> From one enraged man, on the mead-bench,
> from the ale-swiller one, the sword's edge takes life,
> the warrior had more than enough wine,
>   he spoke too quickly before;
> Another shall, through beer poured by the cup-bearer's hand,
> become over-excited by mead; when he knows no measure
> to his mouth or his mood but quite wretchedly he loses his life,
> losing all his lord's favour, he's deprived of happiness
> and men make mention that he killed himself,
> they openly blame what the mead-madman drank.[2]

The *khal*'s authority over his *khalasar* is determined by his health
and strength; when the other warriors sense that Drogo is failing, they are quick to abandon their loyalty to him: 'A khal who
cannot ride is no khal,' advises Jorah. 'This isn't Westeros where
men honour blood. Here they only honour strength; there'll be
fighting after Drogo dies,' he warns Daenerys. 'Your boy will be
plucked from your breast and given to the dogs' (1.9). And indeed
on Drogo's death most of the *khalasar* depart, leaving Daenerys
with only a few slaves as the basis of her horde.

For all their apparent barbarism – for the Dothraki are barely allowed to speak for themselves – their language has a wonderfully metaphorical turn. Drogo uses kennings, short metaphorical phrases, to communicate unfamiliar concepts to his followers. Thus he calls the sea 'poison water', for horses cannot drink it. In Vaes Dothrak, the city ruled over by the widows of dead *khals*, the *dosh khaleen*, Daenerys triumphantly forces down the raw horse heart, convincing even the sceptics that the child she is carrying could be the prophesied 'stallion that mounts the world'. Drogo responds with a wonderfully vivid vow to his *khaleesi*. He swears that he *will* invade Westeros and give his yet unborn son 'the iron chair'. 'I will take my khalasar west to where the world ends, and ride the wooden horses across the black salt water […] I will kill the men in iron suits and tear down their stone houses'; these words, 'I swear before the Mother of Mountains as the stars look down in witness' (1.7).

So too the endearments that the Dothraki use to one another: 'blood of my blood', 'my sun and stars', 'moon of my life' have a poetic ring that suggests that there's no impoverishment of imagination among these people who live so intensely in the natural world. And although her words are borrowed from Mirri Maz Duur's hate-filled revelation that Drogo – though alive and healed of his wounds – has, thanks to her dark blood-magic, lost his mind, Daenerys bids a beautiful farewell to her husband, telling him that they will meet again, 'when the sun rises in the west and sets in the east, when the seas go dry, when the mountains blow in the wind like leaves' (1.10). Daenerys's words, repeated when she sees husband and child again in the House of the Undying (2.10), echo the traditional verses of English ballad which express impossibility or eternity: 'till the sun and moon dance on the green / and that will never be', or the Scots poet Robert Burns's 'till a' the seas gang dry, my dear, and rocks melt wi' the sun'. In the context of the Known World, the idea that the seas might dry up and the mountains blow in the wind seems less of an impossibility and more a reference to the terrible fate of Valyria – on which there's more below.

The Dothraki's religious beliefs, unsurprisingly, centre on a Horse God: the Great Stallion. They believe that on death a man must be burnt along with his horse, so that he may ride with the fiery *khalasar* of his god in the sky, the stars:

> When a horselord dies, his horse is slain with him, so he might ride proud into the night lands. The bodies are burned beneath the open sky, and the *khal* rises on his fiery steed to take his place among the stars. The more fiercely the man burned in life, the brighter his star will shine in the darkness. (*GT*, 72)

Those who are not burned will not achieve that afterlife; Drogo threatens Mago with the most dishonourable treatment when he has killed him: 'I will not burn you, but leave you in the ground with beetles in your eyes and worms in your lungs' (1.8). The sacred mountain, the Mother of Mountains, is a cult centre near the city of Vaes Dothrak, pointing to a specific role for the feminine in this intensely patriarchal society. Indeed, the *dosh khaleen* have real power, of healing and of prophecy, and it is they who identify Daenerys's son Rhaego as: 'the stallion who mounts the world; the Khal of Khals. He will unite the people into a single khalasar, and all the people of the world will be his herd' (1.7).

Vaes Dothrak is a sacred place where weapons may not be carried nor blood be spilt, a necessary warrior-culture precaution at the centre where many *khalasar*s come together. In pre-Christian Iceland the end of the Althing, or annual Assembly, was known as the *vapnatak*, or 'weapon-take', and signified that men could now bear arms once again. In Old English the term 'wapentake' refers to an administrative area of land, smaller than a Hundred and much smaller than a shire; the term probably originated in the constituency of a smaller local assembly. Thus the Dothraki legislate for peaceful intermingling within the sacred city, a custom which Viserys, drunk and desperate, flouts. Jorah warns him very specifically, 'Don't let them see you carrying a sword in Vaes Dothrak; you know the law' (1.6). And Drogo gets around the prohibition on bloodshed by giving Viserys his golden crown in the most horrifying way imaginable. Just so, among the Mongols, it was not the custom to shed the blood of noblemen but rather to put bags over their heads and either drown them or have them trampled by horses.

The Dothraki have much in common with the Mongol tribes who were unified by Temüjin (Chinghis or Genghis Khan, the first Great Khan), who lived from around 1162 to 1227. He founded what would become the largest contiguous land empire ever seen, across Asia and Europe – from the Pacific Ocean to the Caspian Sea – in the thirteenth and fourteenth centuries. Although they raided into modern-day Poland and Hungary, the Mongols did not seek to colonise or subjugate these kingdoms; the western limit of the khanate was the Black Sea area. We know quite a bit about the Mongols, for a succession of western travellers, usually churchmen, went to visit them in the mid-thirteenth century and chronicled their experiences. Like Jorah, these men interpreted what they saw for their readers and for the potentates (the Pope; the Holy Roman Emperor) who had sent them, and their descriptions chime with the view of the Dothraki that the Westerosi form. But, unlike the horselords of the Known World, who don't seem to be literate, the Mongols also wrote their own history, the so-called *The Secret History of the Mongols*, which recounts Temüjin's rise from the perspective of his descendants.

One of the first to visit the *orda* (court, although the word gives us the modern idea of the *horde*) was Johannes de Piano Carpini, who began his journey in 1245, when he was sent by Pope Innocent IV to the new Great Khan, Güyüg. Johannes relates how extreme the climate was as he and his companions travelled eastwards from the badly damaged city of Kiev, almost destroyed by Mongol raiders. Johannes writes of the thunderstorms and dust storms, of hail so

36. A sculpture of Genghis Khan

intense that 160 men drowned when it melted, of scorching heat and savage cold, howling winds and the lack of rain. He describes the difficulties of travel in the mountains and over the endless grasslands, the fires made of horse- and cattle-dung, and observes how little the Mongols wash. Nor do they have towns or cities, he notes, but rather they live in tents, or *gers* (yurts). The Mongols seem to be a friendly and amiable people among themselves (if greatly given to drunken binges fuelled by fermented mare's milk, or *kumiss*), and their women are chaste. Like the Dothraki, they scorn all other nations. They are very keen on being given gifts: the first enquiry of each new *orda* that Johannes comes to is what gifts he and his followers are bearing. The men shave their heads like western monks, and have long braids coiled up behind their ears. We learn too a little of their beliefs: they worship the moon, which they call 'the Great Emperor', and women play a part in cer- emonies around the new and full moons, when men and beasts are purified by passing between two fires. The women stand on either side, casting water over the supplicants and chanting. Impressed by their discipline and comradeliness – there is no fighting and no thieving – Johannes cannot help but contrast the regard that they have for one another with their predilection for killing members of other ethnic groups and their lack of respect for the great men of other nations: Russian dukes and the son of the King of Georgia are not given the deference that Johannes would expect.[3]

Having first arrived at the *orda* of Batu Khan, not very far east of Kiev, Johannes was sent onwards to the Sira Orda, the court of the Great Khan, quite close to the Mongol capital city of Karakorum, a journey which took him across what's now Kazakhstan and Uzbekistan, through the northern part of Xinjiang in China, and on into Mongolia. Johannes notes that widows had a great deal of authority on the death of their husbands and that the Emperor's mother was given the power 'to execute justice' in his absence, a parallel to the authority of the *dosh khaleen*:

> For it is a custom among the Tartars that the courts of their princes and nobles are not broken up (on their death), but some women are always appointed who govern them, and the same proportion of presents are given them that their lord had been in the habit (during his life) of allowing them.

At the Sira Orda, Johannes is impressed by 'a huge tent of fine white cloth [...] of so great quantity that more than two thousand men might stand within it, and round about there was a wall of planks set up, painted with divers images.' Here the party witness the election of Güyüg as the new Great Khan, and are invited to drink *kumiss*. This the Europeans can't stomach; fortunately, they are offered ale instead. Johannes finally manages to deliver his letter from the Pope to the Khan and is given letters to take back. The Great Khan considers sending some of his men back with Johannes as ambassadors, but the Europeans are uneasy about this plan, fearing that the Mongols might be killed en route – bringing down the wrath of Güyüg on them and the offenders – or that they might turn out to be spies. Or, intriguingly, 'lest they, seeing the dissensions and wars which are among us, should be the more encouraged to make war against us.' Seeing the west through the eyes of the easterners – as constituted by a Christian population whose religion is honoured more in the breach than in the observance, where drunkenness, blasphemy, theft and sexual misbehaviour are rife – is the basis of anxious self-criticism among some medieval writers. The author of the *Travels of John Mandeville* recounts how embarrassed he is when the Sultan of Babylon reveals that, from the intelligence he receives from the merchants of his country, who travel widely across Europe to trade, Christians prefer to go to the tavern instead of to church, to fight and steal, to sell their women's honour for a small amount of silver, and to wear ridiculous and indecent fashions. Poor Mandeville is confronted with the Sultan's messengers, who all speak fluent French, and is forced to admit both the truth of their claims and that the Muslims of the Sultan's realm are far more devout and godly in their abstinence from alcohol, their modest clothing and their assiduousness of religious practice.[4] What the folk of Essos think of Westeros (if they think about Westeros at all) might be very similar.

A more detailed description survives of Karakorum, the capital city in the north-east corner of modern Mongolia, walled by Temüjin's son Ögedei in 1235 and later expanded by his cousin Möngke. William Ruysbroeck journeyed there in 1253, bringing letters from King Louis IX of France. William adds a great deal of further information about the Mongols to what we know from Johannes. He gives a strong sense of the size of the *orda*: the chief wife may have 200 carts' worth of possessions. In summer the people drink only *kumiss*, or 'cosmos', as William calls fermented mare's milk. He recalls his first experience of it, quite early in his expedition: 'That evening the man who was guiding us gave us *cosmos* to drink, and at the taste of it I broke out in a sweat with horror and surprise, for I had never drunk of it. It seemed to me, however, very palatable, as it really is.'[5]

William is impressed by how the Mongols eat all parts of the animals they herd, including cows, oxen and camels as well as the horses, sometimes wind-drying the meat, or eating it raw and minced finely. Their horse sausages are particularly to be recommended. Cow's and mare's milk is churned and fermented into both black and white *kumiss* and varieties of butter, cheese and curds. The Mongols dress more sensibly than the Dothraki, in garments made of skin, fur or leather and padded with cotton or silk for warmth and lightness. Duels are often fought, in which no man is permitted to intervene – just as Drogo and Mago battle one another, or as in the fights at the wedding. William had hoped to bring Catholicism to the court of Möngke, and is dismayed to find that he has been forestalled by Nestorians. These practised a kind of Christianity originating in Syria which had spread eastwards throughout Asia. William's troubles are compounded by his interpreter, whose grasp of Mongol is not as good as he had claimed, and he is annoyed at being sent on ever further eastwards from one *orda* to another, until he finally reaches Karakorum and Möngke's court. Here he finds more congenial company – other Europeans who had come to trade or to work there, including the nephew of an English bishop; a woman from Lorraine, who cooks William's Easter dinner; and a French silversmith, making ornaments for the Khan's women and altars for the Nestorian Christians. He finds a lively curiosity about his homeland among the men at Möngke's court: 'And they began to question us greatly about the kingdom of France, whether there were many sheep and cattle and horses there, and whether they had not better go there at once and take it all.' So too Khal Drogo has little doubt that he will achieve victory over the Westerosi, once he sets his mind to crossing the Narrow Sea and embarking on his campaign of conquest. Möngke sends a self-important letter back to Louis, asking that he send formal ambassadors to make clear whether the French desired peace or war against the Mongols. William bears it back with him, and sees that it is delivered.

The Secret History of the Mongols was composed after the death of Temüjin between 1240 and 1260, probably as a family chronicle.[6] It traces Genghis Khan's birth and rise to power within his own clan, his overcoming of the Merkits and the Tatars (a Turkic-speaking people), assumption of the title Genghis Khan and his unification of the different Mongol tribes through his marriage to Börte, the mother of his most important sons, and through swearing blood-brotherhood (*anda*) with various powerful leaders. That a man calls another 'blood of my blood' does not prevent him from double-crossing his friend when the opportunity arises, as both Genghis Khan and Drogo discover. The *Secret History* relates how male captives were usually killed, especially if they failed the 'measure of the linch-pin'. If men were taller than the pin at the end of the axle of the Mongol cartwheels, they were executed; children and women were kept as slaves. They had to demonstrate their loyalty by remaining close to the yurt; for, the *Secret History* advises, 'let them be the slaves of your felt-door. Should they depart from your felt-door, cut out their livers and cast them out'; 'Should they leave your wide felt-door, trample their hearts and cast them out.'⁷ Sheep-neck was served at betrothal feasts, for it was hoped that the ensuing marriage would be as tough and enduring as that chewy dish; the ceremony perhaps inspires Daenerys's heart-eating ordeal. Temüjin has a redoubtable mother to whom he gives a great deal of executive authority, chiming with the information given by Johannes de Piano Carpini. The Mongol religion as practised by Temüjin is a shamanistic one, incorporating ancestor-worship, though the Great Khan's sons would marry wives who brought the practice of Nestorian Christianity into the Mongol nobility. Archery was extremely important, and warriors were capable of firing from horseback at full gallop; arrows were made of fire-hardened and sharpened wood. Knowledge of metal weapons and how to manufacture them was only acquired during the wars with the Chinese at the beginning of the century. Here too the Mongols discovered the advantages of steel plate over their normal breastplates, and helmets made of boiled leather – perhaps the Dothraki leather garments are tougher than they look.

Genghis Khan made it his life's work to unify the different clans and tribes of the Mongol heartland, and, through strict promotion on merit and a genius for military organisation, he welded the three Mongol armies into an unstoppable force. Whether Khal Drogo wielded such authority, despite never having been defeated in battle and finally dying with his braid uncut, whether he could have united all the other *khalasar*s in his vision of western conquest, isn't at all clear. In the books, Drogo and Daenerys make their way to Vaes Dothrak for the Targaryen heiress to be acclaimed as *khaleesi* by the *dosh khaleen*; this journey might have allowed Drogo to recruit new members to his *khalasar* in preparation for his campaign. He is the leader of the largest *khalasar* among the Dothraki nation, some 40,000 strong, and he pledged 10,000 of them to support Viserys's claim to the throne in return for Daenerys's hand. At his death, Drogo has journeyed even further east than Vaes Dothrak; his raiding among the Lhazareen was intended to obtain sufficient slaves to exchange for the 'wooden horses' (warships) that will carry his *khalasar* to Westeros.

Might Drogo have been successful in his conquest, had he lived? Even if, as he vows after Daenerys survives the assassination attempt by one of Robert's agents, he had brought all his forces across the Narrow Sea, it's a moot question as to whether his 'screaming Dothraki savages' could have overcome the Lannister and Baratheon armies. Certainly the strategists of King's Landing are relatively unconcerned about the threat the Dothraki pose while they are confined to the east of the Narrow Sea. Cersei is swift to dismiss the threat: 'The Dothraki [...] don't have discipline, they don't have armour, they don't have siege weapons' (1.5). She is right, though in this scene she is more interested in scoring points over her husband than in demonstrating her grasp of geopolitical fact. And Robert makes the point that while the royal family cower in their castles, the Dothraki would slay everyone in King's Landing; the nobility would lose all the support of the smallfolk in thinking only to save themselves. Daenerys's rather sorry-looking *khalasar*, those who survive the treacherous attack of the Warlocks of Qarth, does not look like an effective fighting force. Dany's investment in the Unsullied (all 8,000 of them plus the trainees) is well worth making.

THE CITIES OF SLAVER'S BAY

Astapor, Yunkai and Meereen are all remnants of the Ghiscari Empire, and all dependent on a slave economy. Astapor transforms its slaves into eunuchs, and then into a military elite, the Unsullied; Yunkai specialises in sexual slaves, while Meereen uses slaves for almost every kind of labour within the city and has a thriving slave market.

Presided over by their guardian statues of harpies, with their pyramids and fighting pits, these old, old cities of the Ghiscari Empire now live on past glories and the present misery of their slave populations: 'Our empire was old before dragons stirred in Old Valyria,' boasts Razdal mo Eraz of Yunkai (3.7). These decadent city states are ripe for the taking by Daenerys once she has acquired the unstoppable military force of the elite Unsullied army. Just as Volantis has five slaves for every free man or woman, the cities of Slaver's Bay are largely populated by slaves, kept in check by a small elite which rules through terror. There are few economic alternatives

37. Saint Adalbertus liberates Slavic slaves

available here: the copper mines are all but exhausted and the felling of the mighty cedars in the time of the Ghiscari Empire has led to desertification and soil erosion: 'Once the trees had gone, the soil baked beneath the hot sun and blew away in thick red clouds' (*DD*, 16). The cities are barren and unproductive, like the harpies who emblematise them. For the harpies – part woman, part bird, Zeus's agents of punishment – are utterly unproductive; in their most famous role they constantly swoop down to snatch the food from the table of unfortunate King Phineus and befoul what is left, rendering it inedible. So too the cities prey on their neighbours, destroying their human resources and making life impossible.

Can Daenerys win the battle for hearts and minds and establish a democratic, just rule in the cities whose populations she has liberated? In this respect the liberal dilemmas which she faces, with her superior military power and above all the growing threat from her dragons, are more reminiscent of contemporary flexing of American political and military muscle in the Middle East than of the kinds of experiences faced in the medieval world. Yet the cities' problems do strike a medieval chord: first with the difficulties faced by the Angevin and Plantagenet dynasties in England and France in the centuries after the Norman Conquest, and second with the short-lived French kingdom of Outremer, the Crusader kingdom established in the Holy Land in the eleventh and twelfth centuries, as we'll see below.

After the sack of Astapor by the Unsullied, Daenerys leaves a Council of Three in charge: a scholar, a healer and a priest. It's not long, however, before they are deposed by a populist and butcher named Cleon who stirs up the populace by claiming that they intend to institute slavery once more. Sharing his name with a violent Athenian statesman and demagogue who advocated mass slaughter and stirred up war against the Spartans, Cleon is soon beginning to train new Unsullied. Once Daenerys has left the Yellow City of Yunkai the slave merchants (the self-styled 'Wise Masters') immediately mobilise, hiring companies of sellswords and sending word to the Free Cities which are involved in the trafficking of humans to inform them of the damage that the Mother of Dragons intends to do to the slave trade. This time Daenerys has not tried to establish a new regime in the wake of the city's surrender. However, it's clear that she can only exert authority over one city at a time: the one in which she, the dragons and the Unsullied are present. Daenerys boldy declares to Xaro Xhoan Daxos, 'If they [the Yunkai'i] should dare to attack me, this time I shall raze their Yellow City to the ground.' However irritating Xaro is, he doesn't lack strategic understanding: 'And whilst you are razing Yunkai, my sweet, Meereen shall rise behind you' (*DD*, 16). Once Daenerys moves on, the old order reasserts itself and new kinds of sectarian killing and guerrilla warfare emerge in resistance to the changes she tries to bring about.

Holding on to authority and to territory in the monarch's absence is a difficult trick. The English kings who followed William the Conqueror were forever trying to balance maintaining their rule in England with holding on to their extensive possessions in France. They managed to retain, even to expand, the territory conquered by William I: when the Angevin Empire reached its largest extent, Henry II ruled from Ireland to the Pyrenees. In 1154 the Plantagenets held more than half of France, though of course they did not rule it directly. But the rising power of the King of France, the death of Richard I 'Lionheart' in 1199, and, more fundamentally, the logistical difficulties of keeping a close enough eye on lands on the other side of the Channel, made it impossible for Henry's son John to retain the majority of his French provinces. He lost Normandy and Anjou to Philip II of France in the Anglo-French war of 1202–14, retaining only Gascony. English efforts during the Hundred Years War to recover the lost provinces were ultimately unsuccessful; by its end only Calais, seized by Edward III in 1346 after the Battle of Crécy, remained in English hands.

If Daenerys had had trusted deputies – and the military power to support them – whom she could have left in charge of the other cities, her dominion in Slaver's Bay might have been more effective and the liberation of the slaves a permanent revolution. But, as coalition forces have found in Iraq and Afghanistan in recent years, unless the invaders are successful in persuading a broad swathe of the population of the need for democracy and sweeping social change, the imposition of a new regime can only be maintained through military force. Once that is withdrawn, old tribal politics, new sectarian coalitions and the covert interference of neighbouring powers will bring down the new governments. As Qavo the Volantene observes to Tyrion:

> This arrogant child has taken it upon herself to smash the slave trade, but that traffic was never confined to Slaver's Bay. It was part of the sea of trade that spanned the world, and the dragon queen has clouded the water. (*DD*, 22)

To interfere with the forces of capitalism and globalisation, to intervene against the market, is a dangerous business, and Daenerys's city of Meereen is paying the price.

Another parallel to Dany's situation is the establishment of the Latin Kingdom – sometimes known as Outremer or 'Beyond the Sea' – in the Holy Land as a result of the First Crusade. Despite the divisions between its leaders and the difficulties of capturing two of the best-defended cities in the Middle East, the Crusaders had succeeded by 1099 in taking both Antioch and Jerusalem. Thereupon, having fulfilled their vows, most of the Europeans turned for home, leaving Godfrey of Bouillon in charge. On his unexpected death in the following year, Godfrey's brother Baldwin was summoned to Jerusalem and assumed the title of king. Baldwin and his successors were able to expand their holding along the Mediterranean coastline, north to Antioch and south along the Jordan Valley. But eastwards lay the Muslim cities of Damascus and Aleppo; no further inland expansion was possible, and thus the kingdom remained as a narrow coastal strip, fortified in the east by the great Crusader castles such as Krak des Chevaliers in Syria. By 1144 Edessa was lost to a Muslim attack; the Second Crusade, partly because of a foolish decision to attack Damascus, collapsed, and the northern territory of the Latin state could not be recovered. With the rise of Saladin in the later part of the twelfth century, the Crusader state became encircled by a unified Muslim force; the defeat of the Byzantine emperor by the Seljuk Turks meant that no help might be looked for from the eastern Christians. Near civil war broke out among the lords of Jerusalem, and thus, after Saladin's definitive defeat of the Christians at the Horns of Hattin in 1187 and the capitulation of Jerusalem and other Latin cities, almost the whole kingdom vanished. The Third Crusade established a second kingdom, centred on Acre, but Jerusalem could not be retaken. After this, despite the activities of Louis IX of France, who spent over four years (1250–4) in the Holy Land, the kingdom remained a piecemeal collection of cities. For almost a century, the cities of Antioch-Tripoli and Acre were ruled by absentee lords until they finally fell to the Mamluk armies of Egypt and the Levant, in 1289 and 1291 respectively. The Mamluks were a slave army, originating in Crimea and the lands north of the Black Sea; once the Mongols had conquered these territories, taking service with the Muslim forces of the south (who were also hostile to the Mongols) was an important move for them.

It was the Mamluks who had earlier halted Mongol incursions further south in the Middle East, defeating Hulagu Khan at the Battle of Ain Jalut in south-eastern Galilee in 1260. The First Battle of Homs in the following year saw the Mongols expelled completely from Syria.

It's tempting to see in the confrontation between Mamluks and Mongols a reflection of the legendary victory of the Unsullied over the Dothraki, the Battle of Qohor, in which 3,000 Unsullied faced up to a *khalasar* of 50,000 Dothraki 'screamers'. Only 600 Unsullied survived this battle, but 12,000 Dothraki fell. The defeated horselords cut off their braids and threw them in front of the

Çarrarriǵ ǵ ic porroñr cõliuc œri   cǿcleǵ tǿc cinfn fir'perr ǿnúr
fnǿciǿǿṛ lc tieiǵ ioi eǵmǿǹn cñiſ   cñíſ.r mǿc cǿ mcmieilneñr

38. Mamluks and Mongols fighting at the Third Battle of Homs, 1299

Unsullied to honour their achievement. The defeated Mongols, it's fairly certain, did not cut off the braids coiled so carefully behind their ears. They retreated to lick their wounds, with the intention of returning as soon as possible to avenge their defeat. However, internal division had begun to fracture the Mongol Empire into separate khanates; Hulagu's cousin Berke Khan, leader of the Golden Horde, who had converted to Islam, was horrified to see Hulagu turn his forces against the sacred places of Islam in Syria and Palestine, thereby bringing down the Abbasid Caliphate, which had ruled the Near East for almost 500 years. Hulagu was recalled to Karakorum, the Mongolian capital, before the Battle of Homs because Möngke Khan, the reigning Great Khan, had died and Hulagu was a potential successor; by the time he was able to return to his own lands in Iran, Berke, by now allied with the Mamluks as fellow Muslims, had declared war upon him.

Just as in Slaver's Bay, the Crusader states were unable to survive once support from the west dried up. The original foundation of the state had depended on dissension among the Muslim leaders in neighbouring territories and on the cultural confidence of the First Crusade and its leaders. But with the geopolitical shift caused in part by the incursions of the Mongols, and not least by the Latins' sack of Constantinople in 1204 – driving a wedge between eastern and western Christianity that was never subsequently overcome – and brought down finally by the infighting of the Jerusalem barons, the new polity could not survive.

EUNUCHS AND THE UNSULLIED

The making of eunuchs, whether through castration or the removal of all the genitals ('pillar and stones'), is relatively common in Essos; in Westeros castration is virtually unknown, encountered only in extreme circumstances. So Ramsay Snow's total castration of Theon registers as a horrific torture; castration as a judicial punishment does not seem to be part of the Westerosi legal system. In medieval Europe men might be castrated for sexual crimes: rape and bestiality. The great twelfth-century thinker and churchman Peter Abelard was (extra-judicially) castrated for his affair with his gifted student Héloïse, a young woman who was the niece of Fulbert, a powerful canon of the cathedral of Notre-Dame in Paris. Abelard and Héloïse contracted a secret marriage after she had given birth to a son; when Fulbert made this public, Abelard denied it (for marriage would have spelt an end to his promotion within the Church). He sent Héloïse away to a convent to protect her from her uncle's wrath, but this seems to have been precisely the wrong move. Fulbert assumed that Abelard was trying to repudiate his wife, and paid a gang of men to break into the philosopher's lodgings and castrate him. Abelard wrote about his terrible experience in his *Historia Calamitatum* ('The Story of my Calamities'):

> Violently incensed, they laid a plot against me, and one night while I all unsuspecting was asleep in a secret room in my

lodgings, they broke in with the help of one of my servants whom they had bribed. There they had vengeance on me with a most cruel and most shameful punishment, such as astounded the whole world; for they cut off those parts of my body with which I had done that which was the cause of their sorrow. This done, straightway they fled, but two of them were captured and suffered the loss of their eyes and their genital organs.[8]

Abelard became a monk, giving up his dazzling Church career, but he continued to write and teach, weathering accusations of heresy from his enemies. He died in 1142, aged around 63.

In Essos, eunuchs perform a number of functions. Varys, born into a slave family in Lys and castrated as part of a magical ritual in Myr, rose to become Master of Whisperers. As he tells Tyrion, from his penurious childhood begging, thieving and prostituting himself on the streets of Myr, he learnt that 'the contents of a man's letters are more valuable than the contents of his purse' (3.4) and he sets about buying and selling information. Varys's network of spies and informers, his 'little birds', are the foundation of his power: 'The birds sing in the west, the birds sing in the east if one knows how to listen,' he tells Tyrion when he materialises in Meereen to help the Imp hold together this 'grand old city, choking on violence, corruption and deceit' (5.10). In this, he has much in common with the Chief Black Eunuch in the Turkish Ottoman court. This office (the *Kizlar Agha*) was created in 1594, and thereafter held by black eunuchs of African origin, usually Nubians from upper Egypt or northern Sudan.

They had oversight of the imperial apartments and the quarters of the palace women, the *harem*. The Chief White Eunuch, in contrast, supervised only the male pages. The closeness of the Chief Black Eunuch not only to the Sultan but, as importantly, to the Valide Sultana, the Queen Mother, embedded him deeply in dynastic politics, supported by his network of spies, who were

39. *'Kisler Aga', Chief of the Black Eunuchs and First
Keeper of the Serraglio (c.1763–79)*, by Francis Smith

(primarily but not exclusively) the other black eunuchs. The Chief
Black Eunuch was third in importance among the officials of the
empire, after the Grand Vizier and the main religious authority, the
Sheikh ul-Islam. No wonder then that Varys plays such a crucial
role on the Small Council and that he regards himself as having
a major king-making role. Just as eunuchs were felt to be more
loyal and trustworthy because they were not seeking to promote
members of their family or scheming on behalf of their heirs, we
may perhaps believe Varys's altruism when he answers Ned's question, 'Tell me Varys, who do you truly serve?' with 'The realm, my
lord, someone must' (1.9).

The most notable role for eunuchs in Essos is as warriors: the
Unsullied. It seems strange to castrate young men who are intended
to make their careers as fighters; the reduced levels of testosterone

that result would, one might expect, not be conducive to aggression and killing potential in the victims. This view partly relies on our modern understanding of the effects of sex hormones, but the view that eunuchs did not make good fighters was common both in late classical and early medieval times. Narses (who lived around 478–573 CE), the Byzantine eunuch general sent by the Emperor Justinian to campaign against the Goths in the Italian peninsula, was regarded by contemporary chroniclers as effective and strategic ('for a eunuch', they often add) – he conquered Rome and drove the Ostrogoths from Italy. But Narses's success was down not to the kind of unflinching courage shown by the Unsullied on the field, but rather to the logistical and administrative skills that he demonstrated in organising armies, as he had organised the civil service at home in Constantinople. He did not drink to excess or indulge in debauchery after battle, and made sure that his men also exercised self-discipline, but just as important was his capacity to make sure that they got paid on time and that their rations were delivered.[9]

During the reign of Nikephoros II Phokas of Byzantium (963–9 CE), Peter Phokas was a leading general, and 'abounded in bodily strength and spirit beyond people's hidden suspicions about him', says the chronicler Leo the Deacon. When the Russians invaded Thrace, Peter led his legion against them and arrayed them for battle. The enormous Russian leader, armed to the teeth and carrying a spear the size of a log (or so the story goes), rode out in front of his men, challenging the Greeks to single combat. And Peter,

> quickly spurring his horse and strongly brandishing his lance in both hands [...] threw it at the Scythian [Russian]. So powerful was the blow that he split his body from front to back, the breastplate didn't make any difference, and the great enemy fell to the ground without a word. The Scythians were so surprised they ran away.[10]

This initiative recalls the tactic of the (decidedly uncastrated) Daario Naharis in his duel with the Meereenese champion in 'Breaker of Chains' (4.3). Such personal daring is, as the Byzantine chroniclers often make clear, both unusual and uncalled for in eunuchs. Since the Unsullied are cut at the age of five, they ought to have a non-muscular build, high voices and – as in fact they do – a tendency to run to fat. It's not physical strength which is their most important characteristic, but rather their discipline and obedience. Their capacity to stand firm, to lock shields and hold the line, to fight with shield and spear, is reminiscent of the fighting techniques of Roman legionaries; their ruthless training, designed to suppress all emotion and sense of individuality, has more in common with the regime used in ancient Sparta to create highly trained soldiers. Well-born Spartan boys were taken from their mothers at the age of seven and sent to boot camp. Here they were given little food or clothing and were encouraged to learn how to steal without being caught. They were taught to read and write so that they could read maps, to sing patriotic songs and, above all, to exercise and practise their skills. Being divided into small groups instilled loyalty to their comrades from a very early age; the proverbial utterance of the Spartan mother as she presented her son with his heavy hoplite shield (the long shield of the infantry): 'Return with it or on it [that is: dead]' indicates the central importance of the military elite within Spartan culture.

Her command of the Unsullied is all that keeps Daenerys in power in Meereen; they are a highly effective force in the particular conditions of Slaver's Bay. But, as debated by Jorah and Barristan, there's an argument to be had about how effective they would be in Westeros, particularly since they do not ride horses. 'There's a beast in every man,' says Jorah, 'and it stirs when you put a sword in its hand'; the Unsullied have the discipline which other soldiers lack. 'The Unsullied are better, they won't rape and kill innocents,' he argues. Barristan is unconvinced; he thinks that Daenerys can only regain the Iron Throne if she has support from within Westeros itself, not by seizing the Throne with a slave army, and he counters Jorah's argument by citing the example of Rhaegar, Daenerys's noble brother who commanded a large army of Westerosi nobility. 'Rhaegar fought valiantly, Rhaegar fought nobly, and Rhaegar died,' retorts Jorah (3.3). Whether the Unsullied will be shipped to Westeros, and whether Daenerys will take power with or without their help, remains to be seen.

VALYRIA AND THE TARGARYENS

The sea journey to Slaver's Bay takes us through dangerous waters, past the Smoking Sea and the ruins of the great empire of Valyria. 'The Doom still rules in Valyria' (*FC*, 29), observes the Reaver, one of Victarion Greyjoy's men, when the voyage to Slaver's Bay is mooted. Tyrion moralises on the Doom as the *Selaesori Qhoran* sails at a safe distance from the smoke and fires still smouldering on the horizon: 'An empire built on blood and fire. The Valyrians reaped the seed they had sown' (*DD*, 33). Valyria was indeed a mighty force in Essos, subjugating all around her, destroying the rival Ghiscari Empire and, as Rome did to Carthage in the Third Punic War (149–146 BCE), razing its fields and sowing them with salt and sulphur so that nothing should ever grow again. Valyria's power depended on her capacity to raise and command dragons, whom the Valyrians used to rain fiery terror from the skies on their enemies. But theirs was also a slave economy; beneath the great chain of volcanoes extending across the neck of the peninsula, the Fourteen Flames, slaves laboured in wretched conditions, mining gold and other valuable metals. Perhaps it was the greed and inhumanity of Valyria's economy that prompts Tyrion's reflection, or perhaps the aggressive foreign policy that destroyed Ghis and invaded the Rhoynar, causing its people to flee westwards to Dorne. At all events, the Valyrian freehold, like the Roman Empire, was the greatest power that the Known World had ever seen.

Until, that is, the day of the Doom: the eruption of Vesuvius in 79 CE, the tsunami that may have destroyed the Minoan civilisation, the volcanic eruptions of Iceland, Mount St Helens and Krakatoa, all rolled into one. The cataclysm was intense; an almighty shudder beneath the earth, earthquakes, eruptions, the sun turning black: a combination of the eschatology of the Christian Judgement Day and the Norse Ragnarök. Was this an ecologically driven catastrophe, caused by the sacrifice of endless slaves to the Valyrian greed for metals in the mines of the Fourteen Flames? Their digging ever deeper and awakening the firewyrms in its depths may have been a contributory factor in the destabilisation of the terrain. Was it a punishment for hubris sent by the gods (but which ones?), or simply a natural seismic event? On that terrible day, the Fourteen Flames erupted, hurling fire and brimstone, boulders and ash into the air, and a mighty tsunami swept across the Summer Sea, engulfing all in its path:

> every hill for five hundred miles had split asunder to fill the air with ash and smoke and fire, blazes so hot and hungry that even the dragons in the sky were engulfed and consumed. Great rents had opened in the earth, swallowing palaces, temples entire towns. Lakes boiled or turned to acid [...] to the north the ground splintered and collapsed and fell in on itself and angry sea came rushing in. The proudest city on all the world was gone in an instant. (*DD*, 33)

This description is the basis of the poem that Tyrion and Jorah recite as they sail among the astonishing ruins of Valyria, with its crumbling towers and dilapidated temples, rather like those at Angkor Wat (5.5). The poem tells of two lovers who chose to spend their last moments gazing into one another's eyes as their whole world was destroyed behind them:

> They held each other close and turned their backs
>> upon the end,
> The hills that split asunder and the black that ate the skies,
> The flames that shot so high and hot that even dragons burned.

Originally composed, we might suppose, in High Valyrian, the poem must have been learnt by all noble children in their school-days, an imaginative reconstruction of the horror that fell on the city. For no one from Valyria survived to tell the tale of the Doom – any more than there were eyewitnesses to the famous destruction of the legendary continent of Atlantis, alluded to by Plato in two dialogues: the *Critias* and the *Timaeus*, written in 360 BCE. Unfortunately the *Critias* is incomplete and breaks off before Atlantis's fate is described, but in the *Timaeus* we learn that 'violent earthquakes and floods' came upon the city, 'and in a single day and night of misfortune all [...] warlike men in a body sank into the earth, and the island of Atlantis in like manner disappeared in the depths of the sea.' Plato adds that for this reason 'the sea in those parts is impassable and impenetrable, because there is a shoal of mud in the way; and this was caused by the subsidence of the island.' Mudbanks are of course easier to sail around than the fiery winds and boiling waters of the Smoking Sea. In Plato's account of Atlantis it's notable that, unlike the Valyrians, the Atlanteans were at first a highly cultured people of great virtue, caring nothing for gold or luxury. This was because their ancestor was the god Poseidon and they had divinity running in their veins, but as time passed the divine element became tempered by the human. Avarice and unrighteousness overtook them, and Zeus determined to make an example of the city.[11]

We might think also of the biblical Cities of the Plain, of Sodom and Gomorrah, on which 'the Lord rained brimstone and fire [...] and lo, the smoke of the country went up as the smoke of a furnace.'[12] God was angry with the people of the Cities for their disobedience and sinfulness, both in sexual matters and in their failure to observe the laws of guest-right. The destruction of Sodom was more powerful in the medieval imagination than the fall of Atlantis, since the works of Plato were not generally known then. Pilgrims to the Holy Land could visit the site where the cities had stood, contemplate the desert around the Dead Sea and try the curious 'apples of Sodom' which looked like normal fruit but tasted only of ash, mentioned both by travellers and by the fourteenth-century poet of the Middle English poem *Cleanness*. He describes the fall of Sodom in vivid terms, with thunderclaps, a rain of fire and thick flakes of sulphur, 'smouldering smoke smelling very horrible':

> For when Hell heard the hounds of heaven,
> he was very glad, opened up quickly;
> the great barred gates of the abyss he burst open
> so that all the region tore apart in great rifts
> and the cliffs everywhere were cleft into little clumps
> Like loose leaves of a book that leaps apart.
> The breath of the brimstone was mingled with it,
> all the cities and their suburbs sank into hell.[13]

The closest we have to an eyewitness report of the Doom is Pliny the Younger's account of the destruction of Pompeii in 79 CE, in a letter to his friend Cornelius Tacitus written a few years after the event:

> Ashes were already falling, hotter and thicker as the ships drew near, followed by bits of pumice and blackened stones, charred and cracked by the flames: then suddenly they were in shallow water, and the shore was blocked by the debris from the mountain [...] Meanwhile on Mount Vesuvius broad sheets of fire and leaping flames blazed at several points, their bright glare emphasized by the darkness of night.

In a second letter Pliny relates how

I looked round: a dense black cloud was coming up behind us, spreading over the earth like a flood. 'Let us leave the road while we can still see,' I said, 'or we shall be knocked down and trampled underfoot in the dark by the crowd behind.'

[...] then darkness came on once more and ashes began to fall again, this time in heavy showers. We rose from time to time and shook them off, otherwise we should have been buried and crushed beneath their weight. I could boast that not a groan or cry of fear escaped me in these perils, but I admit that I derived some poor consolation in my mortal lot from the belief that the whole world was dying with me and I with it.[14]

The Valyrians perished utterly from the face of the earth, but they left behind a number of legacies: the straight roads (like Roman roads) which connect some of the major cities of Essos, 'a broad stone highway that ran straight as a spear to the horizon' (*DD*, 5) and their daughter cities – now the Free Cities which we visited in the last chapter. And of course their language, High Valyrian, which functions rather like Latin in the cultures of Westeros

40. *The Destruction of Pompeii and Herculaneum*

and Essos. High Valyrian is in effect a dead language, studied by learned men such as the maesters and the well-educated sons of the nobility, like Tyrion:

> He had learned to read High Valyrian at his maester's knee, though what they spoke in the Nine Free Cities … well, it was not so much a dialect as nine dialects on the way to becoming separate tongues. Tyrion had some Braavosi and a smattering of Myrish. (*DD*, 1)

Westerosi women don't seem to be taught Valyrian, any more than most medieval girls were taught Latin – Daenerys's peculiar lineage explains her fluency in the tongue. Arya, as a girl and perhaps as a northerner, struggles with the Valyrian-derived tongue of Braavos. Whether Maester Luwin had taught the language to her brothers isn't clear: neither Jon nor Robb find themselves in a situation where they might need to deploy it. Unlike Latin, Valyrian is written in a different script from the Common Tongue: in glyphs, perhaps like Egyptian hieroglyphics. This must make access to the literature preserved in Valyrian very much more difficult; it also seems that Valyria used scrolls rather than manuscript codices like the great books we see Tyrion poring over in Westeros, and thus most of these must have vanished in the Doom.

Low Valyrian has survived in different variants across the Free Cities; in the Slaver's Bay cities there's a strong admixture of words of Ghiscari origin. This makes the dialects of Slaver's Bay very different from the languages of the Free Cities; speakers of Braavosi or Pentoshi can't understand the speech in Astapor or Yunkai. Tyrion's knowledge of High Valyrian helps him to make sense of the languages spoken across the Free Cities, just as a familiarity with Latin makes it easier to understand the languages descended from it: the romance languages of French, Spanish and Portuguese, Italian and Romanian. Daenerys has been brought up speaking Valyrian, a remnant of Targaryen cultural heritage which stands her in good stead when she's negotiating in Astapor. Remember the insults heaped on her by Kraznys mo Nakloz, who does not realise that Valyrian is her mother tongue and that she understands every foul thing that he says about her? Daenerys's itinerant childhood has given her a grounding in some of the languages of the Free Cities as well as the version of Valyrian that survived on Dragonstone where she was born. Just as there were changes between classical and medieval Latin, so Valyrian has changed in the 400 years since the Doom, especially as it is now spoken only by a small group: the Targaryen dynasty. Daenerys must have a natural facility for language; she picks up Dothraki very quickly and she can also speak the Common Tongue.

The Targaryens were the sole survivors of the Doom of Valyria. Warned by a prophetic premonition of the disaster twelve years before it occurred, they flew with their dragons to Dragonstone on the coast of Westeros. It was from here that the invasion and subjugation of Westeros was launched. Dragonstone is now Stannis's seat, somewhat to his annoyance, as we saw in Chapter Three. The Targaryens are prone to prophetic and enigmatic dreams, beginning with that of Daenys the Dreamer, maiden daughter of Aenar Targaryen, who foresaw the cataclysm. Medieval Europeans believed that dreams were often meaningful, sent by God (or, confusingly, the devil) in order to impart knowledge to the dreamer. Some were visions: a figure of authority appeared and spoke directly to the dreamer, warning them of perils to come or urging them to a particular course of action. Others were known as *ænigmatica*: as the name suggests, these were symbolic dreams, requiring skilled interpretation if sense were to be made of them. Classical literature and the Bible offered precursors for such meaningful dreams; Joseph and Daniel built their careers on dream-interpretation for Pharaoh and Nebuchadnezzar. The dream-vision became an important literary genre in medieval French and English, allowing free rein to the poetic imagination. Dreams were perceived as authoritative – if someone claims to have dreamt something, no one else can disprove it – and often prophetic. Daenerys's dreams, like her visions in the House of the Undying, often involve dragons and are frequently violent or sexual, but usually they are so highly coded that neither she nor the reader can readily interpret them.

Another key characteristic of the Targaryens is their custom of preserving the purity of the dynastic bloodline through incestuous marriage. Brother–sister marriages are common, but aunt–nephew, uncle–niece and cousin marriages are also possible. This inbreeding means that Targaryens keep their recognisable physical characteristics of silver-blond or platinum hair and violet eyes, but their children are often born sickly and die young. If they survive into adulthood, they may manifest madness. Tyrion counters Cersei's defence of incest – 'Targaryens wed brothers to sisters for 300 years to keep the blood-lines pure' – with the comment, 'Yes, I know, half the Targaryens went mad. What's the old saying, every time a Targaryen is born the gods flip a coin?' (2.7). Mad King Aerys with his obsession with fire was just the last in a series of monarchs, among them Aerion Brightflame and Prince Daeron, who suffered from insanity. Viserys's instability seems likely to be a product of his genetic inheritance, though the unhappy circumstances of the 'Beggar King' must have compounded his obsessive behaviour, cruelty and impetuosity: 'Who can rule without wealth or fear or love?' he asks Jorah (1.6). It's hard to feel too sorry for him when he eventually meets his fate: one which combines the punishment of a pretender to the Iron Crown of Slovenia, who had a red-hot crown placed on his temples, with the torture of having molten silver poured into eyes and ears, supposedly visited on Inalchuq, Governor of Otrar (in modern Kazakhstan) by Genghis Khan in 1219. Yet, despite his bullying of his sister, there is something pitiable about Viserys's unhappiness and desperation.

Cersei and Jaime's incest, the incest of twins, is aberrant by Westerosi norms, despite Cersei's impassioned justification of her love for her brother and the dubious suggestion put forward by Ellaria Sand, playing a deep double game, that such love would not be frowned upon in Dorne. In medieval literature noble children are occasionally imagined as turning to one another as sexual partners. Siblings would often share a bed, though moralists advised that this practice should be abandoned after the age of seven; particularly where the family was traumatised by early parental death and when well-born children weren't closely enough supervised, brother and sister might cling unhealthily to one another. There's a kind of narcissism in twin incest; neither Cersei nor Jaime can truly relate to a sexual partner outside the twin-dyad. Medieval legend knows of one incestuous set of twins, Signy and Sigmund in the *Saga of the Volsungs*, but here Sigmund is deceived into sleeping with his sister, who has exchanged shapes with a sorceress. Signy is desperate to conceive a child who will be courageous and relentless enough to take vengeance on her husband, the man who murdered her father and all her other brothers. Signy conceals the secret of her son Sinfjotli's parentage until the moment that the vengeance comes to fruition, when Sigmund and his nephew/son have burned her husband in his hall. Admitting her deception, and knowing that the shame of incest is unsurvivable, Signy walks into the flames to die with her hated husband.[15] Wagner's treatment of the story in his opera *Die Walküre* (1856) changes the moral impetus; brother and sister have been separated for a long time and are instantly attracted to one another. Although they realise that they are blood relatives, their passion drives them towards consummation, a sexual union that ultimately causes both their deaths but which results in the birth of the hero Siegfried. In the Norse legend, Sinfjotli is both heroic and monstrous: he cheerfully kills his two little half-siblings when they look likely to betray his presence to their father, but he makes a loyal brother to Sigmund's later-born legitimate son Helgi, and he is taken away by Odin to Valhalla, the hall of heroes, when he dies.

Medieval writers deplored incest as a terrible and unnatural sin, but they did not necessarily regard the offspring of incest as monstrous or hideous. Rather, since the parents were usually good-looking and well born, it wasn't unusual for the child of incest to be handsome, heroic and talented. Roland, the nephew/son of the Emperor Charlemagne, and the Irish hero Cú Chullain were both remarkable heroes and the secret products of incest; both die young, however, and without surviving children, for no one wants to be descended from such prodigies. Mordred, Arthur's son, begotten on his half-sister the Queen of Orkney, is an exception; he is not a particularly effective knight, nor does he have his father's charisma, though he usurps the throne and tries to marry his father's wife, Queen Guinevere. His treachery isn't connected to his incestuous origin in the medieval sources; rather, his usurpation is opportunistic once he's left in charge of the kingdom and its queen.

Is Joffrey's sadism and erratic behaviour an outcome of his incestuous birth? It's hard to say; Tywin blames Cersei's poor mothering for Joffrey's appalling nature, though he doesn't know who Joffrey's father is. Other members of the family, such as Ser Kevan Lannister, have a low opinion of Cersei's influence on her children. Kevan is adamant that he will only serve as Hand if Cersei withdraws from King's Landing entirely and goes to live in Casterly Rock. Yet Myrcella and Tommen seem to have escaped the taint which marred their brother; although we've seen little of Myrcella, good-hearted Tommen dearly loves his cat Ser Pounce (Joffrey, by contrast, was a kitten-murderer) and he adores Margaery too. Will he make a good king once he escapes his mother's influence? That very much remains to be seen.

QARTH AND THE FARTHER EAST

The final phase of our expedition through Essos leads us through the Red Waste, that huge desert which almost kills off Daenerys and the remnant of her *khalasar*, towards the mysterious city of Qarth. Ruled by the Thirteen, and subject still to the malevolent influence of the strange blue-lipped Warlocks, Qarth is a huge port city, owing its prosperity to the great guilds (the Ancient Guild of Spicers, the Tourmaline Brotherhood) and the merchant princes who trade in spices, saffron, silks and other exotic wares from further east beyond the Jade Sea. Qarth lies on the Straits of Qarth connecting the Summer Sea and the Jade Sea, occupying a geographical position similar to Istanbul, or, further east, Singapore.

> Qarth was one of the world's great ports, its great sheltered harbor a riot of color and clangor and strange smells. Winesinks, warehouses, and gaming dens lined the streets, cheek by jowl with cheap brothels and the temples of peculiar gods. Cutpurses, cutthroats, spellsellers, and moneychangers mingled with every crowd. The waterfront was one great marketplace. (*CK*, 63)

In the show Qarth somewhat resembles Petra, that 'rose-red city half as old as Time', but with its bustling souks and formal peacock-haunted pleasure gardens, its smooth-walled towers without visible entrance, it also has a look of Marrakech. The merchant-prince Xaro Xhoan Daxos and the warlock Pyat Pree are the most significant figures in Qarth; Xaro recognises the value of Daenerys and her dragons and invokes an ancient guest-right and blood-oath to bring her and her tottering *khalasar* within the walls of the city. And Pyat Pree has observed how the waning power of the Warlocks has become re-energised since the hatching of Daenerys's dragons.

It's not easy to draw clear parallels between the Qartheen – with their white skins, their reliance both on trade and magic and their belief that they are at the centre of the world – and the medieval past of Europe. Qarth, like China, 'the Middle Kingdom', in its first contacts with the west, regards itself as superior to the rest of the world, and considers that every territory beyond its shores should acknowledge its greatness:

> Qarth is the greatest city that ever was or ever will be. It is
> the center of the world, the gate between north and south,
> the bridge between east and west, ancient beyond memory
> of man and so magnificent that Saathos the Wise put out his
> eyes after gazing upon Qarth for the first time, because he
> knew that all he saw thereafter should look squalid and ugly
> by comparison. (*CK*, 27)

So claims Pyat Pree to Daenerys, and indeed Qarth is wondrous,
brimming with riches and precious objects. Glowing amber and
dark dragon-glass from Asshai, whole chests of yellow saffron
from Yi Ti, lace from Myr, silver rings and chains, a zorse (a kind
of zebra/horse cross) from the Jogos Nhai, a nomadic people living
north of Yi Ti who practise skull-binding on their children and thus
have pointed heads: all these are brought in tribute to the Mother
of Dragons. So too is an embalmed corpse of a warlock, which, like
the *mumia*, or mummy, used in medieval medicine and magic, was
thought to have extraordinary powers. Everything is available here,
and everything is, it seems, for sale. Even human life, for of course
Qarth is a big player in the slave trade, and it's also the base of the
Sorrowful Men, a sect of assassins who whisper their apologies as
they murder their victims.

In the show, the Spice King, whose actual name, he says, is
unpronounceable, enters into negotiation with Daenerys, as a
representative of the guild of spicers. Xaro jokes that the Spice
King's grandfather was only a lowly pepper merchant who married
above his status, and the Spice King concurs. 'Unlike you,' he says
to Daenerys, 'I do not have exalted ancestors; I make my living by
trade and I judge every trade by its merits' (2.6). Although he has
no noble ancestry, he has a mighty fleet of ships which he refuses
to lend or lease to Daenerys, and he has made an even greater
fortune than his grandfather.

Spices were indeed among the most valuable of commodities
traded in the medieval period. Western Europe could not get

enough of pepper, cloves, galangal, ginger, nutmeg, allspice, cin-
namon and all the other richly redolent ingredients of our store
cupboards. It's been mooted that the European diet was otherwise
bland, or that the spices were needed to disguise the taste of meat
or fish that was past its first freshness, but this is unlikely to be
true. Medieval people knew how to preserve meat and fish through
drying and salting, and eating such food when it had gone off was
understood to be dangerous to the health. It seems clear that medieval folk loved spicy flavours just as much as we love curries and
chilli. Chaucer's Cook, who accompanies the Guildsmen and their
wives in the 'General Prologue' to *The Canterbury Tales*, uses galangal in his chicken dishes, we're told, while the hospitable Franklin
chides his chef if his sauce is not 'poynaunt [piquant] and sharp'.
Spices also were thought to have medicinal value; their heat chimed
with theories about balancing the humours in the body, and they
could make the breath smell sweet. Absolon, the clerk who wants
to woo the carpenter's wife, the lovely Alison, in the 'Miller's Tale',
chews 'greyn and lycorys' to perfume his breath, and he addresses
her as his 'sweet cynamome'. All these items had to be imported
from the Orient through the Middle East via the Mediterranean
ports; no wonder then that the merchant princes of Qarth's Spice
Guild could afford ships the size of palaces.[16]

Our sojourn in Qarth poses some difficulties, however. This is
the first truly eastern culture we encounter in the series, and the fact
that there is no native character whose point of view we share, no
insider who can mediate the Qartheen to us, makes understanding
this eastern city of wonder impossible. The cultural critic Edward
Said identified the practice of western writers of regarding the east
as unknowable, exotic, inscrutable and always Other as 'orientalism',
a mode of reading which paid little attention to the perspective
of the non-European, which assessed eastern culture according
to western norms, and which was capable of marvelling at and
despising the east at the same time. So too, in our encounters with
these eastern cultures, we find that the people of Qarth, Asshai and

Yi Ti remain unknowable. We are presented, for our enjoyment, with their exotic accoutrements, their treasures and luxurious ways of living. We know that none of them are to be trusted, that they intend to exploit Dany and her dragons just as much as she intends to make use of them. Wily and inscrutable, operating according to moral codes which are not easily aligned with Daenerys's sense of right and wrong, the easterners combine a love of beauty with terrible cruelty, a paradox which Xaro (himself an immigrant from the Summer Isles) justifies. The social inequality of Qarth must be measured against its aesthetic and intellectual attainment:

> The magnificence that is the Queen of Cities rests upon the backs of slaves. Ask yourself, if all men must grub in the dirt for food, how shall any man lift his eyes to contemplate the stars? If each of us must break his back to build a hovel, who shall raise the temples to glorify the gods? For some men to be great, others must be enslaved. (*DD*, 16)

So too in the Slaver's Bay cities, particularly Meereen, the elites are duplicitous and untrustworthy, while the former slaves who come to power in Astapor are no better than their erstwhile masters. The Yunkai'i bedslaves with their knowledge of the way of the seven sighs of pleasure echo a well-established stereotype of the east as sexualised. It's notable that the only 'Point of View' character who originates from Essos is Areo Hotah, the captain of Doran Martell's guard in Dorne. Areo was born in Norvos and trained by the Bearded Priests, but he has been so long in Dorne that he seems thoroughly acculturated to Dornish ways: while he recalls his difficulty in adjusting to the fiery pepperiness of Dornish food, he doesn't make any further cultural comparisons.

The further east we journey in Essos, the less information we have and the more alien the cultures seem. Melisandre the Red Priestess hails from Asshai, and her weird otherness, marked by her red eyes, her capacity to give birth to shadow-assassins and her fanatical devotion to the Lord of Light, is perhaps accounted for by her origin. Quaithe, the masked shadowbinder who prophesies to Daenerys on more than one occasion, is one of the few other Asshai'i we encounter; her hexagonal-patterned face covering links her to Melisandre, who wears a hexagonal necklace of red stones; hexagons are significant in the Kabbalah and have a particular connection to the act of creation. The city itself, so close to the Shadowlands, is a strange, dying place, built in a dark stone greasy to the touch and where light seems to flicker and vanish, extinguished by unending greyness. Here flows the Ash River; strange, blind and deformed fish can be found in its waters, and warlocks and necromancers practise their art freely. Yet, despite the sense of the place as moribund and sinister, the city's immediate neighbours have no qualms about trading with it.

And that is as far east as we may care to journey along the south coast of Essos; Asshai is no place to linger. Let's turn our ship's prow back westwards towards Westeros and leave the lands of the Shadow behind us. It's time to go home.

EPILOGUE

Unsullied, beware! Serious spoilers ahead!

So we return from the farthest eastern shores of the Known World to familiar Westeros, but as ever it's a Westeros in turmoil. As Tyrion argues:

> The Seven Kingdoms will never be more ripe for conquest than they are now. A boy king sits the Iron Throne. The north is in chaos, the riverlands a devastation, a rebel holds Storm's End and Dragonstone. When winter comes, the realm will starve. (*DD*, 22)

Is there hope for Westeros? Will Daenerys finally turn her back on trying to break the eastern slave trade, and the apparently hopeless task of imposing her own values on rebellious Meereen? Is she, as Benerro believes, Azor Ahai reborn, 'born in smoke and salt', the one who will save the Known World from political chaos – and can her dragons vanquish the White Walkers? Or must the lands north of the Wall simply be abandoned to them? Bran, deep beneath the Haunted Forest, has apparently relinquished any thoughts of pursuing an active life in Westeros. Like many a medieval contemplative – hermit or anchoress – he has retreated into the life of the spirit and is, it seems, harnessing mystical power under the training of the Three-Eyed Crow. But to what end? And what of Jon Snow? Once the mystery of his lineage is solved, will the bastard boy, grown into an impressive man, a Commander of the Night's Watch with political courage and wisdom, be revealed as someone who can achieve more in this troubled continent? His task in securing the northern borders of the Seven Kingdoms, his humanitarian vision for the Free Folk, has been an important theme in the drama at the Wall, and that task is not yet complete, despite the conclusion to Season Five.

Or is there yet another possibility? Consider the young man whose life is imperilled by the usurper who seizes his rightful throne when he is a very young child and who murders his sisters in front of him. A faithful thrall, ordered to kill the little boy, is astonished by the signs of kingship manifest in him. So he fakes the boy's death and smuggles him away to the other side of the sea. There he is reared in poverty, living from his foster-father's trade as a highly successful fisherman. When grown the young man works as a porter. His fortunes begin to turn when he is married; his real status is revealed to his bride, and together they work to recover his throne and depose the usurper. This narrative relates most of the history not of that new candidate for the Iron Throne who emerges in *A Dance with Dragons*, but of the legendary Havelok the Dane, the hero of a late thirteenth-century English romance, based on a predecessor composed in Anglo-Norman French. Havelok succeeds in recovering his throne in Denmark, but, since his wife Goldeboru is the rightful heiress to England, he returns to her kingdom, restores her rights and rules with her there, leaving his ally Ubbe in charge in his native land.

The triumph of the rightful king over the usurper is a powerful narrative in medieval Europe, and parallels to Havelok's history abound in legend and folklore. Like Havelok's foster-father, Theon cannot bring himself to hunt down Bran and Rickon, although sparing them entails the deaths of the two orphans in their place. Those who are charged with the killing of children in myth or folklore often baulk at the task. In 'Snow-White', a deer is substituted for the princess; in the myth of Oedipus the baby is abandoned rather than murdered. Theon's oath-breaking has its limits, and the murder of his sworn brothers lies beyond it. The Targaryen complexion – the purple eyes and silver hair – functions as a kind of 'king-mark'; in the romance this is a light that shines out of Havelok's mouth, 'als it were a sunnebem'. Like Jon Connington, Havelok's foster-father Grim flees with the child over the seas, and raises him as his own. As a former serf, Grim can't educate Havelok in the skills thought necessary for a knight and future king; the young man nevertheless grows up strong, hardworking, good-looking and kindly, his innate nobility shining through.[17]

Havelok as a proto-Targaryen? Well, it's an interesting parallel. Here's what Varys has to say about the young man who's just raised his standard in the Stormlands at the end of *A Dance with Dragons*:

> Aegon has been shaped for rule since before he could walk. He has been trained in arms, as befits a knight to be, but that was not the end of his education. He reads and writes, he speaks several tongues, he has studied history and law and poetry. A septa has instructed him in the mysteries of the Faith since he was old enough to understand them. He has lived with fisherfolk, worked with his hands, swum in rivers and mended nets and learned to wash his own clothes at need. He can fish and cook and bind up a wound, he knows what it is like to be hungry, to be hunted, to be afraid. Tommen has been taught that kingship is his right. Aegon knows that kingship is his duty, that a king must put his people first, and live and rule for them. (*DD*, 72, Epilogue)

What distinguishes *Havelok* from other medieval romances is that its hero does not forget the lessons learnt from a youth spent in poverty. 'Whil he was litel he yede [went] ful naked', says the poem. He discovers at first hand what it is like to be a member of the labouring classes, and once he is raised to the throne he freely rewards the good folk who helped him on his way. He marries his foster-sister Gunnild to the Earl of Chester, despite her lowly birth. Bertram, the earl's cook and Havelok's former employer, weds another foster-sister and is made Earl of Cornwall; he is given the lands of the traitorous steward who had prevented Goldeboru from taking her throne once she reached an age of majority. Havelok's Danishness does not matter to the poet, for his union with the English princess echoes the royal politics of pre-Norman Conquest Britain, when Danish kings ruled in England. That Havelok reigns for 60 years, and he and Goldeboru have 15 children – 'Hwar-of [whereof] the sones were kinges al [...] and the douhtres alle quenes' – suggests continuing peace and prosperity, strong alliances at home and abroad, and dynastic success.

Who should occupy the Iron Throne is the series' key question. The themes of good rule (defined by Varys as 'duty', not 'right'), of learning to use power, to administer justice and to win the battle for hearts and minds have been central to the stories of a good many 'Point of View' characters. So too have themes of gender and rank: masculinity as performed through killing and rape; femininity as trying to resist the coercive forces of patriarchy. What is a life worth, how should it be lived, and what makes a good ending? These are questions to which some answers may be found in the House of Black and White. Freedom and subjection, conquest and trade: these and many more pertinent questions have been raised during our journey.

At the beginning of *Havelok*, before the death of Goldeboru's father, England was so justly and effectively ruled that 'a man that bore / wel fifty pund [...] or more / Of red gold upon his back' could travel the length of the country without being molested or robbed. So too, recalls the nameless Liddle, encountered by Bran and his party, 'When there was a Stark in Winterfell, a maiden girl could walk the kingsroad in her name-day gown and still go unmolested, and travelers could find fire, bread, and salt at many an inn and holdfast' (*SS*, 27). Did such a golden age for the smallfolk ever exist in Westeros – and could it return? Would the restoration of the Targaryen dynasty achieve lasting peace: an ending in which the Targaryens rule 'happily ever after'? Tyrion's offer of his loyalty to Daenerys in the show is predicated on her being, as Varys had claimed, 'the best last chance to build a better world' (5.8). Daenerys seems to be formulating a more radical approach than either her track record in Meereen or the normal ideology of kingship would suggest. To Tyrion's doubts that any of the Great Houses would support her claim, she retorts that the Houses are just 'spokes on the wheel. This one's on top, then that one's on top [...] I'm not going to stop the wheel; I'm going to break it.' The ever-revolving wheel brings a candidate from one or other House to the top of the cycle; yet inevitably that candidate – Renly, Joffrey, Robb, Balon Greyjoy – will plunge downwards, his hopes of holding the Iron Throne destroyed.

This cyclical pattern underlies medieval thinking about tragedy: the fall of a great man is predicated on the first Fall, that of Adam from the Garden of Eden. And Daenerys calls here, I think, on the powerful medieval concept of the Wheel of Fortune. Spun by Fortune, a capricious female figure, the Wheel revolves constantly, pitching those in prosperity down into the depths and raising up those in a miserable estate: from rags to riches, but, inevitably, back down to death. Daenerys's claim that she can break the system seems an extraordinary one: many a medieval monarch hoped that he could place a clog under the Wheel to stop it turning, and every one was proved wrong. The cyclical nature of Known World history and the fortunes of the Westerosi Houses is echoed by the revolving cogs and wheels, the rising and falling figures in the title sequence of the show, as one of my students pointed out to me.[18] It will take something absolutely extraordinary – more extraordinary than dragons or White Walkers – to break that sequence, to arrest the pattern of history. And that suggests that the history of the Seven Kingdoms – unlike that of Tolkien's Middle Earth – will come to an end only after we are no longer reading its chronicles.

Martin's title for the series, *A Song of Ice and Fire*, may allude to Robert Frost's little poem 'Fire and Ice' (1920). Frost speculates about which elemental power will bring about the world's end; he rhymes 'desire' and 'fire', and aligns 'hate' with 'ice'. Is the series heading for Ragnarök, that apocalyptic clash between the powers of ice, symbolised by the Others/White Walkers, and the dragons, 'fire made flesh'? Can the dragons, incarnating that first technological discovery that made culture out of nature, prevail over the planet's raw and untrammelled forces? Can the supernatural, in the form of R'hllor, the Lord of Light, or his avatars, the Prince that was Promised or Azor Ahai, triumph over the Darkness? Epic – the establishment of a new polity in Westeros, with a continuation of Known World history beyond the time-frame of the series; comic – the resolution of the narrative through the classic format of a wedding (or multiple weddings); messianic – the rebirth of Azor Ahai and the fiery sword Lightbringer; apocalyptic – the destruction of everything through the power of winter: all these represent possible endings. There are at least two seasons of the show to go, rapidly diverging from the narrative of the books; with two more books in the offing, it's hard to predict how the end will come.

Here – for what it's worth – is how I prophesy the climax of these two powerful mythologies. For the show, I foretell the triumph of the story pattern of medieval romance: something like the tale of Havelok. I predict a comic/epic ending: a Targaryen restoration, a wedding to an heir who's technically Daenerys's nephew, a limited degree of social reform in Westeros, and the suggestion that the new order will survive through the couple's children and grandchildren. Restoration of the fortunes of House Stark to their pre-eminence in the north would also be achieved. Even so, we can't leave the White Walkers out of the equation; their urgent threat to the north can't be negotiated away. Yet there's not enough dragon-glass, Valyrian steel, nor even enough dragons to eradicate or neutralise them. Summer will need to come early and send them skulking back below ground. The books give more space and more credence to the mythological and mystical – we mustn't forget the urgency of Bran's journey to meet the Three-Eyed Raven or the prophecies inherent in the Targaryen and R'hllor traditions. Both these elements portend apocalypse and renewal on a mythic scale; the ice and fire of the series title will meet and extinguish one another, and from the ashes and the meltwater, the smoke and the salt, the new messiah, heir to Azor Azhai, will arise. Who will that be? Only time will tell.

NOTES

INTRODUCTION

1 The Panotii, from 'Wonders of the East', translated in Andy Orchard, *Pride and Prodigies: Studies in the Monsters of the Beowulf-Manuscript* (Toronto: Toronto University Press, 2003), p. 197.

2 *The Travels of Sir John Mandeville*. Middle English text available at http://d.lib. rochester.edu/teams/publication/kohanski-and-benson-the-book-of-john-mandeville. For a modern translation see *The Travels of Sir John Mandeville*, trans. C. W. R. D. Moseley (London: Penguin, 1983).

CHAPTER 1: THE CENTRE

1 Sir Thomas Malory, *Le Morte D'Arthur*, ed. Janet Cowen, 2 vols (London: Penguin, 1986). For Merlin's prophecy, see I: 45–59. For the 'Tale of Sir Gareth', see I: 231–302. Online in an older edition: http://quod.lib.umich.edu/c/cme/malorywks2.

2 *Beowulf*, my translation. But see also *Beowulf*, trans. Seamus Heaney (London: Faber, 1999), ll. 371–5; 456–73; old English text at http://legacy.fordham.edu/halsall/basis/beowulf-oe.asp.

3 On 'sworn brothers', see Carolyne Larrington, *Brothers and Sisters in Medieval European Literature* (Woodbridge: Boydell and Brewer, 2015), pp. 217–27.

4 'Tale of Gamelyn', in *Robin Hood and other Outlaw Tales*, ed. Stephen Knight and Thomas Ohlgren (Kalamazoo, MI: Medieval Institute, 1997). Online at http://d. lib.rochester.edu/teams/text/tale-of-gamelyn.

5 George R. R. Martin quote at http://artsbeat.blogs.nytimes.com/2014/05/02/george-r-r-martin-on-game-of-thrones-and-sexual-violence/?_php=true&_type=blogs&_r=3.

6 *The Book of Margery Kempe*, ed. Barry Windeatt (Harlow: Longman, 2000), pp. 231–2. Online in Lynn Staley's edition: http://d.lib.rochester.edu/teams/text/staley-book-of-margery-kempe-book-i-part-i.

7 For more on Margaret of Anjou, see Helen Maurer, *Margaret of Anjou: Queenship and Power in Late Medieval England* (Woodbridge: Boydell and Brewer, 2003).

8   Geoffrey Chaucer, 'The Merchant's Tale', in *The Canterbury Tales*, *The Riverside Chaucer*, gen. ed. Larry D. Benson (Oxford: Oxford University Press, 2008). Online at http://sites.fas.harvard.edu/~chaucer/teachslf/mert-par.htm.

9   'Sir Gawain and the Carle of Carlisle', in *Sir Gawain: Eleven Romances and Tales*, ed. Thomas Hahn (Kalamazoo, MI: Medieval Institute, 1995). Online at http://d.lib.rochester.edu/teams/text/hahn-sir-gawain-sir-gawain-and-the-carle-of-carlisle#49.

10 Geoffrey Chaucer, 'The Man of Law's Tale', in *Riverside Chaucer*, ed. Benson. Online at http://sites.fas.harvard.edu/~chaucer/teachslf/mlt-par.htm.

11 Chrétien de Troyes, *Yvain*, in *Arthurian Romances*, trans. W. W. Kibler and Carleton W. Carroll (London: Penguin, 1991). Online at http://omacl.org/Yvain/part1.html (trans. W. Comfort).

12 Malory, *Le Morte D'Arthur*, ed. Cowen, II: pp. 373–89; 427–46.

13 *Njal's saga*, trans. Robert Cook (London: Penguin, 2001).

14 *Beowulf*, ll. 2020–69.

15 *Beowulf*, ll. 1455–64; 2677–87.

16 *Ragnars saga*, in *The Saga of the Volsungs, the Saga of Ragnar Lodbrog, Together with the Lay of Kraka*, trans. Margaret Schlauch (New York: AMS Press, 1978); another translation by Chris van Dyke downloadable from www.turbidwater.com/portfolio/downloads/RagnarsSaga.pdf.

17 *Konungs skuggsjá/The King's Mirror. The King's Mirror*, trans. L. M. Larsen (New York: American-Scandinavian Foundation, 1917), pp. 102–5. Online at https://archive.org/details/kingsmirrorspecu00konuuoft.

CHAPTER 2: THE NORTH

1   Snorri Sturluson, *Edda*, trans. Anthony Faulkes (London: Everyman, 1987); binding of Fenrir, pp. 27–9. Old translation online at http://www.sacred-texts.com/neu/pre/.

2   *Egil's saga*, trans. Bernard Scudder (London: Penguin, 2004); an old translation online at http://sagadb.org/egils_saga.en.

3   *The Saga of the Volsungs*, ed. and trans. R. G. Finch (London: Nelson, 1965), pp. 10–12; downloadable from http://vsnrweb-publications.org.uk/.

4   For a typical werewolf tale, see 'Bisclavret', in *The Lais of Marie de France*, trans. Glyn S. Burgess and Keith Busby (Harmondsworth: Penguin, 1986), pp. 68–72. Translation downloadable from users.clas.ufl.edu/jshoaf/marie/bisclavret.pdf.

5   *Edda*, trans. Faulkes, myth of mead of poetry, pp. 61–4.

6   'Math, Son of Mathonwy', in *The Mabinogi and Other Medieval Welsh Tales*, trans. Patrick K. Ford (Los Angeles, CA and Berkeley, CA: UCLA Press, 1977), pp. 91–8. Online at http://mabinogi.net/math.htm (trans. Will Parker).

7   *The Poetic Edda*, trans. Carolyne Larrington, 2nd edn (Oxford: World's Classics, 2014), 'Grimnir's Sayings', v. 20, p. 51.

8   *Hrafnsmál*; an old translation is available at http://www.sacred-texts.com/neu/
    onp/onp11.htm.

9   For Hereward the Wake, see Peter Rex, *Hereward: The Last Englishman* (Stroud:
    Tempus, 2007).

10 Paul Kingsnorth, *The Wake* (London: Unbound Books, 2014).

11 My translation. For another version of Rögnvald's verse, see *The Triumph Tree:
    Scotland's Earliest Poetry, 550–1350*, eds Thomas Owen Clancy and Gilbert
    Markus (Edinburgh: Canongate, 1998), p. 190.

12 *Edda*, trans. Faulkes; on Ran, p. 95.

13 For the story of Alvild the Pirate see Saxo Grammaticus, *History of the Danes*, ed.
    Hilda Ellis-Davidson, trans. Peter Fisher (Cambridge: D. S. Brewer, 1998), p. 210.

14 Rule of the Knights' Templar, online at http://www.theknightstemplar.org/
    rules-from-1128.

15 *Beowulf*, ll. 3180–2.

16 On the savagery of the Prussians, see Desmond Seward, *The Monks of War:
    the Military Religious Orders* (London: Penguin, 1995), p. 104.

17 Geoffrey Chaucer, 'General Prologue', in *The Canterbury Tales*, *The Riverside
    Chaucer*, gen. ed. Larry D. Benson (Oxford: Oxford University Press, 2008),
    ll. 53–5. Online at http://sites.fas.harvard.edu/~chaucer/teachslf/gp-par.htm.

18 'Branwen, Daughter of Llyr', in *The Mabinogi*, trans. Ford, pp. 59–72. Online
    at http://mabinogi.net/branwen.htm (trans. Will Parker).

19 *Grettir's saga*, trans. Jesse Byock (Oxford: World's Classics, 2009). Older
    translation online at http://sagadb.org/grettis_saga.en.

20 Sean T. Collins, 'Game of Thrones Recap: Dawn of the Dead', 31 May 2015.
    http://www.rollingstone.com/tv/recaps/game-of-thrones-recap-dawn-of-the-
    dead-20150531.

21 *Poetic Edda*, trans. Larrington, 'Thrym's Poem', pp. 93–7.

22 *Poetic Edda*, trans. Larrington, 'Sayings of the High One', vv. 138–45, pp. 32–3.

23 Bede, *A History of the English Church and People*, trans. Leo Sherley-Price
    (Harmondsworth: Penguin, 1955), pp. 86–7; old translation downloadable from
    www.heroofcamelot.com/docs/Bede-Ecclesiastical-History.pdf.

24 *Edda*, trans. Faulkes; on the Fimbulvetr, pp. 52–3.

CHAPTER 3: THE WEST

1   Saxo Grammaticus, *History of the Danes*, ed. Hilda Ellis-Davidson, trans. Peter
    Fisher (Cambridge: D. S. Brewer, 1998), pp. 183–95; quotation, p. 190.

2   *Sörla þáttr;* available at http://www.germanicmythology.com/FORNALDAR
    SAGAS/SORLATHATTURKERSHAW.html.

3   *Entertainment Weekly*'s interview with GRRM, 'GRRM explains why there's
    violence against women on *Game of Thrones*, posted 3 June 2015, at http://
    www.ew.com/article/2015/06/03/george-rr-martin-thrones-violence-
    women?xid=IFT-Trending.

4   Asser, *Alfred the Great: Asser's Life of King Alfred and Other Contemporary Sources*, trans. Simon Keynes and Michael Lapidge (London: Penguin, 1983), pp. 70–3.

5   Geoffrey Chaucer, 'The Man of Law's Tale', in *The Canterbury Tales, The Riverside Chaucer*, gen. ed. Larry D. Benson (Oxford: Oxford University Press, 2008), pp. 87–104. Online at http://sites.fas.harvard.edu/~chaucer/teachslf/mlt-par. htm.

6   For Jane Shore, see Rosemary Horrox, 'Elizabeth Shore', in the *Oxford Dictionary of National Biography*, http://www.oxforddnb.com/view/article/25451?docPos=1, consulted 16 June 2015. Thomas More, *The History of King Richard III*, ed. R. S. Sylvester (New Haven, CT: Yale University Press, 1963). Vol. 2 of the Yale edition of the complete works of St Thomas More, gen. eds A. H. Thomas and I. D. Thornley, pp. 54–5. Thanks to Larissa Tracy for this comparison.

7   Geoffrey Chaucer, 'The Clerk's Tale', in *The Canterbury Tales, Riverside Chaucer*, ed. Benson, pp. 137–53. Quote, l. 880. Online at http://sites.fas.harvard. edu/~chaucer/teachslf/clkt-par.htm.

8   Jean Joinville, 'The Life of St Louis', in *Chronicles of the Crusades*, trans. M. R. B. Shaw (Harmondsworth: Penguin, 1963), p. 216.

9   Snorri Sturluson, *Heimskringla*, trans. Alison Finlay and Anthony Faulkes (London: Viking Society, 2011), pp. 18–19. Downloadable from http://vsnrweb-publications.org.uk/.

10   Maurice Keen, *Chivalry* (New Haven, CT and London: Yale University Press, 1984), pp. 83–101.

11   Chrétien de Troyes, *Erec et Enide*, in *Arthurian Romances*, trans. W. W. Kibler and Carleton W. Carroll (London: Penguin, 1991). Online at http://omacl.org/ Erec/ (trans. W. Comfort).

12   Geoffrey Chaucer, 'General Prologue', in *The Canterbury Tales, Riverside Chaucer*, ed. Benson, ll. 119–269; 623–714. Online at http://sites.fas.harvard. edu/~chaucer/teachslf/gp-par.htm.

13   See http://www.westeros.org/Citadel/SSM/Entry/1185/ (trans. Charles Scott Moncrieff).

14   *The Song of Roland*, trans. Glyn Burgess (London: Penguin, 1990). Online at http://www.orbilat.com/Languages/French/Texts/Period_02/1090-La_ Chanson_de_Roland.htm.

15   Béroul, *The Romance of Tristan*, trans. Alan Fedrick (London: Penguin, 1970), pp. 73–5.

16   Robert Henryson, *The Testament of Cresseid* in *The Poems of Robert Henryson*, ed. Robert L. Kindrick (Kalamazoo, MI: Medieval Institute, 1997). Online at http://d.lib.rochester.edu/teams/text/kindrick-poems-of-robert-henryson-testament-of-cresseid. Translation: *The Testament of Cresseid and Seven Fables*, trans. Seamus Heaney (London: Faber, 2009).

CHAPTER 4: ACROSS THE NARROW SEA

1   *The Book of Margery Kempe*, ed. Barry Windeatt (Harlow: Longman, 2000), pp. 155–75.

2   Geoffrey Chaucer, 'General Prologue', in *The Canterbury Tales*, *The Canterbury Tales*, *The Riverside Chaucer*, gen. ed. Larry D. Benson (Oxford: Oxford University Press, 2008), ll. 269–84.

3   Geoffrey Chaucer, 'The Shipman's Tale', in *The Canterbury Tales*, *Riverside Chaucer*, ed. Benson, pp. 203–8. Quotes, ll. 287–9; 266–8. Online at http://sites.fas.harvard.edu/~chaucer/teachslf/shippar1.htm.

4   David Waines, *The Odyssey of Ibn Battuta: Uncommon Tales of a Medieval Adventurer* (London: I.B.Tauris, 2011), p. 181.

5   *The Travels of Sir John Mandeville*, trans. C. W. R. D. Moseley (London: Penguin, 1983), pp. 171–2.

6   *The Poetic Edda*, trans. Carolyne Larrington, 2nd edn (Oxford: World's Classics, 2014), 'Lay of Hamdir', pp. 230–4; 'Poem of Atli', pp. 204–10.

7   Matthew Paris, *English History*, trans. J. A. Giles, 3 vols (London: Bohn, 1854), III, p. 115.

8   Geoffrey Chaucer, 'The Book of the Duchess', in *Riverside Chaucer*, ed. Benson, pp. 330–46. Quote from ll. 653–4; 659–60. Older edition edited by W. W. Skeat online at http://omacl.org/Duchess/.

9   'So the new god devoured the corpse of the old', cf. Deuteronomy 4:24: 'For the Lord thy God is a consuming fire, a jealous God.' Thanks to Mikayla Hunter for pointing this out.

10 'Oisin's Return', in Thomas Rolleston, *Myths and Legends of the Celtic Race* (London, 1911); http://www.sacred-texts.com/neu/celt/mlcr/index.htm.

11 Bede, *A History of the English Church and People*, trans. Leo Sherley-Price (Harmondsworth: Penguin, 1955); the sparrow, pp. 124–6.

12 *The Saga of the Volsungs*, ed. and trans. R. G. Finch (London: Nelson, 1965); Sigurd's sword, pp. 26–7.

CHAPTER 5: THE EAST

1   Johannes de Piano Carpini, cited from 'The Voyage of Johannes de Piano Carpini', in *The Travels of Sir John Mandeville, with Three Narratives in Illustration of It*, ed. A. W. Pollard (1900; New York: Dover, 1964), pp. 213–60, here p. 216.

2   My translation. For another, see *The Fortunes of Men*, in *Poems of Wisdom and Learning in Old English*, ed. and trans. T. A. Shippey (Woodbridge and Totowa, NJ: Brewer / Rowman and Littlefield, 1976), pp. 58–63. Quote from ll. 48–56.

3   Johannes de Piano Carpini, *The Journey of Friar John of Pian de Carpine to the Court of Kuyuk Khan, 1245–1247*, cited from: https://depts.washington.edu/silkroad/texts/carpini.html. Quote from I: ch. xvii.

4   *The Travels of Sir John Mandeville*, trans. C. W. R. D. Moseley (London: Penguin, 1983), pp. 107–8.

5   William Ruysbroeck, *William of Rubruck's Account of the Mongols*, cited from https://depts.washington.edu/silkroad/texts/rubruck.html. Quote from part v.

6   *Secret History of the Mongols: The Life and Times of Chinggis Khan*, ed. and trans. Urgunge Onon (Abingdon: Routledge Curzon, 2001).

7   Ibid., pp. 115–16.

8   Peter Abelard, *Historia Calamitatum*, cited from http://legacy.fordham.edu/halsall/basis/abelard-histcal.asp (trans. Henry Adams Bellows).

9   On Narses, see Kathryn M. Ringrose, *The Perfect Servant* (Chicago, IL: University of Chicago Press, 2003), pp. 132–8.

10 Ibid., p. 138.

11 Plato's Dialogues: The *Critias*: http://classics.mit.edu/Plato/critias.html; The *Timaeus*: http://classics.mit.edu/Plato/timaeus.html. Here quoted from Umberto Eco, *The Book of Legendary Lands*, trans. Alastair McEwen (New York: Rizzoli, 2013), p. 186; see also pp. 205–6.

12 Genesis 19:24 and 19:28.

13 My translation of ll. 961–8 of *Cleanness*. For the Middle English text, see *The Poems of the Pearl-Manuscript*, ed. Malcolm Andrew and Ronald Waldron, 5th edn (Exeter: Exeter University Press, 2007).

14 Pliny's Letters, cited from http://www.eyewitnesstohistory.com/pompeii.htm (trans. Betty Radice).

15 *The Saga of the Volsungs*, ed. and trans. R. G. Finch (London: Nelson, 1965), pp. 9–14. On incest see Carolyne Larrington, *Brothers and Sisters in Medieval European Literature* (Woodbridge: Boydell and Brewer, 2015), pp. 155–80.

16 Chaucer, 'General Prologue', in *The Canterbury* Tales, in *The Riverside Chaucer*, gen. ed. Larry D. Benson (Oxford: Oxford University Press, 2008); on the Cook, ll. 379–87; on the Franklin, ll. 351–2; 'Miller's Tale', ll. 3690, 3699.

EPILOGUE

1   *Havelok the Dane*, in *Four Romances of England*, ed. Ronald B. Herzman, Graham Drake, Eve Salisbury (Kalamazoo, MI: Medieval Institute, 1997). Online at http://d.lib.rochester.edu/teams/text/salisbury-four-romances-of-england-havelok-the-dane.

2   Thanks to Harry Palmer.

FURTHER READING

Grand Maester Pycelle to Eddard Stark: 'I fear it would be of little interest to you, my lord, a ponderous tome.' (1.4)

Don't let Grand Maester Pycelle put you off reading a bit more about the medieval world of *Game of Thrones*. All the books listed in the Notes can take you into a different world: our own world in the long medieval period from 500 to 1500. Most of what's detailed above counts as literature, but there's plenty to recommend among history books too.

The Oxford Very Short Introduction series includes: *Medieval Britain* (2000) by John Gillingham and Ralph A. Griffiths; *Plague* (2012) by Paul Slack; *The Anglo-Saxon Age* (2000) by John Blair; *The Crusades* (2005) by Christopher Tyerman; *The Middle Ages* (2014) by Miri Rubin; *The Mongols* (2012) by Morris Rossabi; *The Norman Conquest* (2009) by George Garnett; and *The Vikings* (2005) by Julian Richards. All these can give you suggestions for further reading on particular topics.

My medieval history colleague Hannah Skoda, whose blog (http://ideasnowandthen.blogspot.co.uk/) is well worth looking at, also recommends Maurice Keen, *The Penguin History of Medieval Europe* (London: Penguin, 1991), Robert Bartlett, *The Medieval World Complete* (London: Thames and Hudson, 2010), which is full of fabulous pictures, and, less seriously, Ian Mortimer's *The Time*

Traveller's Guide to Medieval England: A Handbook for Visitors to the Fourteenth Century (London: Vintage, 2009).

For more on women in the medieval period, there's my source-book *Women and Writing in Medieval Europe* (1995), published by Routledge, still in print and in an e-book edition. My latest book, *Brothers and Sisters in Medieval European Literature* (2015), deals with siblings across medieval Europe and is about to be issued as an e-book. It doesn't talk about *Game of Thrones*, but there are lots of parallels that could be drawn between the stories discussed in it and the series.

Penguin and Oxford World's Classics provide first-rate translations of medieval literary texts, from French romance to Norse poetry (my own *Poetic Edda* translation among them), from the German epic *The Nibelungenlied* (2010), translated by Cyril Edwards, to the *Decameron* (2008), translated by Guido Waldman. The World's Classics catalogue, where you can filter for medieval texts, can be found here: http://ukcatalogue.oup.com/category/academic/series/general/owc.do.

There are lots of sites of varying quality on the net which engage with medieval topics. A good example is the Medieval News blog, which brings together news and links to stories elsewhere: http://medievalnews.blogspot.co.uk/. And the BBC *In Our Time* archive, http://www.bbc.co.uk/programmes/articles/2Dw1c7rxs6DmyKopMRwpMq1/in-our-time-archive, features a good number of broadcasts on medieval topics. I appeared in some of them – on Arthurian legend, the Icelandic sagas and Norse myth, and Chaucer. The medieval programmes are here: http://www.bbc.co.uk/programmes/p01hb3y1, while the Dark Ages ones are here: http://www.bbc.co.uk/programmes/p01hb35l.

And of course there are the invaluable *Game of Thrones*/*Song of Ice and Fire* newssites and wikis, which answer just about any questions you might have about the books and series: http://winteriscoming.net, http://awoiaf.westeros.org and http://gameofthrones.wikia.com.

Happy reading!

What better way to conclude our literary exploration, then, than with a *Game of Thrones* quote? As Varys says to Tyrion, about *An History of the Great Sieges of Westeros*:

> 'Thrilling subject! A shame Archmaester Ch'Vyalthan wasn't a better writer.' (2.8)

INDEX